"I was mesmerized. This amazing journey is full of challenge, adventure, defeat, triumph, hope, and grace. It was a true inspiration and tremendously uplifting. Thank you for reliving this powerful story and reminding me that faith and trust in this most perfect God will take us in directions that are more powerful and more wonderful than we could ever dream."
—Tom Baker, TV Producer, Owner of Cobblestone Entertainment, Author of *One Dog's Faith*, speaker

"Frances has a most effective writing style that is easy to read and tells the essence of daily life without any attempt to overload the reader with unnecessary detail. Her wealth of dialog in the story, which she labels as fiction because some parts of the story are not built exactly on factual circumstances, takes the reader along in the mind of Mark in a way that creates understanding for why he feels God's presence in his life."
—D. Ray Smith, *The Oak Ridger*

"People have said this is an easy read, and they are right. There are lighter moments in the book when Mark talks about the limited food sources. He had a container outside his small apartment where food would be deposited by neighbors and friends. Frozen food. Some unrecognizable."
—Melanie Tucker, the *Maryville Daily Times*

"This book, quite unexpectedly, became a page turner. I quickly became caught up in Mark's day-to-day activities in Alaska and his total commitment and sacrifice to continue his work only to suffer a terrible disappointment! The anger he felt because of this disappointment led him to perilous circumstances (thus the title of this book). An experience that could easily have taken his life turned instead into a life-changing experience. God has a way of doing that. The scripture quoted throughout the book is biblically accurate, which drew me even deeper into the mission adventures of this 19-year-old man. It is ex-

citing to read about his mission activities from building a church from the foundation to completion, running sled dogs, telling Bible stories to the native children, preaching in the church, and ministering in many other ways. Each day brought new problems and new blessings. I was at once struck by Mark's incredible talent in many areas of his young life. Just existing in the 40 degrees below zero weather where there was little daylight was a challenge in many ways. *Cleft of the Rock* is jam packed with excitement and adventure. God's power and might as well as His love and caring are seen on every page. Don't miss reading this book. You'll love it!!"
—Ann Jarrard, Bible study leader,
Sevier Heights Baptist Church, Knoxville, TN

"To say that I recommend this book is an understatement! *Cleft of the Rock* is a beautifully written account of what can be accomplished when we seek Gods will over our own. The authors seamlessly paint a picture of the struggles of everyday life in Nome, while also showing the spiritual journey Mark was on during his time in Alaska. *Cleft of the Rock* takes you through the full range of conflicts you can expect to face when you step into the will of God. The book then shows how those same struggles can turn into the biggest blessings in the end if you are willing to endure as Mark did. Read this book! It will break your heart and spiritually mend it in the best way."
—Sarah Mace
Alcoa, TN

"There are so many books available to assist the Christian walk, but the best are those who show us how to walk by example. As Mark shares his triumphs and struggles, we see how Jesus works in Mark's life to accomplish His Will. Many of us dance the 3-step (2 forward, 1 back) in our walk, but Mark shows us we can keep moving forward instead of backing off, by listening to God's still voice instead of panicking or running away. A very encouraging read, but even more so for young people trying to find God's will for their lives. I highly recommend this book. I read it in two days because I did not want to put it down!"
—Marty Stebbins, Sunday School leader
Sevier Heights Baptist Church, Knoxville, TN

"This is a story that interweaves Alaskan and Christian culture in a beautiful way. It shares eloquently the directing force God has on Mark's life and how Mark recognized and experienced it. It is a beautiful testimony of how seeming insignificant and life-changing events transform our lives. Well worth reading. I'm looking forward to sharing this story with my children."
—Unnamed Kindle customer

"I highly recommend this book for anyone, young or old, seekers and believers. The clear and engaging story of Mark's life in Alaska is exciting and is interwoven with plenty of good Bible teaching written in a way that makes it easy to understand, even for folks who have never read the Bible before."
—Russell L. George
Maryville, TN

"Great book! Tells a true story of how to walk by faith in and witness the presence of the Living God in the midst of storms, dark days, and rejection. At the same time, the reader is caught up in the life of living in a remote part of Alaska during the winter months when there is very little daylight and temperatures are 40 degrees below zero. Thanks to Frances Smith for this great book of adventure and faith."
—Sarah Ebbs
Maryville, TN

"I just finished reading this amazing book. What made it amazing was the way God worked in this young man's life. It is well written and I found myself becoming a part of this young man's life and being in Alaska with him. It is theologically sound and heartwarming. I highly recommend reading this book."
—Rose Goforth
Knoxville, TN

9-26-18

To Sue - thank you!

Book Two in the Ordinary Man trilogy

THORN
in the
Flesh

Based on a True Story

Frances Smith

Fran Smith

Jer. 29:11

Gazelle
PRESS
Mobile, AL

AUTHOR'S NOTE:

This book could not have been written without the testimony upon which it is based. Mark Smith, my wonderful husband, provided the stories told here, and also provided important insights on theological and biblical matters. This, like *Cleft of the Rock*, is his story.

Scripture taken from the New American Standard Bible, copyright 1960, 1962, 1963, 1968, 191, 1972, 1973, 1975, 1977, 1995 by the Lockman Foundation. Used by permission.

ISBN 978-1-58169-647-9
For worldwide distribution.
Printed in the United States of America.

Gazelle Press
P.O. Box 191540
Mobile, AL 36619
800-367-8203

DEDICATION

This book is dedicated, with much love, to our wonderful mothers, Sharon Smith and Myrtle Chapman Walker.

To Sharon from Mark—no one knows everything you went through all those years, bringing up a precocious young boy while taking care of a family of five and being the pastor's wife—which, I know, was a full-time job in itself. I thank you and the Lord that I turned out as well as I did. Your spiritual support and prayer have been key to my growth and development over the years. You're an unselfish, generous, wonderful mother and I love you very much.

To Myrtle from Fran—for a lot of years, it was you and me against the world. When I think back at all you did for me, all the times you took care of me and went to battle for me, it brings me to tears. I remember when you put the last penny we had in the offering plate at church, not knowing how we were going to pay our electric bill the next week. I remember you sending off the deposit for me to go to the college I wanted to go to, having no idea where the rest of the money was coming from. I remember your unconditional love and support throughout my life. We've had some difficult times, but we've stuck together. And the best compliment anyone could give me is that I'm turning out like you. I love you, Mama.

Because of the surpassing greatness of the revelations,

for this reason, to keep me from exalting myself,

there was given me a thorn in the flesh, a messenger of

Satan to torment me—to keep me from exalting myself!

Concerning this I implored the Lord three times that it

might leave me. And He has said to me, "My grace is suf-

ficient for you, for power is perfected in weakness."

Most gladly, therefore, I will rather boast about my

weaknesses, so that the power of Christ

may dwell in me.

2 CORINTHIANS 12:7-9

PREFACE

When *Cleft of the Rock* was published, the prevailing question was, "How could one person, and one so young, do all of that?" The answer is that it wasn't Mark who did all those things at all, but the Lord Himself. And the story doesn't end after his incredible year in the Alaskan mission field. God was just getting started with Mark.

Thorn in the Flesh picks up where *Cleft of the Rock* left off. Mark finds himself in another, much different mission field, one far closer to home but no less important and challenging. And the Lord, once again, proves that He can and will use anyone, at any time He chooses.

Thorn in the Flesh, like *Cleft of the Rock*, is based on a true story. Some names were changed either because I was unable to contact those people to get their permission, or because the people are now doing the Lord's work in very dangerous mission fields, and their very lives could be at risk if their identities were revealed. To further protect their identity, some minor characters are fictitious.

As with *Cleft of the Rock*, I have worked carefully and prayerfully with Mark to present the events faithfully and truthfully. And as with *Cleft of the Rock*, the more I wrote, the more Mark remembered—especially the parts that are most spiritually important. We firmly believe that God gave Mark those memories, some of which had been buried in his brain for years. Some memories were spurred by conversations with Bob Hall and Kenny Duncan, who vividly recall life at the University of Tennessee's Baptist Student Union—now called the Baptist Collegiate Ministry.

Some of the events in this book may seem unbelievable, but those are the parts that live most clearly in Mark's memory. So, this story is told the way Mark remembers it, incredible as it may seem.

I hope you enjoy, and are blessed by, *Thorn in the Flesh.*

PROLOGUE

It feels so good when life is going well. Maybe you eye the horizon warily, wondering when the storm will hit. Where are the clouds? Surely, there must be clouds.

Yes, there are. Always. Even if you belong to Jesus. Maybe especially if you belong to Jesus. It's all about whether you run from the rain, hunker down, or stand out in it with your arms outspread.

Since Jesus cared enough to die for us and then continue to refine us and sculpt us, He obviously thinks we're worth something. Sometimes there's pain and illness that He doesn't take it away. It may seem like our prayers stop at the ceiling. At those times, it's a challenge to keep walking in faith and try to learn whatever it is that God is teaching us.

That's a lesson twenty-year-old Mark Smith had to learn the hard way. He'd been protected all his life, time after time. He'd just completed a life-changing year of mission work in Alaska. He returned home to what looked like a charmed life—a free place to live, a new job, a ministry to begin . . . and then it happened.

Thorn in the Flesh is the story of how one young person learned to trust God, overcome overwhelming pain, and be a key player in God's plan. He learned to persevere and let God use him, and he's still learning the impact he had. People see him at the gas station or the grocery store and tell him that because of his presence in their lives when they were young, they are Christians today.

It seems that we all have our thorns in the flesh. We see them throughout the Bible and in our everyday lives. Sometimes they are literal; sometimes they are figurative. When things are going well and hardship hits you from out of the blue, it may seem worse. When you think you are living in God's will, it can be downright perplexing. That's when you have to remember Romans 8:28. "And we know that God causes all things to work together for good to those who love God, to those who are called according to His purpose." In times like Mark went through, you have to hang onto that verse for dear life, repeating it to yourself over and over, breathing in its promise.

And remember to persevere. Because God can use anyone, at any time, in any situation. The results can be . . . well, miraculous.

PART 1:
SOWING

1

"Our test results are inconclusive, but from your description of your accident and the level of your pain, my guess is that you have a partially severed disc," said Dr. Bill Reed, the top neurosurgeon in Knoxville.

"So what do we do?" my mother asked, barely holding back the tears, grasping my hand tight. My dad stood stoically by.

"If it splits, we can fix it surgically. But until it does, and we know for sure, there's nothing we can do. I could be wrong. He could get better. For now, I'll refer you back to your orthopedist. He'll help you manage the pain."

"How long?" My dad's voice was quiet.

"Could be days, weeks, even months, or years. No way to tell." He turned to me. "You walked in here. Come back when you're crawling."

Our ride home was quiet, until about the halfway point. My dad spoke in a carefully controlled voice. "Did they make you sign a paper before you got on that bull?"

I shifted painfully and sighed. "Yes."

My mother turned around. "You signed a paper? What did it say?"

I sighed again. "That I wouldn't sue anybody if I got seriously injured or killed." Then I had to defend myself. "But everybody else was doing it and nobody got hurt."

Even as I heard the words coming out of my mouth, I knew they were ill-advised. I braced for the inevitable *Would-you-jump-off-a-cliff-if-everyone-else-was-doing-it?* bomb from my mother, but she and my dad just looked at each other and shook their heads. That was somehow much worse than any words. Tears ran down her face, and she reached back and patted my leg carefully.

For the rest of the trip home I lay in the back seat, braced with pillows, wondering how I could live through such excruciating back pain indefinitely. Things had been going so well. I'd just come back from a year-long mission trip to Alaska, was settling in as a resident at the Baptist Student Union at the University of Tennessee, and had just started a job as youth minister at nearby Pleasant Grove Baptist Church. I had no idea how I could do all these things when I was in this kind of pain.

I'd thought the Lord was smiling on me, that He had great plans for me. My confidence had been skyrocketing. Now this.

The car moved slowly toward home, and my thoughts drifted back just a few weeks, to when I came home from Alaska.

2

I sat on a front pew, waiting a bit nervously. I chewed on a hangnail. Beside me sat a carousel full of slides, and the projector stood ready in the aisle. A tripod screen would soon be lit with pictures from the life-changing year I'd just had. The people filling the sanctuary today had helped make that year possible, and I owed them a tremendous debt.

I tugged at my collar and fanned myself with my church bulletin. I'd grown up here in Athens, Tennessee, but this summer seemed a lot hotter than before. Probably it was because my body was still used to the climate near the Arctic Circle. Even in June, it never got above about seventy degrees. Here it was in the nineties. Since I came home, I spent most of my time standing over an air conditioning vent but still could never get cool.

I opened my hymnal, stood with everyone else, and sang "Bringing in the Sheaves." I shared my hymnbook with Miss Nick, which brought back childhood memories of sitting in this congregation when my dad was the preacher, and my mother sang in the choir. At the time, my younger sister, Mellie, was still in the nursery. I would never dream of sitting with my older sister, Lisa, because Miss Nick fed me candies and stroked my back with her long fingernails. That, and the droning of my dad's voice, lulled me to sleep during most every sermon. Everyone said he was a good preacher, but I wouldn't know. I was almost always asleep.

I didn't really need to look at the words in the hymnbook, so I gazed around as I sang. I'd grown up in this church. My dad had built it from the ground up. He had served as pastor here for eleven years, and building this grand facility had been the culmination of his tenure. We had moved to Maryville when I was in the ninth grade, but in a very real sense, this was still home. These people had watched me grow up and considered me one of them.

At twenty, I probably didn't look very much different than these people remembered me. I was a little taller, just shy of six feet, but my weight had never caught up with my height. Even after a year of hard construction work, I still weighed only about 150 pounds. My hair had remained dark brown and very curly; my eyes were still the same vivid blue. Any of these older people, especially my Sunday school teachers, would know me instantly.

So many memories in this church. I looked up at the huge light fixture. My dad loved to tell the tale of the lady who'd lost her balance in the balcony and ended up swinging from the chandelier.

In the Sunday school rooms, I'd pilfered mints while waiting for my dad to finish talking to people after services. He took his time with his flock, but he expected his family to appear and be ready to go home immediately after the last person had left. One day, absorbed in playing with the toys, I didn't hear when my family's car started up and left without me. It was a long walk home.

As a child of ten, I'd walked down that aisle in a public declaration that Jesus was my Savior. And it was to these people I'd turned when God called me to the mission field. The kind of trip I'd wanted to do—to Nome, Alaska—cost money. Most Baptist churches give in an organized way to world-wide missions, but this congregation had given over and above to help make it possible for me to go. From June 1979 until just two weeks ago, I'd ministered to the natives in Nome. Along with two other people, I'd built a new church for them. I'd cried with them, laughed with them, rejoiced with them. I'd taught them, baptized them, married them, and buried them. I'd felt their hurts and their triumphs.

I'd lived through cold like I'd never even imagined. And I'd learned how to catch and cook my own food in ways I never had done as a Boy Scout. When it's a choice between catching food and going hungry, the situation becomes very real.

Most important, I'd matured spiritually in some profound and amazing ways. I was not the same person who'd boarded the plane for Alaska a year ago. On a mountaintop near Nome I'd come face to face with the Almighty during an arctic blizzard. He'd wrapped me in His love and protected me in the cleft of the rock. By the time I came home, my whole plan for my life had changed. Until then I was on a pre-med track at UT, planning to become a dentist so I could make lots of money, have people work for me, and take Wednesday afternoons off to go fishing. Now I planned to finish my degree at UT and then go to seminary and serve God, wherever and however He wanted.

In many ways my heart was still in Nome. I missed those people with a physical ache, but I'd always known my time there was only for a season. Now I wanted to do a good job of telling my home-town people about the year they'd helped make possible. They deserved to know how profoundly my life had been shaped. I wanted to make the Nome people, so dear to me, come alive for these folks. Real people, real life-changing stories.

The singing died down. I looked expectantly at the pastor, who'd succeeded my dad six years ago, but he didn't move from his seat. Instead, down the aisle came Prof Powers, my mentor and former scoutmaster. This was the one man, the only man, who'd believed in me when I was a little ruffian. I'd accepted Jesus, but I definitely didn't act like it. My shady friends and I put firecracker bombs in old ladies' mailboxes and lobbed eggs on cars' windshields. I got in fights, many of which I started.

This man, a nationally renowned scoutmaster, had looked at me and seen something worthwhile. He took me under his wing, spent time with me, and taught me. I finished my Eagle requirements, all except for writing up my final project, when I was thirteen, then moved an hour away to Maryville. I guess he knew I would never finish that last step and get my Eagle rank unless he kept after me. He was right. He kept pestering me, and immediately after I turned fourteen, I finished the last requirement and went back to Athens to receive my new rank.

That award is still one of the most prized accomplishments of my life. It has gotten me jobs. It has gotten me attention, the good kind. And it has helped me in a lifetime of working with young boys like me. I owed it all to this man.

As he passed my pew, he rested his hand on my shoulder for a fraction of a second. When I looked up at him, he winked at me and grinned. He leaned down and whispered, a little too loudly, "Don't worry, I'm not going to tell about the rock throwing at Sand Island." Then he went up the steps to the pulpit. He looked out at the congregation.

"My name's Prof Powers, and I'm here to introduce a young man I admire very much. I've known Mark Smith since he was just a toddler. Now you folks knew Mark as a small boy, so you won't be surprised when I tell you he was precocious. But there was always something about him, some spark.

"Thanks to your generosity and support, he's just spent a year in the mission field in Alaska. He's back now, and he's here today to tell us about his adventure. Please welcome my 144th Eagle Scout, Mark Smith."

I was still trying to force my mouth to shut. I admired and respected this man more than I did anyone else on the planet. And he was saying he admired me? I knew if I got up to speak at this moment, I'd embarrass myself. So I just rose, met Mr. Powers as he came down from the stage, and gave him a big hug. "Thanks," I said hoarsely. "That means a lot."

He patted my shoulder. "It was nothing but the truth." Then he went and sat down next to his wife, Ozelle.

I stepped over to the projector and turned it on, slid my carousel of slides into place, and took my place in the pulpit.

"Thanks, Mr. Powers," I said, looking directly at him.

I looked out at the congregation. There were so many familiar faces—Sunday school teachers, neighbors, people I'd been in classes with as a kid, now all grown up.

"It's good to be home," I continued, "and this is and always will be home to me. I grew up here, and when God called me to the mission field it was you I turned to. You didn't let me down. You stood behind me, financially and in prayer. Because of your support, I have just experienced the most impactful year of my life. I am sure that when I'm eighty years old, if I'm blessed to live that long, I'll still say that. I'm going to try this morning to relate some of it to you."

Today there would be no sermon; my message was the featured part of this church service. That meant I had about twenty minutes to tell my story. I turned to the screen. On it was a picture of Nome from the air.

"When you think of Alaska, you probably think of snow. In the winter you'd be right. But in the summer, it's not much colder than it is here. It's really pleasant. When I flew in for the first time, the temperature was about seventy degrees."

As the slides clicked by, I told about the town, the people, and the church. A picture popped up of a group of old buildings that looked like they were about to fall down. "This is the church site." Several people's eyes widened, and they leaned closer. "We had to clean out these buildings, demolish them, and clear the site for construction."

In the next slide, the buildings were gone and the lot was cleared. In the next, pilings that would form the foundation rose from the ground, driven firmly into the permafrost. Slide by slide, picture by picture, I told about how a vibrant church was erected from nothing.

"God's hand was on it at every step." I told them of George Allen, the saloon owner who treated the church like his pet project. Every time we needed manpower or machinery to get a task done, it appeared.

I told them of Matthew Hawkins, the Texas millionaire who'd come through for us when our funds ran out. Thanks to him, the church was built stronger and sturdier than we could have done it otherwise. And I told them of our pastor, Will West, whose unflagging faith and leadership had inspired me.

The slides switched over to other areas of our ministry. There was the Lighthouse, where kids could go after school to play games, do crafts, and hear Bible stories. There was the state-run group home for abused and neglected children. I told them about one-eyed Paul, adorable Prissy, and charismatic Darren. And as I talked, I suddenly realized I wasn't nervous anymore. I was telling them about people I loved.

"These kids are victims of their culture," I explained. "They're all wards of the state. Their parents are either dead or drunks, usually living on the street or in jail. Alcoholism is, by far, the biggest problem in Alaska. It's an issue anywhere, but it's an especially big issue there. Every part of our ministry was dedicated to fighting it."

The slides flashed by, in chronological order. The weather got colder before our eyes. Snowdrifts were almost up to houses' roofs and completely covered all the vehicles, making cars useless. Snowmobiles ran out of gas so dog sleds were the most dependable way to get around. Pictures of Will's dog team flashed on the screen, and I told the congregation about mushing the dogs and how it felt to whiz across the snow. I'd learned the hard way about whiteouts and snow blindness.

The pictures began to show more people: Charles and Patsy Chandler, the Anchorage couple who'd bought me good, warm clothing and prepared me for survival in the brutal Alaskan cold. Will and his wife, Denise, who'd been friends, mentors, and surrogate parents. Atka, the little native boy I'd befriended while salmon fishing. Jack, my roommate in the tiny, frigid apartment we'd shared. He and I had learned to survive in this subzero climate. Hailing from California and Tennessee, we had to learn fast to catch our own food and protect ourselves from the dangerous, plummeting temperatures. As I talked about survival, I noticed Mr. Powers' proud grin. I looked him in the eye. *Yes,* my look said: *You taught me many of these things. Without you I would have been in deep trouble.*

There were pictures of Connie, the girl who became Jack's wife, and Robert Wallace, the animal skin artist who'd so profoundly affected my life. Although I'd never stop trying to reach people, he'd taught me painfully that not everyone wants to be reached.

As the pictures flicked by, I relived the year. At the end were pictures of the finished church, and me standing outside welcoming people to services during the seven weeks I'd served as interim pastor. The screen went dark.

"This was only scratching the surface," I said. "I could talk for hours. I want to thank you all. I am grateful to everyone who helped me, who prayed for me, who supported me in any way. Thank you. Are there any questions?"

A man on the second row raised his hand. I recognized him as Mr. Pauling, my Sunday school teacher when I was ten years old. He hadn't changed much.

"Hi Mark. That was an amazing story. Could you tell us what your plans are now?"

"Hi, Mr. Pauling. I've learned that it's iffy to make plans too far into the future because my plans aren't necessarily the Lord's plans. But right now, my plan is to go back to the University of Tennessee and finish my degree. I'll be living at the Baptist Student Union, and I hope to be working as a youth minister at a church near Knoxville. When I graduate, I hope to go to seminary for further training."

Miss Nick, whose name was actually Lois Nicholson, raised her hand. "Mark, I couldn't help but hear what Mr. Powers said to you before your talk, something about a rock throwing incident? Could you share that with us?"

I threw Mr. Powers a sheepish glance. "I was afraid someone heard that. And it really is a good example of the punishment fitting the crime."

So I told the story. Mr. Powers was a master of discipline. His boys almost never acted out, and when we did, he acted swiftly and decisively.

During one of many camping trips as a Boy Scout, my group was on a hike at a camp near Watts Bar Lake. I lagged behind, practicing skipping rocks across the water. Mr. Powers had told us not to throw rocks, but surely skipping stones across the lake didn't count. We were on a hilltop overlooking the water, and I didn't often get a chance to skip stones from that height. I was counting how many skips I could get. I didn't notice the fishermen approaching.

Fishermen are serious. When they are on a good fishing hole, they get a little upset when the fish are disturbed. All the men had to do was say, "Hey, what are you doing there!" to get Mr. Powers' attention. He strode back to the end of the line of hikers and assessed the situation in one sweeping glance.

"Smith."

I looked at him with an unflinching, truthfully terrified gaze. "Yes, sir?"

"Were you throwing rocks?"

Lying wasn't an option and I knew it. "Yes, sir."

"What did I say about throwing rocks?"

"Not to."

He measured me with a long look. "Go get a rock, and it better be big enough or I'll pick one out for you myself."

In fear that my rock wouldn't be big enough, I chose one that was almost impossible to lift. It weighed half as much as I did. Mr. Powers gave me an approving nod.

"Now get that rock back to camp and bring it to me. I'll see you when you get there."

The group headed back toward camp, and I stood and thought. In my zeal, I'd picked a really heavy stone, way too heavy to carry. I searched along the bank of the lake until I found a rope, then lashed it around the rock and made a harness that let me drag the rock through the sand back the mile to camp.

About sundown, almost out of strength, soaked with sweat, breathing hard, I finally arrived with my burden at Mr. Powers' tent. He took one look at me and carefully studied the knots in my rope. "Good job, Smith."

At the campfire that night, I noticed his feet were propped up on my rock.

Although I thought I was alone on the trail, he'd had spies who told him of my progress. He was very close to sending someone after me when he got word I was on the edge of camp.

I finished the story to amused guffaws from my listeners. Then I told the congregation what I hadn't mentioned before.

"Mr. Powers is one of the best people I've ever known," I said. "God used him to change my life when I was an unruly little kid. His teaching and discipline and care … they are a major part of my understanding of this world and how to survive in it. Thanks, Mr. Powers."

He nodded at me with moist eyes.

There were other questions, until the pastor started looking at his watch.

"I know you're probably ready for your lunch," I said. "I'll stay around as long as anyone still has questions."

To my surprise, about twenty people did. A few just wanted to tell me how much I'd grown, pinch my cheeks and ask about my mom and dad, but most sincerely wanted to know more about my experience. I spent an enjoyable hour talking with these people and headed home with a smile on my face.

3

I hadn't returned straight home from Alaska. It had been an emotionally, spiritually, and physically draining year, and I needed some transition time. So I'd flown to Norman, Oklahoma, to visit my maternal grandparents. When I was growing up, my family had visited about once a year, and those were some of the happiest times I could remember. My grandparents were wonderful, devoted to each other, so vigorous and full of life. Spending time with them was one of my favorite things.

My grandfather, Don, owned a laundromat on the University of Oklahoma campus. When I was a small boy he often took me to work with him, and I mingled with the college kids as they did their laundry. High-profile athletes, upcoming scientists, actors, artists, future bestselling authors—they all had dirty clothes, and they all found their way to my grandfather's laundromat. He'd hauled in a couple of study desks, and the students studied as they did their laundry. Sometimes he would transfer their loads from washer to dryer if they forgot. Some paid him a small amount in appreciation for this.

He was a classic example of blooming where you're planted, using your position in life to minister. From six in the morning until nine at night, he worked at his business and, over the years, turned it into his own kind of ministry. While kids washed and dried their clothes, he talked to them and really listened to what they had to say. For many of them, it was their first time away from home, and my grandfather turned into a sort of surrogate dad and, in later years, grandfather. He listened without judgment, and the pictures and plaques on the walls spoke of his faith without his ever having to open his mouth. Whenever anyone asked him a question, he was ready to witness.

He came home at night, removed his work clothes, put on his comfortable cotton pants, and got a container of ice cream out of the freezer. He ate it straight from the carton, usually just a few bites, but it was his comfort food. No one else was allowed to touch that ice cream carton.

My grandmother, Viva, was a respected porcelain artist, specializing in birds. She sold her work—pictures, jewelry, jewelry boxes, china—at the laundromat and local craft shows. Students came into the laundromat to buy gifts for the women in their lives. One asked her to paint a pre-engagement ring for his girlfriend. When she asked him what he wanted her to paint, he told her to paint a scoop of ice cream. She took that assignment as seriously as she did a commission from the governor of Oklahoma to paint the state bird, tree, and flower. Last I heard, those pieces were still hanging in the governor's mansion. She practiced several times to get it just right, and one of those attempts is displayed in my home today.

I remember her sitting in her studio, which overlooked the back yard, with all her windows open so she could hear and talk to the birds. She could perfectly mimic each one so well that I sometimes thought there was a bird in the house. Bird feeders hung all over the yard to attract her feathered friends.

One of my fondest memories was traipsing around the back yard with her, looking for nests and checking on the progress of eggs. She knew where each nest was and how many eggs were in each. I wasn't allowed to touch them, but we watched them and knew when the eggs hatched. Whenever any bird died, she dissected it and perfected her craft by studying its feathers. She taught classes in bird painting, and she kept and used these real bird pelts in her instruction.

These were all good memories, but things weren't so good now.

My grandfather had had a stroke and was having an extended time of very bad health, and my grandmother wasn't healthy either. She would be diagnosed several years later with pulmonary fibrosis, but for now she just knew she didn't feel very well, and her eyesight was beginning to fade. She had lovingly chosen to keep her husband at home and care for him herself for as long as she could, but it was not easy. Besides spending time with them, I wanted to give her a break. She had had little time to spend with her paints and porcelain since my grandfather got sick. Maybe I could give her that time.

It didn't work out that way, though. Although I tried repeatedly to take some of the load from her while I was there, she was having none of it. Besides taking care of him, she was determined to pamper me too. She made me apricot pies from scratch, still one of the best things I've ever put in my mouth, and I don't even like apricots. I spent time with my grandfather, playing chess with him during his lucid periods and just talking to him.

I also spent lots of time in prayer and in the Word. I hungered for the intimacy with the Lord that I'd experienced in my tiny, frigid apartment in Nome. For three months, six hours a day, I'd been taught by the Spirit of the Almighty Himself as I studied the Scriptures and grew in my spiritual walk. It was an awesome and humbling experience, and one I knew doesn't happen very often in a person's lifetime. Now as I prepared to start the next phase of my life, I needed to feel His presence.

On my last night in Oklahoma, I knelt beside the bed in my little room in my grandparents' house. "Lord," I prayed aloud, "I'm about to go back into the real world. I know that what happened in Nome was special. Please help me to stay focused on You and do things the way You want me to do them. Help me see opportunities for service. I want to stay in Your will and glorify You. Please fill me and help me and work through me."

I paused. The main thing I needed to always remember was the importance of staying humble, of remembering that it's not about me. It's never, ever about me. It's always about Him. If I could re-member that, and communicate that to others, I knew any ministry I undertook would be successful. I bowed my head again.

"It's all about You, Lord. Help me to always keep that in the front of my mind. I know there will be times when dark forces will do everything they can to get me off track. Help me to put on Your armor, Lord, and claim Your protection.

"Go home with me, Father. Please see me safely there and help me get started. And be with all the people I love. I pray this in Christ's most holy name, amen."

I rose and surveyed my room. It was ten o'clock. My trunk was packed. I was ready to board my early flight tomorrow and move on to a new chapter in my life. A good night's sleep would be excellent.

But the prayer I had just prayed, for humility and opportunities to serve, was answered before I clicked off my lamp. This was one that I couldn't have predicted or, to be honest, ever wanted. My grandmother stuck her head in the door. She looked haggard, despondent, and at the end of her rope.

"Mark?" she whispered.

"Yes, Grandmother?" I was alarmed. I'd never seen her look like this.

"I can't deal with it. It's your turn." And she turned and shuffled away.

"What?" I jumped out of bed and ran after her. "What?"

"Take care of your grandfather. You wanted to help. You can." She trudged woodenly toward her studio.

I started after her, then realized I'd best go find my grandfather, although I wasn't sure I wanted to see whatever had put that look in my steel-spined grandmother's eyes. I started down the hall to my grandparents' bedroom and started seeing brown smudges on the walls. I followed my nose the rest of the way. When I got to the door, the sight and the stench brought tears to my eyes. My proud grandfather sat on the floor next to the wall, covered in his own excrement. The walls, the bed, and the furniture were covered in it. It was so much, I couldn't imagine where it had all come from.

It took hours to clean it all up. I washed down the walls and the furniture with Lysol, put the bedding in the laundry, and gently led my grandfather into the shower. He stood there meekly while I washed him all over, like an overgrown child. My heart broke to see this man, always so robust in my childhood, reduced to this.

I remade the bed. When everything was clean, I tucked him into bed and kissed his forehead. He looked at me with eyes suddenly clear. "Mark?"

"Yes, Grandfather?" Tears in my eyes, I stroked his wet hair back from his face.

"I'm sorry."

"What for?"

"For being like this. I know it's a burden. I'm glad you were here tonight."

"Me too."

"You take care of your grandmother, you hear?"

"Yes, sir."

"Go to her now."

"I think she's in her studio."

"She is? That's good. She needs it."

"You go to sleep now. I love you."

"I love you too."

Some people are huggers. For my grandfather, the equivalent was a gentle pat on the back of the hand. All of us grandkids knew what that meant. When he patted my hand lovingly, the tears I'd blinked back spilled down my cheeks. He turned over and began snoring almost immediately.

I padded down the hall to my grandmother's studio. I had no idea what time it was. The windows were open as usual, and the night birds hooted and called. Sitting in the dark, using a bright lamp, my grandmother painstakingly painted a Boreal chickadee onto a small round piece of porcelain. Its little talons clutched a small pine branch, its feathers were ruffled, and its black, beady eyes looked alert and impudent.

As I watched, she signed her name in the bottom left corner: Viva Abee Smith, 1980.

"This is for you," she said. "I've already fired it several times. I'll put it in the kiln one more time, and it will be ready for you to take home with you."

For my grandmother to give away a piece was unusual. Everyone, but everyone, had to pay for her work. I took a closer look. The little bird looked like my grandmother had when she first came to my room tonight. A little bedraggled, but still alert and proud. I knew I would treasure this always.

She slid it into the kiln and looked up at me with eyes that were now at peace. "Thank you, Mark. I just couldn't have dealt with that tonight. It was God's mercy that you were here."

"How many times has that happened?"

"More and more." She sighed wearily.

"You need some help. You're not well yourself."

"Your grandfather wouldn't want anyone else to see him like that. Can you imagine?"

I couldn't. She was right. But it seemed like way too much for her to handle on her own, and I said so.

"Too much? We've been together for more years than I can even remember. When I see him like that, I remember how he was in our early years. How much in love we were. We still are. I can't let anyone else take care of him when I know how he'd feel about it."

I looked at her with love. "I'm glad I was here to help you this time."

"Me too." She stood and stretched, listened. "I think I hear your alarm."

I listened too. Sure enough, I heard the tones of the alarm telling me it was time to get up, eat breakfast, and leave for the airport. So much for a good night's sleep.

An hour later I had eaten and packed the little bird carefully into my trunk, and the two of us left my grandfather snoring and headed for the airport. I had grown up a little more over the last few hours. I'd always loved my grandparents, but now they were both much more human than they'd ever been, and I loved them even more for their humanness.

4

I wasted no time when I got back to Tennessee. The day after I spoke at my old church in Athens, I drove my new Chevette, which I'd ordered and paid cash for with some of the money I'd earned in Alaska, to UT and walked along the tree-lined street to the Baptist Student Union. Even though it was June, lots of students were on campus taking summer classes. Girls sunned themselves on the lawns. Boys played Frisbee nearby, sneaking sideways glances at the bikini-clad girls. It was hot, dripping hot in downtown Knoxville. I sweated as I walked and wondered if I'd ever get used to the warmer climate again.

The BSU was right across from fraternity row, which I'd always thought was an interesting and challenging place to locate such an organization. It was either a very good thing or a very bad thing. There was so much activity here, too much for a boy who'd lived in Nome, Alaska, for the past year. Time in Alaska moves at a molasses pace; time in Knoxville rushes like a raging river.

The door was open, and I went into the big old stone house. Although kids were on campus, none of them were here. My footsteps echoed in what sounded very much like an empty house. But from the office area I could hear the distinct clicking of typewriter keys and followed the sound.

Bob Hall, the director of the BSU, sat with his back to the door, facing the window, pecking away at the typewriter. His office was organized chaos, a jumble of books and papers that cluttered every flat surface, including the floor. To him, it wasn't messy at all. Somehow, he was always able to put his hands on exactly what he needed.

He wore his usual outfit, casual pants and a long-sleeved dress shirt rolled up to his elbows. His glasses perched on the end of his nose as he typed. What hair he had stood up a little where he'd raked his restless hands through it.

Bob had been one of my mentors since my freshman year at UT. He was only ten years older than I was, but much more spiritually mature. It was he who hooked me up with the tremendous leaders of Campus Crusade for Christ, he who wrote the letter of recommendation to the North American Mission Board that resulted in my being sent to Nome, and he who counseled me on dark forces and how to defend against them. It was also he who was now offering me a free place to live for my last two years at UT, and he who had just recommended me for a job as youth minister at a nearby church. I could never repay Bob Hall for all the things he'd done for me, both tangible and intangible.

It was always amazing to me that he didn't jump when someone came to the door, engrossed as he was in his typing. But he never did, so I didn't hesitate to speak in a normal voice.

"Hey, Bob!" I greeted him. He spun around in his swivel chair, and his face lit with a smile. He rose and came to greet me at the door. Instead of shaking my hand, he gave me a firm, warm hug.

"Mark!" He held me at arm's length and looked me over with a twinkle. "It's so good to see you."

"It's good to see you too. I really appreciate you thinking of me."

"Thinking of you? We've done a lot more than think of you. You've been the object of much prayer here for the past year."

"Really?" I hadn't known that, but it warmed my heart. I'd also found out when I got home that my Aunt Sandra and Uncle Marvin, my mother's sister and brother-in-law, had fasted and prayed for me, off and on, the entire time I was in Alaska. I knew for a fact it had made a difference. For some of the things I'd been through, some of the situations I'd escaped from, the only thing that made sense was the protection of the Almighty.

Bob had called me near the end of my stay in Alaska, just when I was seriously wondering where I was going to live and how I was going to support myself when I got home, and offered me free housing and a chance at a youth minister job.

Now I looked at Bob and smiled as we sat, him behind his desk and me in his visitor's chair. He found it impossible to sit still, so I knew he wouldn't last long behind his desk.

"I've heard of more and more people who prayed for me, and I can tell you, the prayers made a huge difference. The Lord saved my life at least three times that I know of while I was in Alaska. Probably more times that I didn't know of."

He sat back in his chair and shifted. "And now here you are. Ready to get back to the real world."

"Here I am. Although I'm still having a little trouble making the adjustment."

"Better get with the program quick."

"Tell me about it."

"The head of the search committee at Pleasant Grove is expecting you to call him to arrange a time to meet. You'll meet with him, and if you pass muster, he'll arrange for you to interview with the entire search committee. Then you'll preach a trial sermon, probably at a Sunday night service. Afterwards the committee will have a brief meeting to make a decision and you'll find out before you leave the church that night. It sounds like a long process, but it usually goes pretty quick. If you get on it, you could have the job by Sunday night."

"Sunday? This Sunday? That quick?"

"If you get on it."

"Believe me, I will. Who's the head of the search committee?"

"A guy named Roberts. He works at the King Ford dealership on Alcoa Highway. Just give him a call and set something up."

I scribbled down the name and location. "That it?"

"That's it."

"Wait. You said I have to preach a trial sermon? That would be Sunday night?"

"Yep. Problem?"

"No." I'd just preached seven Sundays in a row in Nome, so I had some resources. All I had to do was pick one of those sermons and customize it for Pleasant Grove. I moved on to the next subject—the housing he'd offered me at the BSU. "I'm really excited to have the chance to live here. Tell me about that."

He rummaged through a drawer. "Everyone who lives here is selected through an application process." He withdrew a thick, stapled packet of papers, which he slid across the desk. "This is the application. We have space for four boys and two girls, and we get a couple hundred applicants each school year. I choose carefully, and I select students for a number of reasons. You'll understand when you meet everyone."

I looked at the packet and at Bob, not understanding. "I'd be happy to fill out the form and apply, but I thought you already offered me the room."

"I did. It's yours. Your experience in Alaska gave me more than enough reason to choose you. You're going to make a difference here. But I need the application on file."

I flipped through the packet. It was several pages and would take some thought. "Can I fill it out and bring it back?"

"Just put down your name, address, and phone number."

I stared at him some more, then did as he said and slid the packet back.

"Thanks." He stood and held out his hand. "Welcome to the BSU. How about a tour? You can be the first to pick a room."

*   *   *

This was an unexpected boon. Although I knew I didn't want to be a dentist, I had decided to stay in the pre-med program because I had already completed two years of tough coursework. Changing majors now would mean an extra year at the undergraduate level. I wanted to get my undergrad degree and go to seminary. Being in the pre-med program meant lots of studying, so I needed a place where it was private and I could concentrate.

We walked out of Bob's office, which was in the front corner of the big house, and started our tour at the front door.

"You've been here before, so you know the basic layout," Bob said. "We try to make the common areas accessible and welcoming so people want to come here. We can't reach them if they don't come."

This common room was equipped with comfortable looking chairs, a couple of desks, and lots of open space. Big windows, the kind that cranked open, overlooked the front lawn. Just inside the windows were padded window seats, perfect for a student to sit and watch what was going on outside.

Next we climbed a stone spiral staircase. At the top of the stairs was a small bedroom.

"This is one of your choices," Bob said. I looked around. The top of the stairs would be a high-traffic area, with little to no privacy. I thought this was a no.

"Probably not, but let me see the other choices."

We continued through the house, through another common area—this one with a seating area, a television, and a foosball table—then came to a small room that opened directly into the common area. "This used to be a storage room, but we turned it into a bedroom."

I studied it. "I'm hoping there's a room with a little more privacy. My course load is going to be pretty heavy."

"I think I know which one you're going to choose." He led the way to the side of the house. The noise from the street grew fainter as we went down a short hall. One bedroom was on the right, a bathroom was on the left, and another bedroom was straight ahead and slightly to the left. This was more like it.

"I like this," I said.

"I thought you would. Which one do you like better?"

I walked into both bedrooms and measured them with my arms.

The two rooms were almost exactly the same size. It really was a coin flip. I chose the one on the left because it was closest to the bathroom.

"I'll take this one. Okay?"

"Absolutely. I'll put a sign on the door. Two of the other boys should be here within the next few days. They'll get the next two choices. The other boy and the two girls will be here right before school starts."

"When can I move in?"

"Whenever you want." We turned to head back downstairs.

"Where are the girls staying?" I asked as we walked.

"They have their own apartment at the back of the house, with their own entrance," Bob explained. At the bottom of the stairs was the kitchen, which I'd never really been in before, but it was like the rest of the house—designed to be useful and welcoming.

"So, what do you think?" Bob asked.

"I think I'll be very happy here for the next two years."

"Everyone who lives here has a seat on the Executive Council. I'm thinking of nominating one of the girls, Wanda Wells, for president because she's the only senior and did that job last year. We'll also elect a vice president, a treasurer, a secretary, a mission leader, and a special programs leader. I was thinking of nominating you for the mission job because of your experience."

"That's fine."

"We'll have our first meeting as soon as everyone gets back."

"Sounds good."

We had finished our tour and made our way back to the front door. I stuck out my hand.

"Thanks, Bob. This means a lot to me. I won't let you down."

"I'm not worried about that." He shook my hand. "You just get hold of Mr. Roberts and get that ball rolling."

"I'll do that." I walked down the steps, back toward my car.

5

Driving home along Alcoa Highway, I thought about everything Bob had said. I had a room, which I thought was the best room at the BSU, for the next two years. I had an assignment, one that fit me perfectly. I could move in whenever I wanted, and I decided that would be early next week. I was used to being on my own and really didn't want to move back home.

Hopefully I would get that youth minister job. A recommendation from Bob Hall had to carry some weight. My next course of action was to contact Mr. Roberts at King Ford and set up an interview.

As I thought about this, King Ford came into view on my right. My dad always said, telephone is fine, but nothing takes the place of face to face. Why not? I swung into the parking lot. An attentive young salesman approached me as I got out of my Chevette. Could this be Mr. Roberts? I had no idea what he looked like.

"Hi there. Anything I can show you?" he asked.

"Is Mr. Roberts around?"

The young man looked startled. "Just a minute. Stay right here."

I waited, walked about, and looked at the rows and rows of spiffy new Fords. When I was checking out cars and finding one I could afford to pay cash for, these sleek models hadn't made my list. My little car was the best I could do, but it was fun to look at these anyhow.

Before long, a big man with the build of a football player, a shock of silver hair, and a flash of white teeth came striding up. He wore a three-piece suit, a tie, and shoes shined to a mirror finish.

"Hello. Were you looking for me?"

"Are you Mr. Roberts?"

"Yes, I'm Henry Roberts. I own this place. What can I do for you?"

The owner. I recovered quickly. It was just like Bob not to tell me the man I was looking for was the owner.

"I'm Mark Smith." I stuck out my hand. "Bob Hall at the BSU said I should contact you about the youth minister job at Pleasant Grove. I was driving by, so I thought I'd say hello in person."

Henry shook my hand in a grip that was almost painful. I'd always prided myself on a firm handshake, so I returned in kind. His eyes widened.

"That's quite a handshake you've got there."

"Thanks. My scoutmaster made a point of it."

"Scoutmaster, huh? What rank did you get to?"

"Eagle. It came in handy in Alaska. I just got back from a year of mission work in Nome. Did Bob mention that to you?"

"Yes, as a matter of fact he did. I've been looking forward to meeting you. Let's go into my office."

I followed him inside, where he waved off an approaching salesman and kept walking. We went to the back of the building, where he passed a trim, pretty secretary in a cubicle. "I'm going to be tied up for a few minutes," he said to her. "Please make sure I'm not disturbed."

"Yes, sir."

He closed the door and motioned me to sit in one of two chairs in front of his desk. He took the other.

"Well, Mr. Smith, tell me about yourself."

I gave him the abridged version of my history. I was twenty years old, a preacher's son, and had been a Christian since I was ten. I was called into the mission field at a youth retreat. The North American Mission Board sent me to Nome for the summer to build a church, but that assignment turned into a full year when I was offered a long-term job with the group home. Along the way I'd run youth programs, done prison ministry, and served as interim pastor, as well as doing all sorts of odd jobs to survive when the funding for the group home job was pulled.

Henry listened, eyes widening. "And you're twenty?"

"Yes, sir."

"That's all pretty impressive. Now tell me why you want to work at Pleasant Grove."

"Working with the kids in Alaska was very rewarding. Now I'd like to do the same thing here at home. I'll be going to seminary when I graduate from UT, and I believe youth and children's ministry is where I'd like to concentrate. And, I was told you have an opening."

Henry kept nodding and smiling. "Can you be at Pleasant Grove on Sunday at three o'clock to meet the rest of the search committee?"

"Yes, sir."

"And be prepared to preach a sermon at the seven o'clock service?"

"Yes, sir."

"Then I'll see you on Sunday." He stood and gave me another handshake. He hesitated and then said, "Here's a little advice ... tread lightly with the couple who's been doing this job on a volunteer basis for the past couple of years. They aren't totally on board with hiring someone for the position. You'll have to win them over."

"Thank you," I said sincerely. "That's good advice."

I shook his hand again, then headed down the hall and out of the building. I waited until I was in my car and well down the road before I shot my fist into the air and gave a victory whoop.

6

I worked hard to get ready for my interview and—thinking optimistically—weigh which of my sermons to customize for Sunday. For five days, I'd been on my knees asking the Lord which of my seven sermons I should use. So far, I'd received no guidance. Early Saturday morning I knelt beside my bed and tried again.

"Lord," I prayed, "please give me the words. I want to do Your will and say the things You would have me to say to these people that would please You and plant seeds of faith in their hearts. You have given me all these sermons; please tell me which one will work best for the people I'll be talking to on Sunday."

I fell silent and concentrated. Sometimes I would hear guidance in a small voice inside me, either during prayer or at other times. Sometimes I would get it during Scripture study. At times, I got no guidance until the last minute. Those times were unnerving, and I hoped this was not one of them.

Later in the kitchen I sat at the table with a tall glass of cold milk, raked my fingers through my unruly hair, and tapped my pencil as I tried to think. My dad, Richard, stood at the stove, fixing pancakes, which he did every Saturday morning. I'd already set the table for breakfast. Now, I watched him as he worked.

He looked the same as he had all my life, although he was showing more weight around his midsection. He was a little shorter than me, barrel-chested, and had the booming voice of a pulpit pastor. His hair was white, and his bright blue eyes were like mine.

Looking at him, I gave myself a mental head slap. How to get ready for an interview? Ask someone who's hired people for jobs like this before. It so happened that a person like that was standing in front of me in his wife's frilly apron, fixing pancakes.

"Dad," I began, "can I ask you something?"

"Sure. What's up?"

"What kinds of things did you ask people who were applying for jobs at your church?"

He thought about it as he flipped the pancakes.

"It depends on the job they were applying for. I guess you'd be asking specifically about a youth minister job."

I nodded.

"If I were interviewing you, I'd want to hear your testimony first. If you don't have that down pat, think about it and get it polished. Thirty seconds or less."

"Okay."

"Then I'd want to hear about your experience working with kids. I'd want to hear short, specific stories."

"My work at the Lighthouse and the group home should be enough, right?"

"For a boy of twenty, I would think that's plenty."

"What else?"

"I'd ask you about your plans and ideas for what to do with a youth group of your own. What kinds of things would you do with them? How would you teach them? How would you deal with problem kids?"

I scribbled furiously as he spoke. "I think I can answer those questions. I dealt with all of that in Alaska. Anything else?"

"Your plans for the future. They'd want to know that they're not going to be doing another search anytime soon."

"They'll be doing one in two years."

"That shouldn't scare them too bad. Just be honest and say you're going to seminary when you graduate from UT."

"Thanks, Dad."

"That help?"

"It helped a lot. It gives me a place to start. Now I need to work on those questions and pick out a sermon for Sunday night."

"You're pretty confident."

"I just want to be ready in case this is where God wants me."

He ladled more batter onto the griddle. "How are you coming on the sermon?"

"I'm having a little trouble with that. I've spent the past five days on my knees, asking Him to show me which of my seven sermons I should use. I'm just getting no response at all."

He looked at me. "You've been asking which of your seven sermons you should use?"

"Yes."

"Seems to me the answer is obvious."

"It is?"

"Maybe He doesn't want you to preach one of your seven sermons at all. Have you considered doing something entirely different?"

Another mental head slap. I'd been listening and reading, looking for guidance, but I'd completely neglected a third major way God speaks. He sometimes sends trusted people to give us messages. We see it time after time in the Bible. In Paul's epistles, he counseled the early Christians about the importance of learning from and listening to others, and using and respecting their spiritual gifts. That's what discipleship is all about. I'd never been discipled, or discipled anyone else, until the past year. I was still getting used to it.

"You're right," I said. "I should have asked you a long time ago. Thanks."

"You're welcome." He sat down and looked into my eyes. "Mark, listen to me. You have a chance to be used by the Holy Spirit. That's something incredible. But you have to remember to be humble. It's hard to do, when He has chosen you to do His work. It's easy to feel you're pretty special, right? You have to resist that. Just as quickly as He chooses you to do something, He can choose someone else if your mind and heart are not right. Stay humble, spend lots of time on your knees and in the Word, and don't ever forget that it's all about Him."

I listened, knowing my dad was right. Things were going so well, it would be easy to get full of myself.

"Thanks," I said again.

"No problem. I'm proud of you, Mark."

Tears that had been threatening spilled over. I ducked my face, not wanting him to see. This was the first time in my life my dad had ever said those words to me. I'd heard him say it to my sisters, Lisa and Mellie, but it seemed that his standards for me were always higher and I never quite measured up. We'd spent innumerable hours together as I'd grown up, fishing and working around the house, but he'd never said those words. I hadn't known until this moment that I'd hungered to hear them.

And, of course, I was a guy and couldn't tell him now. I just said, "That means a lot, Dad." I cleared my throat. "I'd better get to work. I have a lot to do to practice these questions and come up with a sermon."

"That's the right attitude. If God has something for you to do at this church, it will all work out. You just do your best and He'll take care of the rest."

When I went to bed that night I was still no closer to knowing what I supposed to preach about tomorrow, but I trusted that I'd wake up with clear thoughts.

7

Morning came, and there were no revelations. Time was getting short, so I decided not to go with my family to church, feeling the morning would be better spent in the Word and on my knees.

"Lord," I begged, "I need some help here. If You don't want me to use one of the sermons You already gave me, then what? What do You want me to say tonight? This is Your church and these are Your people. I want to say what You want me to say."

I studied Scriptures for an hour, then fell to my knees again and listened silently. I still heard nothing, but now, from deep inside, I felt the urge to go to church. Not with my family, but to Pleasant Grove. Ten minutes later, I was dressed and on my way.

I knew where Pleasant Grove was, but this was my first trip there. The road wound past Maryville and straight into the foothills of the beautiful Great Smoky Mountains. The mountains spread out in the distance like an undulating green-grey carpet. There was no end to them, at least not that I could see.

It was almost 11 o'clock. Sunday school was over, but the worship service hadn't yet begun. People milled around outside, and a few were still arriving, both by car and on foot. I pulled into one of the last parking spaces and sat for a moment, watching.

In the parking lot were old pickup trucks, ramshackle cars, and a few new-looking models. They were mostly Fords, which I realized with a smile wasn't surprising at all, since the owner of King Ford was a member here.

Everyone was dressed impeccably, the men in suits and ties, the women in dresses and high heels. The children were spiffed up in their Sunday best.

I felt a kinship with these people. I'd been brought up in the same way to show respect for the Lord's house. Many churches were steering away from that in an attempt to bring more people to the Lord, and that was fine for the unchurched, but I believed that people who came to church every Sunday needed to dress with respect. My family wasn't rich, but my parents always made sure my sisters and I had nice church clothes. I'd had two pairs of shoes, one for school and one for church, and I'd always known I'd better take good care of them. Once, I lost one of my Sunday shoes while playing in a leaf pile. My dad sent me back to that leaf pile and told me not to come home until I found it.

These people looked like good, salt-of-the-earth, country folks. They reminded me of my Uncle Frosty and Aunt Cat, who really weren't my aunt and uncle at all, but we loved them as if they were. My dad's first church was near Louisville, Kentucky. He worked there during seminary and continued after he graduated, until he and my mother moved to Oak Ridge, Tennessee, in 1959. Uncle Frosty and Aunt Cat were among his congregation in Kentucky, and they became good friends. Later, when my parents went out of town for conferences or some other reason, I would beg to be allowed to stay with Uncle Frosty and Aunt Cat on their dairy farm. From them I learned how to collect eggs, milk cows and goats, and all kinds of other things that most kids would have no reason to know.

All the people here seemed to know each other, like one large community. They greeted each other. The men shook hands, and the women hugged. I knew that any stranger would stand out, and people were already staring at me in my car. As soon as I walked in the door, people would crane their necks, looking at me and wondering who I was. I hated being the center of attention, but there was no help for it. I sighed and reached for the door handle.

Just then, a face appeared in my window and thick knuckles rapped on the glass. I jumped, then calmed my racing heart as I rolled down my window. The man looked amazingly like Uncle Frosty.

"Young man? Can I help you?"

I got out of the car and held out my hand. "Hello, sir. I live across town and heard about your church, and thought I'd visit you. My name's Mark Smith."

He shook my hand. "I'm Bob DeLozier. Nice to meet you. You live across town, you say? Whereabouts?"

"On Mountain View, near the high school. I go to UT. Soon I'll be moving into the BSU on campus."

We strolled across the parking lot in the summer sun. Inside the cool, dim sanctuary, Bob and I seated ourselves on a pew near the back, beside an older lady and a quiet young man with alert eyes who appeared to be about my age. I glanced around and noticed a good number of young people of all ages, from toddlers up to high schoolers: Sweet, pink-cheeked little girls in frilly dresses and lacy socks . . . small boys who looked like they'd been stuffed into their Sunday clothes . . . kids in that tough in-between age group, not quite a child but not yet a teenager, looking determinedly bored because that was the cool way to look . . . and a few older kids, who looked like they were about to graduate high school. These years were the final chance to reach them, teach them, and disciple them before they went off to college or work.

Already I felt like these were my people, and I understood why I'd felt the urge to come here this morning. I was learning important things about the church and the way people interacted, things I wouldn't have known if I'd simply shown up for my interview at three o'clock. These people had already wormed their way into my heart, and I didn't even know them yet.

When the pastor, Dan Dunkel, stood up to preach, the last piece fell into place. He was an old-style pulpit pastor who shouted and sweated his way through his message. Just like my dad. I felt like I'd come home. After the service, person after person came up to greet me warmly. One of them was Henry Roberts, who shook my hand firmly and smiled. "Come to check us out?" he asked.

"No, sir. I just felt led to come here this morning."

"What did you think?"

"It feels like home," I said simply. "I hope I get the chance to work here."

"You may just get your wish. See you at three. I'll meet you out front."

"Sounds good. See you then."

8

"Dad, it reminded me of our church in Athens." I swallowed a bite of chicken casserole. My mother had a way of fixing this meal so it melted in your mouth. One day, I told myself, my wife would need to get this recipe.

My family sat at Sunday dinner, my dad at one end of the table and my mother at the other. Across from me sat my sister, Lisa, eleven months older than me. Beside her was my other sister, Mellie, seven years younger. Beside me sat Jerry Lambert, Lisa's fiancé.

"How so?" My dad reached for more mashed potatoes.

"The people all knew each other. They were so warm and friendly. All the hymns were familiar. And the pastor preached just like you."

"Just like me?"

"Yeah. I was sitting at the back of the church, and I could hear him loud and clear even though he wasn't standing at the microphone."

My mom laughed. "Sounds like a good fit." She got up to fetch the pitcher of iced tea and refilled our glasses. "Did you know anyone?"

I swallowed a big bite and washed it down with tea. "Not at first, but by the time I left I felt like I knew everyone."

As soon as the meal was over, I excused myself and went to my room for some final moments of prayer. I still had no idea what I was going to preach about, but I was no longer worried. I felt a conviction that Pleasant Grove was where I belonged, and the situation was in the Lord's hands. I'd done all I could, and He'd tell me what to say when He was ready.

By two-thirty, I was in my car and headed empty-handed back to Pleasant Grove.

*   *   *

When I drove up to the church, Henry Roberts stood out front waiting for me. He looked a little more casual now, in khakis and a golf shirt. As I pulled up, he looked my Chevette over with a smile.

"Nice car," he said as I got out.

"Thanks. I needed something I could pay cash for, and this was it."

"You paid cash?"

"Yes."

"That was a good choice. Next time, though, you come see me."

"Yes sir."

We talked as we walked through the church, and he led me to a conference room. "Everyone's already here," he said. "We had a few other business items to attend to, so they got here thirty minutes ago." He opened the door. "Everybody, I want you to meet Mark Smith. He comes to us from the UT Baptist Student Union, recommended by our friend Dr. Bob Hall. Would everyone please introduce yourselves and tell Mark a little about yourselves and your function on the committee?"

I scanned the faces in the room and realized that I'd met all these people this morning at church. They'd been among those who came up after the service and greeted me. Including Henry, there were four men and three women. One by one, they went around the table and formally introduced themselves.

"I'm Robert Galyon," said one man. He was squat and barrel-chested like my dad. "My wife, Martha, and I have been serving as youth ministers on a volunteer basis for the past two years."

"I'm Martha," said one of the women. She was tall, brunette, very tanned, and had a slightly skeptical look on her face. "Our daughter is a senior in high school and our son is in fifth grade. We originally took the job because we wanted to be sure our children had a good youth program."

This was the couple Henry had cautioned me about. The introductions went on.

"I'm Charlie Timmerman, the church finance director."

"I'm Seth Howard, a member at large from the congregation. I have two older kids in the youth group."

"I'm Shirley Hitch, also a member at large."

"I'm Patsy Pritchett," said the other lady. "I'm the church secretary and receptionist."

"And as you know, I'm Henry Roberts, the chairman of the search committee," said Henry. "Mark, let's start with your testimony."

This part was easy. I'd been giving my testimony for the past year to people who'd never even heard the name of Jesus. Telling who He was to me and how He'd worked in my life was a privilege. This set up the entire interview in a positive way, and the next hour was pure fun. We discussed my upbringing and calling, my experiences in Alaska, and my plans for the future. Then the conversation shifted to how I would fit into the family at Pleasant Grove, and I shared with them about my times on the farm with Uncle Frosty and Aunt Cat.

"I felt at home when I walked into the church this morning," I told them honestly, as the hour came to an end. "Actually, I think I fell in love when I was sitting in the parking lot, watching the people. This is where I'm supposed to be. I'm absolutely confident of it."

The members all looked at each other, nodding, with smiles on their faces, scanning each other without words. Henry watched the wordless interplay with obvious satisfaction and turned to me. "Mark, we feel you've got the job. We feel as strongly as you do that this is the Lord's will. You still have to preach, and we still have to vote, but at this point it's a formality. You have the committee's unanimous support."

I stared around the table, dumbfounded. "Really?"

"Really," said Seth Howard, the at-large member with older kids. "I am completely comfortable having my children's spiritual education in your hands."

"That's huge. I won't let you or your kids down."

As the meeting broke up, I called aside Robert and Martha Galyon, the couple who'd been acting as youth ministers.

"Thank you for your support," I said. "I hope you're not too eager to be done with this job because I'm going to need your help."

Robert said nothing, but Martha said, "We'd be happy to. What do you need?"

"For a while, just do things like you've been doing them and let me watch and learn. I think it would be a mistake to jump in too quickly."

"I think that's a wonderful idea," she said. "You can start by coming to all our meetings and events, and we'll go from there. Just so you know, we have a trip coming up to Myrtle Beach next month. It's been in the works for a while, and all the kids are really looking forward to it."

"Perfect. Thank you." I paused. "Is there a place I can be private for a little while to pray and prepare to preach?"

"Sure," said Martha. She led me down the hall to a small office. "It will be quiet here. I'm looking forward to hearing you preach." And she left me.

Alone, I marveled. *God always knows,* I thought. This whole time I was agonizing and fretting about the sermon, He knew that I would have the job before I even had to preach. He was telling me to trust Him.

The question remained, though—what to say from the pulpit? And in a flash, I knew.

* * *

Sunday evening services are usually sparsely attended, and Pleasant

Grove was no different. To my surprise and pleasure, though, many youth were in the congregation. Since youth groups usually have their own programs on Sunday evenings, I assumed they were there to hear their potential new youth minister. That fit in perfectly with what I planned to say—another way things were falling into place.

After several hymns and the offering, Henry went up to the pulpit and cleared his throat. It rumbled like thunder through the microphone and around the church. Kids giggled.

"I'm here as the head of the youth minister search committee to tell you that we believe we've found our man," he said. "As you know, we've looked for a long time to find the right person. And in the end, God led him straight to us. He's going to speak to us now, and the committee will take a final vote after the service. Mark Smith, would you please come up?"

I rose, climbed the steps to the pulpit, and faced the congregation.

"I'm so happy to have this opportunity," I said. "I want to thank Mr. Roberts and the rest of the search committee for their faith in me. If you do vote to hire me, I won't let any of you down.

"I've spent the past year in the mission field in Nome, Alaska, and I'll tell you I'm really tired of whale blubber and rancid seal oil. I hope you'll treat me to some produce from some of your farms. Anything but Brussels sprouts."

At that everyone in the congregation looked at a little lady on the front row, the same one I'd sat beside this morning. Henry, who sat behind her, leaned forward and said in a loud whisper, "Miss Ina, you've got to feed this boy." I grinned and went on.

"Since it's really cold and dark near the Arctic Circle, I had a lot of time to think and pray. The one thing that was obvious all along was that God wanted me in the ministry. Where and how, I didn't know. I helped build a church, worked with abused and neglected children, mushed dogs, and preached to inmates in the local jail. God saved my life three different times while I was there. Why, I don't know, except that I guess He just wasn't finished with me yet.

"The first eighteen years of my life were spiritually uneventful.

41

I was saved, but I changed very little. I shot fireworks at cows to make them stampede. I lobbed eggs onto car windshields. I hotwired bulldozers and took them for joyrides on construction sites. I shoplifted from stores in town.

"I never gave God a chance to work in me or shine through me. I know now it was because I was ignorant about spiritual education and discipleship. We had a youth group, but it didn't do much for me. I finally got the spiritual nourishment I needed at another church, and when I had that, a light went on in my spirit and a passion caught fire in my heart.

"This morning, before I came into this building, I sat in the parking lot and watched all of you. Just looking at you, I knew this was where I was supposed to be. And I'm confident that teaching and discipling other Christians is what I was born to do. So I pray that the Lord will use me here, to be a light for you.

"I pray that I can do for you what was done for me. For the smaller children, I pray that I can help you love and understand the Bible, and learn to talk to your heavenly Father. I want you to understand exactly what He did for you and how much He loves you.

"For the middle schoolers, this is a tough time. You need someone who understands what you're going through at this point in your life. I do, and your Father does. He made you, so of course He knows everything about you. I want you to learn to lean on Him and trust Him to help you make all the right choices. I want to help you find and use the tools that will get you through these years. The choices you make now will be ones you'll look back on in later years, I promise you. And much of what you make out of your life will be your responsibility.

"For the high schoolers, you're getting ready for the rest of your life. There are big decisions ahead. Maybe you'll be going off to college; maybe you'll be going straight to work. Maybe you just don't know yet. But now is a pivotal time for you. Your Father wants to help you. He wants you to trust Him. He wants to have a relationship with you, and there's nothing in this world that can compare to that. I hope to teach you how to let Him in. He does have a plan for your life, each and every one of you.

"This is a two-way street. You'll be teaching me too, because I find out every day how much more I still have to learn. We'll have two years together before I go off to seminary. It's my hope and prayer that when we study the Bible, it will begin to make sense to you like never before. It's like a manual for how to live your life. There are no problems that you will face, that you won't find the answer to in that Book."

Here I paused and looked directly into the faces of the kids' parents, one at a time.

"I give you parents my word, here and now. I will give everything that is in me to do my best by your children. The Lord can do anything, and I will actively strive and pray every day for Him to work through me for them. My goal is to teach them and inspire them so well that each and every one of them is saved and baptized before they leave this youth group.

"I'll need your help. Let's work together for these kids. I already love them."

* * *

After the service, Henry Roberts was the first one to come up and offer a handshake.

"Excellent job," he said. "If I had a child in the youth program here, I'd be sold. Can you hang around for a little while? We have to vote, but it won't take long,"

"Sure. I'll probably be outside."

"See you in a little bit."

The little lady Henry had called Miss Ina bustled up to me next. She wore a mountain homespun dress and was round, neat and trim. She wore a pale yellow cardigan and a saucy hat on her iron-gray hair that was fixed in a bun at the nape of her neck. "Hello, I'm Ina Gambrell, but everyone calls me Miss Ina," she said. "Welcome to Pleasant Grove. I'd love to hear more about your experiences in Alaska, and I think I can wash the taste of rancid seal oil out of your mouth."

"Miss Ina, I'm happy to meet you. I'm all for that, and I'm available pretty much any weekend."

"Sunday dinner next week?"

"Excellent. Thank you."

I wandered outside, and other people came up and offered their well wishes. At the side of the church, three of the older boys shot baskets through a netless hoop. Another lounged in the shade and watched. *No time like the present,* I thought. When the last person had shaken my hand, I went to my car and pulled a football from the back seat. The boys watched me quizzically. I pointed to a short, dark-haired, athletic-looking young man and called, "Go long."

He sprinted down the parking lot into the grass beside the church and kept going, full speed. I threw a laser and hit the boy in stride, right into his hands. For the next ten minutes I threw the ball with the boys and took the first steps toward getting to know them.

The boy lounging in the shade was Miss Ina's son, Pete. He had just finished high school and was living at home. The one I'd thrown the ball to was named Jimmy. The others were tall, blond Jonathan and John-John, who was stocky and so muscular he looked like a bodybuilder. All three were going into their junior year of high school.

"If any of you decide to go look at UT, come find me at the Baptist Student Union." I fired another pass over Jimmy's head, and he made a diving catch in the grass. "I'll be living there for the next two years and I'd love to show you around."

Just then Henry came out of the church and looked around for me. I waved, and he came over with a big smile. "Congratulations. You're hired. Unanimous vote. Even the Galyons. I think your sermon was what they needed to hear."

"That's so good. Thanks a lot, Henry. When do I start?"

"Next Sunday. Okay with you?"

"More than okay. I'll see you then."

"You have a good week." And he strode across the parking lot to a new, top-of-the-line Ford and drove off.

I walked back to the boys. "Guess you've got yourselves a youth minister."

Jonathan shuffled his feet and eyed me. "We're not going to be doing lame stuff, are we?"

"No lame stuff."

"What then?"

"If you heard my sermon in there, you know what I'm all about. Living and working for the Lord is not lame, and it's never boring. You'll see. Just give it a chance."

Leaving the boys with curious looks on their faces, I hopped in my Chevette and headed home.

9

Bob had said I could move in whenever I wanted, and I took him at his word. I arrived at the BSU before noon Monday, with a mattress strapped to the top of my car and a dresser wedged in the trunk. One suitcase sat in the back seat. The room was small, and I didn't need much.

I pulled up in front of the BSU and sat for a moment, looking at the house and thinking about how greatly I'd been blessed. *Thank You, Father, I prayed silently. You have taken care of me. You provided a place to live and a job for the next two years. Help me to glorify You. Use me. Work through me. I'm Your vessel, here for You.*

As I sat and debated how best to get my mattress off the car and up the steps, two wiry young men emerged from the building. One was brown-haired, barrel-chested, muscular and tall; the other was dark with a medium build and wore what looked like a blue skirt knotted at the waist. I guessed these were two of my housemates.

"You're Mark." The dark-headed boy stuck out his hand. "Bob saw you from the window upstairs and said we should come give you a hand. I'm Brandon Payne."

"I'm Kenny Duncan," the red-headed boy said.

"I'm Mark Smith." I shook hands with both of them. I tried not to stare at Brandon's apparel. "I like your dress, Brandon."

"It's not a dress, it's a sarong and it's really comfortable. You should try it sometime. This is what all the people in Indonesia wear."

Kenny guffawed and slapped his thighs. "Looks like a dress to me, too. I've already been kidding him about that."

"How do you get it to stay up?" I wanted to know. It didn't look like it had any snaps, buttons or zippers.

"You just have to know how to tie it," he said and demonstrated expertly.

"Wow," I said and changed the subject. "I do appreciate the help. I was just wondering how I was going to get this mattress up those spiral steps."

"You should have done it the easy way," said Kenny. "I'm sleeping on the floor."

"And I only brought a hammock," Brandon put in.

For the next few minutes we wrestled the mattress off the car and up the steps to my room. Brandon was right; his sarong thankfully stayed securely in place throughout the very physical process.

Afterward as we drank ice water in the kitchen, I discovered that both Brandon and Kenny were missionaries' sons. They were American citizens but had spent their entire lives in the mission field. Brandon's parents were in Indonesia, while Kenny's were in Kenya.

"You're going to have the opposite problem from me," I told them. "You probably think Knoxville is cool, but I've been in Alaska for the past year, and I've been hot and miserable since I got home."

"Nah, this is nothing," said Brandon. "You want to see heat, come to Indonesia."

Brandon and Kenny had both moved in on Friday of the previous week, the day after I'd been here and picked out my room. Kenny had chosen the large closet-like area just off the common room upstairs. Brandon had hung his hammock in the alcove at the top of the spiral staircase. Neither of them had chosen the second room in the small suite where I was, so I supposed I would have some quiet time there for the rest of the summer, but that would turn out to be incorrect.

Our first week at the BSU, they remembered my statement

about the heat and challenged me to an endurance contest. Never one to back down from a challenge, even if I have no chance of winning, I accepted. In those days, the BSU had a flat roof that was accessible from the big closet next to my room. Kenny and Brandon wanted to see who could stay on the roof, in the hot sun, the longest. We stripped down to our briefest shorts, spread out towels, and clicked a stopwatch. Never have I lost a challenge so completely. Kenny and Brandon, used to the hot sun in Kenya and Indonesia, basked in our Knoxville heat. I wilted within thirty minutes. After two hours, as I watched from the coolness of the house, they finally tired of the contest and declared themselves double winners.

As I got to know them over the next few days, I realized that missionaries' kids don't have the option of being shy or withdrawn. Both Brandon and Kenny were outgoing, outspoken, and gregarious. Kenny loved to play practical jokes, and since Brandon and I were the only ones there at the moment, we got the brunt of it. Brandon was the comic relief of the group. He could find humor in everything. The next two years were going to be fun.

10

My first Sunday as youth minister, the preacher introduced me to the congregation and announced that there would be a potluck meal after church the next week to welcome me. All members were asked to bring a dish for their families with enough to share. If this church was anything like the other churches I'd been to, the women would compete to see whose fried chicken, or potato salad, or pecan pie, or chili, or deviled eggs, or just about any Southern delicacy you could think of, was the best. Judging would be very subjective and eventually determined by how much of each dish was left at the end. For the ones whose food was wolfed down, it would mean unofficial bragging rights until the next potluck.

But that was next Sunday. This was now, and I followed the Gambrells home after church. In the car ahead of me were Miss Ina, her husband, Pete Senior, and her son, Pete. We drove for about twenty minutes. Maryville is nestled at the base of the Great Smoky Mountains, but the Gambrells lived high in the hills, up winding dirt roads so narrow that trees scraped the sides of the car. On we went, deeper into the mountains, then climbed up and up on a road so steep that the only view from my windshield was the sky. Finally, we emerged into a clearing and a log house came into view. Ageless, hewn out of solid pine logs, it perched on stilts on the side of the mountain. The side facing the driveway was one story, but based on the steepness of the mountain, the other side had to be at least three stories. And I'd bet the view from the deck was stunning.

Another car was already there, and a young woman bustled out of the house, wiping her hands on her apron. One look told me this had to be Miss Ina's daughter, so alike were they.

"Hi, Mom, I knew we were having company so I started lunch for you. You must be Mark." She offered a small hand, still dusted with flour. "I'm so glad to meet you. You're the new youth minister?"

I shook her hand gently. "Yes, ma'am."

"I'm Liz."

"Liz is my oldest child," Miss Ina said to me as we made our way inside. She gestured to a young man seated at the table and two toddlers on a blanket on the rough wooden floor. "This is Todd, Liz's husband." Todd stood and shook my hand. "And these little rascals are Hope and Grace, their twin girls."

"They're really cute." Kids this small were a bit out of my comfort zone. The girls were cute, though.

Miss Ina shooed her husband, Todd, Pete, and me onto the front deck while she and Liz watched the kids and finished lunch. My first impression had been right—the view was breathtaking. The mountains rolled out before me in an undulating vista of smoky blue. Sometimes I'd wondered why people would choose to live so far out in the country. This was why.

"This place is incredible," I said sincerely. "How do you ever get anything done when you can just sit here and look at this?"

"My great-granddaddy knew what he was doing," Pete Senior said with a strong Tennessee mountain twang. He took out a pipe and lit it. "He built this house with his own hands, more than a hundred years ago. Couldn't 'a been easy. Lugged all these logs in here by mule. And take a look at these beams and supports. Ain't nobody does work like this anymore."

We went down a flight of stairs from the deck to the ground, and I took a closer look. These logs were hand-hewn, notched, and nestled together so that no nails were used. The supports were more pine logs, carefully leveled to hold firm against the mountain storms, which I heard could be considerable.

"Amazing." I touched the outside wall admiringly. "This is craftsmanship, all right." After building the Nome church, I had a true appreciation for the skill and time this cabin had taken. And when we went back up to the deck, Pete Senior pointed out the deck chairs. They too were hand-built and melded together with no hardware.

One chair looked special. It sat off by itself, at the corner of the deck. It had comfortable looking, well-worn cushions. A handcrafted ottoman sat before it.

"Who uses that one?" I asked.

"That's Ina's prayer chair."

"Prayer chair?"

"Yeah." Pete Senior drew on his pipe. Unsatisfied, he relit it and drew it again. "People're always asking her to pray for this, that, and t'other. She spends two solid hours every day in that chair, talking to God. Sometimes she even skips meals."

"She prays for everyone who asks her to?"

"Not ever' body. Some things she won't waste the Lord's time on."

"How does she know what to pray for and what not to?"

"She just knows. She and the Lord understand each other pretty well. People ask her to pray for them because they say when she asks, God listens."

*　　*　　*

We lounged and looked out over the mountains in companionable silence. Inside the open screen door, the women chattered as they cooked. The toddlers clattered their toys and chortled. Pete sat on the steps with a pine straw between his teeth and watched. I was coming to understand that this was his manner. He was always watchful but seldom participated. I'd bet he had a lot to share, though. Mountain people always did.

I was still thinking about Miss Ina and her prayer chair. I'd heard of prayer warriors. My mother's sister, Sandra, was one.

When you ask a prayer warrior to pray for you, he or she doesn't take it lightly. If they say they will, they really do. And they usually seem to have a more direct line to God than other people do. It's a gift. Prayer warriors seem to get their prayers answered, so people ask them to pray for them. A lot. I was intrigued and wanted to spend some time talking with Miss Ina about this.

Looking around, I saw something I hadn't noticed before. Sitting against the front wall of this treasure of a cabin were two rifles, a .22 and a .270. The .270 looked as old as the cabin itself. Like everything else here, it was ancient but beautiful and looked well-used. It was just like the one my grandfather had used to teach me to shoot when I was about ten years old. Memories raced through my mind of my grandfather taking me out in the woods hunting. He taught me to shoot game in the head and not damage the meat. We brought home mess after mess of squirrels for my grandmother to cook, always shot straight through the eyes. Jack Barker and I had used a newer version of this gun to shoot ptarmigans in Alaska. Like the squirrels, the shot had to be precise; otherwise, we'd just get a bunch of feathers.

As I gazed at it, Pete reached over, picked up the .270 and started cleaning its already glossy stock.

"That's a beauty," I said.

"It belonged to my great-granddaddy, the same one that built this place," said Pete. "It's mine now. Still shoots just like it did back in the day. Straight as an arrow. We don't use it much, though. Usually use that one." He gestured at the .22. "That's Dad's."

"What do you use it for?" I asked Pete Senior.

"Target practicin' and varmint killin'."

"What kind of varmints?"

"Coyotes. Come right up and eat our chickens. Ina hates 'em. All the farmers do."

"Mind if I give it a try?"

"Sure."

Pete Senior went inside and fetched a box of shells. The .22 held thirteen rounds, and we took turns picking off cans stacked on a rock at the edge of the yard. The whole time, Pete sat and cleaned the .270, never even looking up.

Then I saw a movement at the edge of a clearing at the bottom of the hill, and I focused on it. My eyes narrowed. Not taking my eyes off the movement, I asked, "Does anybody around here have a big gray dog?"

"Nope. Why?"

"What's the .270 sighted for?" I asked Pete.

"A hundred yards."

"Can you hand me a round and sight it for one-fifty?"

"Sure."

Wordlessly he adjusted the sight, then handed me the gun and a shell. As I lifted the priceless old gun to my shoulder, I sent a prayer of thanks heavenward for the wonderful old man who'd been my grandfather and for my experiences in Alaska. Both were about to come in very handy, and might just save some chickens.

In a seamless move, I chambered the round and brought the gun to scope level. Then I could clearly see my quarry. It seemed to realize it was in danger and sprinted away. I tracked it across the clearing and pulled the trigger. A large coyote dropped in its tracks, just before it entered the woods.

All the men stared. Pete Senior found his voice first.

"Well, goll-darn it. Didn't even see that thing sitting there. If that's the one that's been eating Ina's chickens, she's going to be real happy."

"I saw it sitting there but I thought it was out of range." Todd shook his head. "Good shooting, Mark."

"Thanks." I handed the old gun back to Pete just as Miss Ina called us to lunch.

*   *   *

"Dangedest thing I ever saw." Pete Senior sat down at his place at the table while Liz brought platters of long, juicy ears of corn, crispy fried okra, sliced tomatoes, tender cabbage, thick gravy, and steaming biscuits to the table. "One minute old mister coyote is planning his next raid on our henhouse, the next he's dead as a doornail. Never knew what hit him. Your chickens're safe now, Ina."

"I'm so glad." Miss Ina came to the sink where I was standing, washing my hands, and hugged me around the waist. The top of her head came to just under my chin. "Thank you, Mark." She went back to the counter and resumed ladling stew into bowls. When she finished, she placed the bowls in front of us, then took her place at the opposite end from her husband. "Would you pray?"

Pete Senior asked the Lord's blessing on the food, and we all dug in. I'd grown up in Tennessee and was used to country cooking, but this food was at a whole new level. "Miss Ina, did you grow these vegetables yourself?" I asked.

"We sure did. Got a garden right down the hill. We'll be bringing in vegetables on into the fall. Then we can them and put them up for the winter. We'll sell them at the market too. Nothing like fresh vegetables."

"These are terrific." I ate with gusto. "What kind of stew is this?"

"That's from a possum Pete brought in yesterday. He slow-cooked it all night so it'd be nice and tender."

"Brought in?"

"From the road. Pete's always bringing me things for the table. Long as they're still warm and haven't been run over too bad, they're just fine."

"And what's this gravy?"

"Squirrel. My husband shot it early this morning."

I was conscious of Pete grinning and everyone watching me to see how I'd react to this, but after a steady diet of ptarmigan, arctic hare, walrus, and whale blubber, my stomach wasn't going to rebel at possum road kill or squirrel gravy. The stew was actually very tasty. Besides the possum meat, it had potatoes, onions, carrots, corn, tomatoes, cabbage, and squash. I kept shoveling it in. "Tastes just fine to me. You definitely got the taste of rancid seal oil out of my mouth."

As we ate and talked, I learned about the Gambrells and they learned about me. Todd worked construction for a company in Maryville. Pete Senior had worked at the Alcoa aluminum plant for thirty years before retiring last year. Liz sometimes substitute taught in the elementary school, but she'd reduced her work time when the girls were born. Miss Ina spent her time here at the house, taking care of her chickens and putting up vegetables, and praying. Pete Senior had been wrong when he said she spent two hours a day in her prayer chair. Lots of times it was even longer than that.

"That's incredible." I slathered a hot biscuit with fresh honey from the bees Miss Ina kept at the edge of her garden. "I've heard of prayer warriors. My Aunt Sandra is one. She and her husband fasted off and on and prayed for me the entire time I was in Alaska. It worked too. The Lord saved my life at least three different times while I was there."

"He'll do that." Miss Ina measured everyone's tea glasses with eagle eyes and then, apparently satisfied, looked back at me. "Like you said, He just wasn't finished with you yet."

"That's what I think."

The meal wound down, and Liz rose and began to gather the dishes. Miss Ina started to get up and help, and Liz said, "No, Mom, I've got this." She gave her mother a meaningful look.

Miss Ina sighed. "Thank you, Liz. Mark, would you walk outside with me for a minute? I want to show you something."

"Sure." We got up and walked outside into the hot sunshine. The mountains were a little cooler than the city, but it was still hot. "What did you want to show me, Miss Ina?"

Safely away from the house, she turned and looked at me with eyes filled with pain and a sheen of tears. "It's not so much something I want to show you, as something I want to ask you."

"Anything."

"I'm so worried about Pete."

"Pete? Your son?"

"Yes." She gave a watery laugh. "I know it's confusing, having a Pete and a Pete Senior. It's my son I'm worried about."

"Why are you worried? What can I do?"

"I'm worried about his salvation." She paused, and I waited. "With Liz it was so easy. All her life, she's loved the church. She accepted Jesus when she was just seven years old, and I've never had a reason to worry. I know her eternal soul is safe."

"But Pete?"

"There's just something about him that seems to resist the Lord. He goes with us to church, but it's almost like he's immune to the Gospel."

I sure hoped not. I'd had some experience with that in Alaska, with Robert Wallace, and it was the most painful thing I'd ever been through. "Why do you think that?"

"You've been around him. What do you think?"

"I think he's young and searching. Some people just need more time to search and find out on their own."

"Will you help him find the answers? Will you pray for him?"

"Of course I will. Does he come to youth group?"

"He's too old."

"I'm the youth minister, and he's only too old if I say he's too old. Pete is welcome anytime. He can help me." I was already thinking about youth and discipline, and knew that Pete could be very helpful.

11

For the next three weeks, before the Myrtle Beach youth trip, I got used to my new life. I added another job when Emmett Vaughn Lumber Company, where I'd worked as bookkeeper before I left for Alaska, heard I was back and called to see if I'd come work for them when I wasn't in class. Sure, I said. More money in my pocket. It was just a matter of time management, right? Morning classes and afternoon work.

I spent my weeks in Knoxville, either getting to know Bob, Kenny, and Brandon or working at the lumber company. Weekends were devoted to my Pleasant Grove job. Youth activities and Bible studies were on Saturdays, and church and youth group meetings filled my Sundays.

Miss Ina's inviting me to Sunday lunch had started a good-natured war. When people found out that I was free all afternoon between church and youth group, they lined up to invite me to eat with them after church. My lunches were scheduled through September.

These were invaluable opportunities to get to know the families of Pleasant Grove, but I also managed to make myself useful. Some of these ladies were either elderly widows or single moms. In those cases, I made a point to look around the house and help in any way I could. Maybe a step was uneven or broken, or maybe an appliance didn't work just right. Thanks to my dad, I could usually figure out how to tackle any small household task.

The Pleasant Grove community was an unusual blend. Most

were locals, but there were some who traveled from nearby Knoxville, which is a good-sized city. A large number were from smaller towns, such as Maryville, Alcoa, Walland, and Townsend. Those people worked either in Knoxville or at smaller businesses closer to home. Plenty of people worked farms and some were genuine mountaineers. The farmers grew and sold produce, soybeans, cotton, and grain. The mountaineers shot, trapped, and fished for most of their food. They also grew and sold produce, tanned hides, and did woodworking for cash and in trade. I could relate. It was, in a way, like the subsistence ways of Alaska. These people stuck together, I learned. You mess with one, you mess with them all.

I also watched Robert and Martha Galyon and began making mental notes on how I wanted to run this youth group. About twelve kids attended regularly, in grades seven through twelve. One was the Galyons' daughter, Angie, who was drop-dead gorgeous with thick blond hair and hazel eyes. She had to know how pretty she was, but she had a humility and maturity that was unusual for girls her age. Their son, Travis, was a little too young for youth group but attended anyway because his parents and sister were there. Robert was quiet and capable, while the two women of the family were outgoing and gregarious.

Travis seemed as if he weren't quite sure where he fit in this family of strong personalities. My heart ached a little for him as I watched him try to find his way. Before long, I began arriving early enough to throw a football with him in the backyard while his parents prepared food and the older kids milled around waiting to be fed. Travis looked unsure at first, as if he didn't know what to think. I treated him like part of the youth group, and soon he began to accept my presence. And, although I didn't know it at the time, this helped me gain his parents' trust and confidence.

The younger kids of the church were served through a choir program led by Greg Wilson, a new music minister my age who was hired the same time I was. Jimmy, Jonathan, and John-John were always there, along with four other boys and five girls. Some younger girls began coming after the first week, and they looked at me in a moony-eyed way that let me know they didn't have Scriptures on their minds. The new youth minister, evidently, was fresh meat.

As far as I could tell, the Galyons ran this ministry like a social group, which was fine in the beginning, but now it was time for more. Saturday gatherings were always at their house, and the Scripture lessons were pretty elementary. I knew firsthand how impactful a good youth group could be, and I saw this as a real opportunity to make a difference in these young lives. As soon as we got back from Myrtle Beach, I told myself, I would begin to take the reins.

* * *

All of us have pivotal times in our lives, times upon which the rest of our lives turn in one way or another. That Myrtle Beach trip would change my life forever.

We left on Thursday, July 17, a group of seventeen in a caravan of cars, vans, and trucks. We looked like exactly what we were, a bunch of country folks headed to the beach. All the moms had pressed food upon us—sandwiches, fried chicken, chips, and such—and we didn't have to stop at all for meals. The trip was more than four hundred miles and took about seven hours. So as to spend time with more people, I hopped around among cars that had extra seats when we stopped for gas and restroom breaks.

We arrived on Thursday afternoon and spent an hour checking in, unpacking, and getting settled. I shared a room with Pete, Jimmy, and Jonathan. There were two double beds, but in the manner of all males over ten years old, none of us shared a bed. Seniority ruled. I got one bed, Pete got the other, and Jimmy and Jonathan occupied the floor.

We spent Thursday night and Friday on the beach. The boys were all hard muscle from farm work, and they had true farmers' tans—mahogany-dark arms and ivory-white upper arms, chests, and backs. They were a step ahead of me, because after a year in Alaska,

I had no base tan anywhere. After a day in the water and on the beach, our white parts were all lobster red. Martha was well prepared with bottles and bottles of green aloe goo, and we slathered it on ourselves after our showers Friday night.

Myrtle Beach is one of the vacation capitals of the South. The area stretches for about fifty miles and includes Murrells Inlet, Garden City, Surfside Beach, Myrtle Beach, and North Myrtle Beach. The Myrtle Beach area is more than just a beach. Even back then it had amusement parks, shops, putt-putt courses, carnival games, teen dance clubs, and anything else a teenager might like to do. On Saturday, we all traipsed from our hotel to the downtown area and scattered, with instructions to meet at six o'clock for supper. The area isn't that big, so our paths crisscrossed throughout the day.

About three o'clock, some older boys and I happened upon an area near the ocean where people were trying their luck on a mechanical bull. The movie *Urban Cowboy* had just come out, causing a wave of interest in mechanical bull riding. A sign declared that if you could stay on the bull for eight seconds or longer, you got a free t-shirt. We stood and watched for several minutes as person after person got on the bull, and person after person was thrown off after just a couple of seconds.

I studied the contraption. It didn't look that hard. The sign offering the t-shirt listed basic instructions and a diagram of how it should be done. Hold the padded strap with your non-dominant hand and use your dominant hand for balance. Move your legs forward and squeeze with your lower body, relaxing your upper body. Keep your eyes on the bull's head for clues as to directional changes. Lean back when the bull's head moves down and forward when its head moves upward. And, if you are concerned at any time, say stop.

As I stood reading the sign and critiquing all the riders, Robert Galyon came up behind me and nudged my shoulder. "You should try it," he said encouragingly.

"I was thinking about it."

"You're an athlete. How hard can it be? All you have to do is stay on for eight seconds. These kids would be so impressed if you beat that bull."

That did it. In a snap, I ignored the little warning voice in my brain and made up my mind. "I think I will. It looks like fun."

Motivated to impress the kids, and with too much pride and confidence in my own athleticism, I paid my money and filled out forms—including one that said I wouldn't sue if I got seriously hurt. The word spread and members of the youth group came running to watch. I settled on the bull, clamped my legs tight, wrapped my left hand snugly underneath the padded strap, and nodded to the operator. The bull began to move, slowly at first, and I couldn't see what the big deal was. It was just a matter of physics. After a couple of seconds it began to move faster and buck harder, and I had to concentrate more. Eight seconds suddenly seemed like a long time, but they passed and I was still on.

The operator yelled, "The record for this bull is forty-five seconds! Do you want to keep going?" I nodded, not taking my eyes off the bull.

Robert continually shouted encouragement. "Hang on! Hang on! Beat that thing!" The kids fed off him and screamed their heads off, urging me on. And so, spurred on by their adulation, I stayed on . . . and stayed on. . . and stayed on. Forty-five seconds came and went. The bull bucked harder and faster. I clamped down and hung on for over a minute. My back twisted and my rear end banged into the bull, but it was bearable. Finally the operator slowed it down and let me off.

At first I couldn't tell that anything was seriously wrong. My back was sore and stiff, but that made perfect sense. I'd just done something I'd never done before. Of course my muscles would be sore. At supper, the pain got worse, but I just needed to lie down I thought. But when I finally got back to my room and was able to do that, my lower back literally froze in place. When I tried to move, it caused such excruciating agony that I screamed. And I am not a screamer.

Frightened, Pete ran for Robert and Martha, who came immediately. The looks on their faces quickly turned from concern to terror when they saw how much pain I was in. Then followed a trip to the emergency room and a series of x-rays that showed nothing wrong. The doctor said I'd strained my back muscles and released me with some pain pills. I gobbled them, but they didn't make much of a dent in the excruciating spasms.

I spent the next day on a lounge chair on the beach, in incredible pain but trying to enjoy our last day. The seven hours back to Maryville on Monday were the most agonizing of my life. I lay, humiliated, on the back seat of a truck, tears streaming down my face, trying not to shriek every time we hit a bump.

I had left my car at the church but was in no condition to drive, so late that day we pulled into my parents' driveway. Martha had alerted my parents, and they came running out to the car. Robert and my dad carefully helped me out of the truck and into the house.

"I'm so sorry," Robert kept saying. "I'm so sorry. I feel like I'm responsible for this." My mother, fussing over me and getting me settled, got a steely-eyed "mom" look on her face. I wanted to tell Robert he'd best hush, but he kept on. "I'm the one who encouraged him to do it. If I hadn't, he might not have stayed on so long."

My mom, I could tell, was too angry and upset to talk. My dad said, "Mark loves a challenge. He would have stayed on until they had to pry his cold, dead fingers from that bull. We'll get him to a doctor tomorrow."

"Will you let us know what he says?" Martha asked.

"Of course we will."

12

Four days later, my parents and I sat in the office of one of the best neurosurgeons in Knoxville. They'd taken me to my family doctor, who'd referred me to an orthopedist, who'd referred me to Dr. Bill Reed, who'd ordered an MRI. Now we sat in his examining room, getting the bad news.

"Have you ever been told you have degenerative disc disease?" Dr. Reed asked me.

"No."

"It's partially because of that pre-existing condition that the bull ride affected you like it did. You have what we call a compression injury." Dr. Reed showed us some pictures from the MRI and pointed to a spot. "You have some bulging and slight herniation in one of your discs. I'd say from your symptoms that you've also probably got a disc that's partially severed, but that wouldn't show up on an MRI until it actually splits open."

"What does that mean?" my mother asked.

"For now, it means medication and rest. The bulging could calm down and move back into place."

"How long will that take?" my dad wanted to know.

"It could take up to three months. And your athletic days, I'm sorry to say, are over. No tennis, no running, no lifting. Nothing that puts strain on your lower back. With injuries like this, added compression could be devastating."

"How about the severed disc?"

"There's nothing we can do about that until it gets worse. Then we'll be able to see for sure what's wrong. And that could take a long time. Years."

"Years?" I spoke for the first time. There was no way I could stand this pain for years. "There has to be something we can do."

"Like I said, medication and rest."

"When do you want to see me again?"

"Do you have any pain in your legs?"

"No."

"Can you walk?"

"Yes."

"Come back when you're crawling. That will mean the disc has snapped. For now, go back to your orthopedist and get some good painkillers."

*   *   *

And so a new era in my life began. Always an athlete, I slowly began to adjust to the reality that I wasn't one any longer. I lived at home for a couple of weeks and indulged in a massive pity party. I spent hours in prayer, pleading with God to take this pain away. There was no answer.

Early one morning I was sitting at the kitchen table after a horrible, pain-filled night, feeling sorry for myself. I was about to start on a new life and a new ministry, one I felt strongly that I'd been called for. Then why? Why did this happen to me? And why wouldn't God help me now?

My dad came in and sat down across from me. "Bad night?"

"The worst."

"Tell me."

"I can't find any position that doesn't hurt. Even the painkillers barely take the edge off."

"I know how that feels. Remember, I had back surgery a few years ago. But you've got something else on your mind, other than the pain. Don't you?"

I looked my dad in the face. "I'm wondering why this had to

happen to me. I'm a good person, aren't I? I'm praying and praying, and it's like my prayers stop at the ceiling. I don't feel as if I'm getting through. I'm certainly getting no comfort."

"And you're angry at God."

"A little, yes. It's more like I'm hurt and confused. Why did He let this happen? All I want to do is serve Him."

My dad leaned forward and folded his hands together on the table. "Son, I've been praying for you too, and I'll keep praying. But sometimes the answer is just no."

"But why?"

"Because God gave us good brains, and He expects us to use them. Bad things sometimes happen to good people, but this isn't even one of those times. You had clear and complete control over what happened to you, but you let your pride lead you right down the wrong path. You said you had to sign a waiver before you rode that bull."

I remembered the forms I'd hurriedly scrawled my name on before I entered that ring, and sighed. "Yes."

"Exactly what did it say?"

"That riding a mechanical bull could cause serious injury or death, and I wouldn't sue if that happened to me." I looked at him imploringly. "Those kids were looking at me, and Robert was challenging me, and I just made a snap decision."

Dad nodded. "Your pride got the better of you. Here's a good rule of thumb. If you have to sign a form like that, you probably don't want to do it."

I knew he was right but resisted. "Everyone else was doing it, and none of them were getting hurt."

"How long did they stay on?"

"A few seconds."

"And how long did you stay on?"

I sighed again. "Over a minute. I set the record." That statement, even to my own ears, sounded empty and prideful.

"I bet none of those other people have degenerative disc disease."

"But Dad, I didn't know I had it. If I'd known, I definitely wouldn't have done it."

"Did you feel any kind of warning before you got on that thing?"

I remembered the feeling I'd had right before I'd made the decision, the little voice in my head that I'd ignored. "I guess I did. It sounded a little like Mom."

"That was the Holy Spirit telling you not to do it. That was your chance to not go through what you're going through now."

"So now what?"

"Now, we deal with it. As for the Lord not listening to your prayers, you're wrong. He absolutely is, but you're not the first person to feel that way. We've all felt it. Look back through the Bible. You see it over and over again. You're not alone.

"You have to be ready for the very real possibility that the answer to your prayers may be no. This may be something you have to deal with and make something good out of it. The apostle Paul had an affliction, something he dealt with every day of his life. Some people think it was back pain, but we really don't know. He prayed to be delivered from it, and finally God told him in essence that he might as well save his breath."

"I don't remember that."

My dad pulled out his Bible and flipped to the book of 2 Corinthians. "Look at chapter 12, verses 7-10."

I read it silently, then aloud. "Because of the surpassing greatness of the revelations, for this reason, to keep me from exalting myself, there was given me a thorn in the flesh, a messenger of Satan to torment me—to keep me from exalting myself! Concerning this I implored the Lord three times that it might leave me. And He has said to me, 'My grace is sufficient for you, for power is perfected in weakness.' Most gladly, therefore, I will rather boast about my weaknesses, so that the power of Christ may dwell in me. Therefore I am well content with weaknesses, with insults, with distresses, with persecutions, with difficulties, for Christ's sake; for when I am weak, I am strong." I looked up at my dad. "So weakness can actually be a good thing."

"It's something you can use for the glory of God, either now or in the future. I can guarantee you that if you let Him use it, He will."

I sighed yet again. "This is not what I wanted to hear. I'm still going to pray about this, and I know someone else I'm going to ask to pray for me too."

"Your mom and I will be praying right along with you."

*　　*　　*

The next time I was at Pleasant Grove I sought out Miss Ina. She, of course, knew all about my situation from Pete. I asked her to pray for me.

"Of course I will. What, specifically, do you want me to pray for?"

"That my back will be healed."

"Why?"

I thought about it. Why? The answer seemed simple. "So I can do my job."

"Does your back need to be healed for you to be able to do your job?"

I hedged. "It would make it a lot easier."

She looked at me knowingly. "The good Lord knows what's best, Mark. I heard all about how you got hurt, and I suspect your pride got the better of you. The devil whispered in your ear, and you listened. God had no part in your decision to get on that bull, did He?"

"No, ma'am." I hesitated, then added honestly, "Something inside me told me not to. I didn't listen."

"I'll pray for you, Mark, but my prayer will be that the Lord will help you deal with your suffering and that He'll use it for good in your life."

For the next few days I thought about what my dad and Miss Ina had said. It reminded me a lot of something Will West had told me after my experience in the arctic blizzard on top of Anvil

Mountain. He'd said God expects us to use our brains, and it's unusual for Him to spare us the consequences for our actions. Generally He lets us live with what we've done. He uses it for good in our lives if we let Him, but He doesn't spare us. So, I slowly began to accept that this was life now. I didn't stop praying about it, but I began to live with it.

Everywhere I went, I carried a chair that reclined because I couldn't stand to sit down. When I had to drive, I put a small pillow behind my back. So many little things I now discovered I could not do. And the doctor was right about running. When I had to move quickly, I walked fast because running was agony. When I had to bend over, I squatted instead. With the ever-present pain, solid hours of sleep became a distant memory. I learned to survive on about two or three hours of fitful sleep a night. It was embarrassing to live in the body of an athlete, but move like an eighty-year-old man. And the best doctors could do nothing.

I moved back to the BSU in time for school to start. My decision to bring only a mattress turned out to be a good one because the solid floor gave my back more support than a bed with box springs would have.

Robert Galyon was devastated. He felt so bad that he had egged me on like he had. It wasn't like him at all. But I assured him it wasn't his fault. I was too proud, trying to fit in with the kids and not listening to the right voices. Now I could blame no one but myself.

Pleasant Grove gave me time to recover. I continued to attend all youth events and meetings, contribute, and form my own ideas about how I wanted to do things, and I set August 31 as the date when I would formally take over.

13

My twenty-first birthday came and went. One Saturday after youth group, about two weeks after my accident, Pete and I stood by our cars, outside the Galyons' house. This shared experience had brought us closer, and I had found in this quiet young man someone I believed could be a true friend. His character went much deeper than the road kill scooper I'd first met.

"How you doin', man?" he asked in his usual direct way.

"Making it."

He gave me a look. "How you really doin'?"

I sighed, as I'd been doing a lot lately. "Not good. Awful, really. Everything was going so well, and now my whole life is different. It hurts all the time, and I can't even think about being like this for years."

"That stinks."

"Yeah." We stared at the sky in companionable silence. "Know what I miss the most?"

"What?"

"Fishing."

"Fishing?"

"Yeah. I used to get my dad's truck and boat and go out whenever I wanted to, but he's preaching revivals all summer and there's no way I can handle the boat by myself. I have a canoe, but I can't even manage that by myself. I miss just being out on the water."

"Well, heck, you can go fishin' with me anytime. You don't have to do nothin' but sit there."

"Seriously?"

"Sure. How 'bout tomorrow after lunch?"

"Will you let me pay for gas and bait?"

"No need. We'll just slip a boat in the river, and I'll catch us some lizards."

The next day, and every day for the coming week, Pete and I were out on the river. We caught lizards, dug for night crawlers in the rich mountain soil around his house, and ate Miss Ina's mayonnaise sandwiches while floating down the river and catching fish after fish. River fishing was new to me, and I found that I loved it. Slowly Pete's companionship and the time on the water began to heal my aching spirit.

I learned more than I ever could have otherwise about Pete and the mountain culture. In ways, it was very close to the subsistence system used by the natives in Alaska. Every part of everything Eskimos caught was used in some way. Big catches, like whales and walrus, were celebrated. The mountain folk were similar.

Although Pete was quiet and had no formal job, I was quickly impressed with his work ethic. He worked as hard as anyone I'd ever known. When he fished, there was no catch and release. His catch went either to his family's table or to the market. He shared some with me every time, and I filleted the fish and put them in the freezer at the BSU for the times I had to cook.

Whenever Pete saw an animal dead in the road, he stopped and inspected it. If it were warm and unsquished, it went into his truck and, subsequently, his mother's supper pot. When he hunted, it wasn't for sport. The squirrels and other critters he killed served not only as food, but their pelts also kept his family warm or brought in money for other essentials. The coyote I'd shot was a much bigger deal than I'd realized at the time. I wished now that I'd gone down the hill and fetched the carcass. The Gambrells could have used the money.

Pete had learned woodworking in the tradition of the generations before him. His wooden creations were as good as anything in any furniture store. He, like the others in this area, used the fruits of his labor for barter.

As we spent day after day together, Pete at first looked at me as if wondering when the "God pitch" was going to come. I could only imagine how much time his mother spent talking to him about his salvation. But I said nothing, valuing this door of friendship, sincerely enjoying our time together, and hoping that the Lord would somehow use me. Soon he began to relax, and we both began to open up. I told him about some of my experiences in Alaska, and how the Lord had been at work there.

This part of the river was mirror-smooth at the end of the day. The sun dipped behind the trees, making multi-colored ribbons in the sky and on the water. Pete looked pensive. "You really believe all that stuff?"

"Absolutely, beyond any doubt."

"I don't."

"Why?"

"I've seen too many bad things happen. It just doesn't make any sense how any God who cares about us would let stuff that like that happen. The things I heard in school make a lot more sense. There was a big bang, and everything since then has just happened. Then when we die, that's it."

"A lot of people think that."

"But not you."

"No."

"Why?"

How to explain something I simply knew and felt down deep inside? God had reached out and grabbed my heart when I was ten years old, and my spirit had caught fire at a youth retreat when I was a little younger than Pete. He had had a good, Christian upbringing, the same as I had. His mom was a prayer warrior, for crying out loud. Faith just had not taken root in him, at least not yet. I thought hard before I answered.

"I could give you all kinds of scientific answers, Pete, but it really comes down to faith and if you believe Someone put us here, or that it all somehow cosmically came together in one big accident." I reached into the bait cup and pulled out a night crawler. "Look at this fella. He's so little, but so complex. We dissected these in biology in high school." I deftly threaded the worm onto my hook and tossed it near the bank. The line jerked almost instantly.

"Yeah, we did too."

"Remember how complicated they are inside?" I reeled in a good-sized, indignant large-mouthed bass. He panted in the bottom of the boat and glared at us. I removed the hook from his mouth and slid him onto the stringer hanging in the water beside the boat. "And think about ants, and ladybugs, and birds. Even blades of grass. And it all works together perfectly. How can you look at all of that and think it was an accident? The only thing that makes sense to me is that Someone who knew exactly what He was doing made it all."

"In school they teach evolution."

"That's just a theory. No one knows all the answers. As I said, it comes down to faith. I just know it in here." I tapped my heart.

"If there's a God, He let you get hurt. Aren't you mad at Him?"

"No, I got hurt all on my own. You were there; you saw it. God actually tried to tell me not to get on that bull, and I didn't listen."

He discarded that notion almost immediately; I could see it in his eyes. "He could heal you."

"Why? I have a perfectly good brain. He saved my life three times in Alaska, and two of those times were when I did something stupid. This time, I have to deal with the consequences. I can't blame Him at all."

"I wish I could be so sure. But I just don't feel it like you do. And, I figure that if I'm wrong, I've been good enough that I'll get into heaven anyway."

"Pete, there's only one way to heaven, and that's Jesus. No one gets there without believing in Him. And I didn't feel it like this until I was eighteen. Maybe one day you will too."

"I doubt it."

We fell silent until almost dark, then began catching bass one after another, and there was no time for talk.

14

In the two days before classes began, my other three housemates
showed up. Vernon Douglas, who would be living in the room next
to mine, moved in without a ripple. I was in my room one afternoon, trying to get comfortable on my mattress, when suddenly a
boy about my size, but bulkier, stood in the door. He had blazing
red hair, a red mustache, and alert brown eyes. His muscled arms
and legs were covered with red hairs that were sun-bleached orange.
He wore baggy gym shorts and a tattered t-shirt that said North
Carolina State Football and had sweat rings under the armpits. "Hi,"
he said, and stuck out his hand. "I'm Vernon."

I got painfully to my feet and shook his hand. "I'm Mark. Good
to meet you."

"You from here?"

"Grew up about an hour down the road and lived in Maryville
ever since. You?"

"The North Carolina high country. Ever heard of Boone?"

"My church youth group went skiing there one year," I said.
Pretty place."

"Yeah, it is."

"What year are you?"

"Junior. I lived in the dorms my first two years."

"Me too. The BSU is a lot better."

"I'll say."

We spent the next few minutes talking companionably about life

73

at the BSU. I told him how everyone would take turns cooking meals for the whole group. There were no janitors here, so we had to clean the place ourselves, including the kitchen and the bathrooms in the public area. This was especially important because when people walked through our door, we wanted them to feel comfortable and at home. A stinky toilet was a complete turnoff.

"What kind of ministries do we do?" Vernon asked.

"I'm not sure yet, but I think we'll all stay pretty busy. I mean, look where we are, right across from fraternity row. That's a big opportunity. We can support each other and teach new Christians and come up with new and exciting stuff to bring people in … sorry, I get carried away sometimes."

"No, keep going! That's all good stuff."

"I guess we'll find out some details at the first Executive Council meeting. We'll all have jobs. We have to be elected, but I think that whatever Bob thinks we'd be good at is generally what we get. He wants to nominate me for the mission job. A girl named Wanda was president last year, so I guess she'll do it again this year. She's a senior."

Vernon and I had a lot of time the next day or so to get to know each other. I helped him unpack and showed him around, and we talked nonstop. He was an education major and wanted to coach and teach high school physical education. He had a quiet, steady, but confident and authoritative way about him that I believed would inspire respect in the kids he taught and coached.

Vernon had been a high school quarterback and could have played for a small college if he'd wanted to. But when he tallied up the prices, even with the football scholarships he'd been offered, the University of Tennessee was cheaper.

When Vernon found out about my injury, he instantly became my personal fitness trainer. "Just because you're hurt, doesn't mean you can't stay in shape," he asserted. "We'll strengthen the rest of your body so you can get back to doing at least some of the things you did before." That sounded great to me. I was eager to get back to some semblance of the life I'd known before.

The girls arrived the day before school. Wanda Wells had just finished a summer job in her home town. She blew into the BSU like a small tornado, bustling about and giving people tasks in advance of the Executive Council meeting, which would be the next week. Soft and plump, she was a few inches shorter than me. Her light brown hair frizzed about her damp face and her blue eyes snapped as she whizzed from place to place.

Susan Bryant, a junior like Vernon and me, was brunette, petite, and sweet. She had a quiet understanding in her dark brown eyes that would be a perfect foil for Wanda's vivaciousness. She went unobtrusively about getting her room set up and organizing a schedule for chores and kitchen duty. By the end of her first day, we all knew when we had to cook and clean.

That first week, before classes started, there was way too much time for mischief. Summer was now over, and kids swarmed the campus. Kenny, the practical joker, went into overdrive with so many new victims around, and Brandon and I were his eager accomplices. Vernon could take a joke but didn't like to dish them out. The fraternity directly across the street from us was perfect fodder, especially in the evenings when young girls sashayed down the street for parties, dressed in their high-heeled finest.

Every old house, especially one inhabited by several young people, is prone to vermin, and the BSU was no exception. One day Kenny found a rat in a trap in the kitchen and came up with a brilliant idea. He tied a strong string to the dead rat's tail and went up on the flat roof, with Brandon and me on his heels. Eyes fastened across the street, he began to whirl the rat over his head like an African native would have done.

When I saw what he was about to do, I stopped him. "Hold on, man, let's do this right." And I went to my room and came back with a strong fishing rod and a big bass hook. I tied the hook onto the rod, with both my housemates looking on with delighted comprehension, and set it securely in the rat's rump. "Now give her a toss."

Kenny threw the rat as far as he could, the fishing line whirring.

The rodent bounced to a stop on the sidewalk across the street, just on the other side of a row of parallel-parked cars. It sat innocently on the dark sidewalk until several girls approached, chattering to each other and not even looking where they were going. Just as they got close to the rat, Kenny gave the line a twitch. The result was a cacophony of shrieks and scattering coeds that had Brandon and me hysterically collapsing out of sight on the roof. Kenny, muffling his own hilarity, hastily reeled the rat to a safe location on our side of the cars, out of the girls' sight. But by then they were long gone, having scurried into the fraternity house. By the time the boys burst out the door, the rat was safely into the bushes beside the BSU and the three of us were rolling around on the roof, holding our sides. That rat was used so much that he eventually fell apart and we hit on the idea of using a rubber rat that I had in my tackle box, which served just as well and lasted much longer.

The fraternity boys quickly caught on to what we were doing, and at first they were a little surprised that the goody-two-shoes Baptists across the street knew how to have fun. There evolved a good-natured competition of whose prank was best.

Kenny and Brandon climbed a big tree in front of the BSU and threw nuts at people, then hid behind the branches. That tree was also a good vantage point for watching the sunbathing girls on the BSU's roof. They shot peas through straws at the frat boys and howled at them looking wildly about to see where the barrage was coming from. Those pranks weren't for me; I was in no shape to climb a tree.

One contest with the frat boys required stealthy feet and focused awareness. We sneaked up to their house and, if our luck held, inside and up to their bedrooms. If any of them came to their room and found one of us sitting on their beds, we won. If we found any of them on our beds, they won. After a couple of days everyone in both houses grew to know everyone else, and sentries were posted to identify and apprehend intruders. Winning grew more and more difficult, but we were very good.

Brandon stepped the game up a notch when he filched one fraternity boy's car keys and sneaked back to the BSU undetected. The girls were horrified, but Kenny and I thought Brandon was a genius—until we found out that the boy had to go to a family member's funeral and couldn't find his keys. Brandon, contrite, went to the frat house the next day, keys in hand, and confessed. We called a truce after that.

Surprisingly, the prank competition turned into a kind of weird ministry, because it opened a door between the BSU and the fraternity that wouldn't have been there otherwise. I learned that anything, absolutely anything, can be useful to the Lord.

15

As the time for the EC meeting grew closer, I became more and more excited. Ministry opportunities were everywhere. All of us had our strengths, and together we could do amazing things. Wanda had given us tasks based on our expected roles, and I had already jumped into action. When she called the meeting to order, I sat eagerly with my report on my lap. The six residents, plus Bob and two at-large members that Wanda had picked because the by-laws required it, were there.

The first order of business was to elect officers and committee chairs. As expected, Wanda was elected president for a second year and I was chosen as mission chair. Vernon was vice president, Susan was secretary, and Brandon was treasurer. Kenny was special projects.

Next, Wanda called for reports on tasks she'd already assigned.

"Susan, what's the status of the open house?" Susan had the job of organizing an open house that would showcase the BSU and our ministries, and would hopefully entice people to want to come back. The open house was tentatively scheduled for one week from today.

Susan looked harried and apologetic. "Wanda, I've been so busy getting this house organized that I haven't started on it yet. There's time, though."

"I'll pitch in and help if I need to."

"I'd appreciate it."

As Wanda went around the room and asked for reports, person

after person had no report and had excuses about why they hadn't done anything. Time after time, she accepted their excuses and offered to do the work herself. And time after time, they accepted. Bob chimed in and offered his help, as well.

I sat, flabbergasted. This was a group of gifted people, all seemingly energetic and dedicated. And it looked very much like Wanda and Bob were going to end up doing all their work. I was the only one with a report, and mine was more ideas than actions because the mission job was a relatively new one. The main thing I wanted to do was get the ball rolling for a mission trip to Nome next summer. The idea was discussed and adopted. Finally, as the meeting was about to end, I couldn't stand it any longer. I raised my hand and Wanda called on me.

"Yes, Mark?"

"I'm sorry, Wanda, but this is crazy."

She looked startled. "It is? How?"

"There's so much we can do here, and this meeting is just the beginning. But people are going to have to be accountable. I know everyone wants our work to glorify the Lord."

People murmured agreement and nodded their heads.

"I think that's a given," Wanda said.

"Mark, what's your point?" Bob asked.

"My point is that Wanda had some good ideas and gave people jobs to do, and no one did them."

"Everyone's busy," she began.

"Yes, everyone is busy. But that just means we all have to share the load. You and Bob are busy too, but I sat here and watched you both offer to do all the work. You're the president and he's the director. You have to give us jobs to do and then expect us to do them. Hold us accountable. If we're too busy, we can get help from other people. I think we all want to work, but we need leadership."

Wanda's eyes were snapping blue fire by now. "You think you can do better?"

"That's not what I was saying."

"That's sure what it sounded like." She threw her clipboard on the floor. "You think you can do better, here's your chance." She stalked toward the door as we all watched, openmouthed.

Just as she put her hand on the doorknob, Bob stopped her. "Wanda, for the sake of the record, can you be clear here? You're resigning the presidency of the BSU?"

"Absolutely. And for the record, I make a motion that Mark Smith be elected president. And I hereby resign from the Executive Council." She turned furious eyes on me. "This is a hard job. I can't wait to watch you crash and burn." And she sailed out and shut the door firmly and loudly behind her.

Silence fell. "Well," Bob said, and cleared his throat. He gathered his thoughts. "Vernon, you're the vice president. There's a motion on the floor. Can you take over here and let's elect a new president?"

"I second Wanda's motion to make Mark Smith president of the BSU."

"Wait," Bob said. "Before this is final I think we need to ask Mark what he thinks. All he did was make some suggestions. He never asked to be president."

I thought about it. There wasn't time for a long private prayer session, so I had to go with what felt right. "I'll do it, if we're all on the same page."

"What page is that?"

"There are so many ministry opportunities here, so many ways to witness and serve God. If everyone agrees with that and is willing to work, then I accept."

Everyone nodded, and Vernon called for the vote. "All in favor?"

"Aye." Everyone approved.

I looked around. "Okay then. Everybody hit your knees."

Startled, Bob and the four remaining residents slowly got to their knees in front of their seats, closed their eyes and folded their hands. At that point, the two at-large members had evidently had enough, because the door slammed two more times. I took a deep breath and shut my eyes.

"Lord, this is Your place," I said. "We're here to serve You. I pray that we do Your will and that everything we do here glorifies You. I pray that we find the right opportunities and the right ministries. I pray that Christians will be empowered and strengthened, and that more people will be brought to You. We're all accountable to each other and to You. Show us, Lord. Help us measure up to Your standards. Show us what You want of us. We're Your servants. Give us the wisdom, the discernment, and the courage to be all that we can be in Your service. In Christ's most holy name we pray, amen."

Finally, Bob and I were alone in the room. He shook his head and gave me a wry smile. "Well, you really stirred up a hornet's nest, didn't you?"

"I didn't mean to. I just couldn't stand to watch how things were going. No one was being held accountable for anything. I wasn't raised to operate that way."

"Wanda is good at getting things done, but she's not so good at making other people get things done. I think she'd agree that's true."

"I hope she's not too mad at me."

"Oh, she is. I've never seen her that mad. But she'll come around."

"Do you agree with me?"

"I never thought about it that way, but yes, I agree with you. We can do a lot more than we've been doing. You've made me excited in a way I haven't been since I've been here. Good luck. I'll be right behind you all the way."

"Luck's not what we need. We need the Lord's blessing."

"That's what I'll be praying for."

Vernon was waiting for me when I got up to my room. "Who would've thought that?"

"What?"

"You and me, president and vice president. I was thinking the same thing you were, but I didn't have the guts to speak up. We're going to get some things done around here now!"

* * *

Things didn't look so good over the next couple of weeks. The entire house seemed to be holding its breath, waiting to see what would happen with Wanda. The air simply pulsed with animosity. There was no way we were going to get anything done with this darkness permeating every corner. Finally, in desperation, after days of having Wanda glower at me every time our paths crossed, I asked Bob's advice.

"Bob, should I talk to her?" I asked him.

"That's the worst thing you can do. It would just blow the lid off again. I've known Wanda for a long time. She'll come around. I can't guarantee what will happen when she does. She may be helpful, or it may just ease up so it's possible for you two to be in the same room. Just pray for God to handle it in His way and sooner rather than later."

In the meantime, people sniped at each other. The open house was a miserable failure. No one showed up, not even our regulars.

In the past, the BSU had held noontime events on Thursdays, where we offered free food and speakers for anyone who wanted to come. It was time for that to crank up, but I couldn't imagine how it would get done with things like this. Every time I sat down to work on it or talked to Kenny about it, we seemed to spin our wheels.

All my wonderful ideas seemed to be for nothing. I wanted to disciple people, to help them grow in their spiritual walk. In my mind's eye I could see seasoned Christians working with freshmen, helping them pray and study the Word. I could envision Bible studies in the dorms. Local churches could partner with us, which would be a win-win.

Bob was completely supportive, but it didn't help. Unless we all were a team, we were nothing. I read Scriptures that talked about all the parts of the church being one body, and none more important than the other. When one part is out of joint, nothing works right. Still, I heeded Bob's counsel, held my tongue, and prayed. And tiptoed around, like everyone else.

The one good thing that developed during that time was my fitness regimen with Vernon. He mandated that we set our alarms for six a.m. every day, and when they went off, we both had to instantly hit the floor for twenty push-ups. Whoever set foot in the hall first was the day's winner. The loser had to fix the winner's breakfast, or clean his room, or do his laundry, or some other detested chore. We synchronized our clocks to the second, so neither had an advantage.

At first he skunked me. As my alarm went off I could hear him, just a few feet away, hitting the floor and counting out his push-ups. After a few days, though, my body clock adjusted and I woke up seconds before the alarm went off. I had a slight advantage because I had only the mattress, not an entire bed, so I had less distance to the floor. The instant the clock hit six, I was off the mattress and on the floor. I became adept at quick pushups, and rarely lost our competition after the first few days. This gave me one thing to focus on in the midst of the misery that was the BSU until Wanda stopped being angry.

Finally, two weeks into the term, she came to see me. I sat on one of the window seats in the front room, propped against the wall, a pillow at the small of my back and an organic chemistry textbook open on my lap. I watched her a bit warily from the corner of my eye as she came into the room. She perched on the other side of the window seat and folded her hands in her lap.

"Hi," she said.

I looked up at her. "Hi."

"I just wanted to apologize for storming out of the meeting the other day."

"It's no problem. I'm sorry I upset you."

"How's it going?"

"You were right. It's a lot of work." I hesitated, then went with my gut. "I could really use your help."

"What do you need?"

"The noonday program is kicking my rear. Would you consider taking it over?"

Her eyes began to sparkle and take on their usual blue gleam. I could almost see her mentally rubbing her hands together in anticipation. "That's my favorite program. What's the problem?"

"I think that's the key to everything else we do, and Kenny and I are both new here. We just can't to seem to get any traction. I think it needs your experience and connections. Once that's going well, everything will begin to click."

"I completely agree."

"I'd like to make that a committee position, if it's okay with you. That's how important I think it is."

"You want me on your team after the way I acted?"

"I can understand why you reacted that way to what I said. There were probably more tactful ways for me to say it. I'm just glad you're willing to take this on."

"I'd love to. Truce?"

"Truce. Pinky swear?"

"Pinky swear."

We both held out our pinkies and solemnly made it official.

16

As August 31 drew nearer, my plans for the Pleasant Grove youth began to solidify. No longer would it be primarily a social group, but we would do honest-to-goodness Bible studies and real mission work. As I did with the kids in Nome, I would pick stories that were relevant to their lives and would use the Bible as a how-to manual for everyday living. We would still have fun; I had always been a goofball myself. But I was determined that the kids would learn something and grow spiritually.

No longer would we meet week after week at the Galyons' house. My limited experience at Pleasant Grove told me these kids' parents, and even other adults in the church, would be more than willing to host our weekly meetings. Getting into the homes would be an invaluable way to understand the kids and show me best how to approach them.

They had already wormed their way into my heart, and I promised myself—as I had promised their parents weeks before—that I would do my best to plant seeds of faith in their minds, hearts, and spirits. Every day I prayed that God would show me how He wanted me to work with these remarkable young people.

They were all bright, each in his or her own way. There was Jimmy, who never talked about his home life, but he haunted the church and hovered at my side. Any time we had a youth event, he was there. His dad told me in the beginning that if Jimmy misbehaved, I was to let him know immediately. But there were no behavior issues. I didn't know the whole story and still don't, but I know from firsthand experience how it feels to have a dad who believes in firm, physical discipline. I could see myself in Jimmy. Prof Powers had been the positive male influence in my life; without him, I'd have turned into someone totally different.

He got good grades, but this was just because he cared so much. He had to scratch, claw, and sweat for every A and B. College was what he wanted, but he was unsure if he'd get to go. In 1980 there were no state-funded lottery scholarships, and money was tight.

He was a natural athlete, as I had noted in June when we'd first thrown a football in the church parking lot. Fearless and competitive, he threw his body into whatever sport we were playing. Football, basketball, volleyball, baseball—he constantly had scrapes and bruises from diving for a ball in some sport or other. He found joy and escape in competition, and his friends were all very willing to oblige.

Jimmy and Jonathan were inseparable, a classic example of opposites attracting like poles of a battery. Where Jimmy was dark, short, muscular and compact, Jonathan was tall, blond, slim, and flexible. Jonathan had the look of a kid born into wealth. His mother always wore flawless makeup, had a perfect hairstyle, and played bridge. His dad wore white, crisply ironed dress shirts to work. Jimmy teased Jonathan about paying teachers for top grades; that's how easy school work seemed for Jonathan. He was the confident golden boy headed for the Vanderbilt engineering program. It was simply assumed that he would be a great success in whatever he did. He bossed his younger sister, Laura, around incessantly. Although she was several years younger than Jonathan—about Travis Galyon's age—she came along with him to youth group meetings.

John-John was, in every way, a farm boy. His parents were hard-working, salt-of-the-earth people, outgoing and hearty. They hallooed when they saw you in town, and they offered to host the youth group whenever needed. John-John and his younger brother, Danny, constantly wore overalls and t-shirts, and when he put on a swimsuit for water events, his chest and upper arms shone ivory white. In these hot days of August, the white became lobster red and then peeled, and then he did it all over again.

College was a pipe dream for him, so much so that it was simply assumed he'd be staying on the farm after high school to help his dad. The farm was what he knew; it was his future. His muscles bulged and rippled from hard farm work. Loads that other people couldn't budge were effortless to him. His biceps were literally rock hard, as I discovered one Saturday during our youth group meeting. We were playing basketball in the parking lot, and finally I asked him something I'd been dying to since the day we'd met.

"John-John, can I punch you on the arm?"

He looked startled, then gave me a flash of white smile. "Go for it."

I gave him a medium punch directly in the bicep. He didn't even brace, didn't even rock off the firm foundation of his feet. I stared. "Can I hit you harder?"

"Give it all you've got." This time he did brace.

I reared back and gave him my hardest punch. He grinned at me. "That the best you can do?"

I had to give it to him. "Yep. You've got muscles like Samson. That actually hurt my fist."

The Galyons stared in stunned amazement at the youth minister punching one of the kids. But it created a new camaraderie between the kids and me. And from then on, John-John was known as Samson, and the other kids took turns punching him on the arm.

* * *

It was time to begin putting all my plans for the youth program into motion. The Galyons' experience was invaluable in this ministry. *Empowerment,* I thought. *That's the key.* They are important. Let them know it. But how? I dedicated some prayer time to this question, and the answer came at the youth group meeting on August 23.

Since I first came to Pleasant Grove, the young girls had been much more focused on the boys, including me, than on what I was saying. They flirted and pranced. They wore short shorts and tank tops that showcased their budding breasts. When we had water activities, they wore tiny bikinis and left themselves uncovered when they emerged from the pool or lake. Martha Galyon had no patience with this; she had ample experience with Angie, her gorgeous daughter.

"Put on a cover-up," she would tell the pubescent ones sternly. "You have all the time in the world to show off your stuff. This is a Bible study."

They obeyed, but their minds clearly weren't on what we were doing. Their preoccupation with males was becoming an impediment to the entire youth program.

As we began a study on Samuel in the Galyons' living room, it seemed especially extreme. Giggles and flirtatious looks escalated. And I noticed, as if my eyes were newly opened, how very effective Martha was with the females.

"Girls, listen to Mark." She stood in the kitchen doorway and gave them a steely *don't-make-me-come-out-there* look. "This is important."

I continued. "We're going to talk today about Samuel, who would turn out to be a very important part of Israel's history. The story begins with a woman named Hannah, who was one of two wives of a man named Elkanah. The other wife was named Peninnah, and she had lots of children. Hannah had none. Back then, having children, especially sons, was the most important thing women could do. It made them valuable to their husbands and sometimes kept them from being thrown out onto the street. It's hard for us to imagine today, but that's the way it was.

"Elkanah loved Hannah, so she didn't have to worry about being thrown out of the house, but she wanted very badly to give him sons. The other wife made it worse by making fun of her and putting her down. Poor Hannah. She was miserable. It got so bad that she cried all the time and wouldn't eat. Elkanah hated to see her so upset. He said he loved her and couldn't that be enough?

"Hannah went to the temple to pray about it. She cried and

rocked back and forth and prayed for the Lord to give her a son. She told Him that she would give the boy to Him for his entire life, and a razor would never touch his head. That was a big deal back then. Devout Jews never cut their hair.

"Put yourself in Hannah's sandals. How badly did she want a son? It ate up her insides and made her sick. She was even willing to give the child to God before he was even born. A priest, Eli, was sitting by the door and saw her praying. The Bible says she was 'speaking in her heart, only her lips were moving, but her voice was not heard.' It must have looked pretty weird. Eli thought she was drunk and told her to put away her wine. Hannah told him she wasn't drunk, just pouring out her soul to God.

"Then Eli told Hannah in a nutshell to go home and quit worrying about it, that God would answer her prayer. So she stopped crying, went home, and started eating again. Soon she became pregnant. She had a son and named him Samuel. And as soon as Samuel quit nursing, she took him to Eli at the temple and gave him to the Lord.

"This is Hannah's story, and this is the last major section of Scripture about her. But how important was she? God used her to bear one of the most important prophets in Israel's history. He would be the one to find and anoint a young shepherd boy named David, who would be one of God's most important servants and an ancestor of our Lord Jesus. We'll talk more about Samuel next week and his life growing up in the temple with Eli. At first it was probably pretty boring, but one night everything changed."

"What happened?" Jimmy asked.

"We'll talk about it next week. But he did hear voices, and they weren't coming from a person. Everybody be sure to bring your Bibles next week. You'll need them."

Finally, when all the kids were gone, the adult Galyons and I attacked the mess. Robert ran the vacuum while Martha and I washed dishes. Angie and Travis were doing homework, which was substantial in these first days of school.

Martha washed a big pot that she'd used to make spaghetti for everyone and handed it to me to dry. "So, you're taking over next week, right?"

"Right. A week from tomorrow. I wanted to talk to you about that." I dried the pot and set it on the counter.

"Okay. What's on your mind?" She took a plate and dunked, soaped, and rinsed it with a practiced hand.

"I think we have a little problem with the younger girls." I dried the plate and took another that she held out.

She snorted. "You think?"

I gave her a relieved look. "I'm glad you agree."

"It'd be hard not to."

"I have an idea what to do about it."

"I'm all ears. I've fought this fight for over two years."

"We need to get serious for the kids to be able to get anything out of this. What if we split them up, just for about twenty minutes for the Bible study? We'd still socialize before and after."

"I like that, but how do you propose to do it? There's just one of you. What are you going to do with one group while you teach the other?"

"I was watching you tonight, and the answer just came to me. What if you take the girls and I take the boys? You're a lot better with them than I am, anyway. I'd still organize and plan everything. Sometimes the studies would be the same, but sometimes they could be different. You could tell them stories they'd be interested in. You and I would work together on that."

"I think that's a fantastic idea." Robert spoke from the kitchen doorway, where he stood with his shoulder propped against the jamb. "Martha can crack the whip with the young girls like no one else I've ever seen. She'll keep them in line and teach them something at the same time."

"I like it," Martha said. "Let's give it a try."

I spent the next week contemplating lessons and activities for the coming weeks. It was a challenge. I wanted to make the social time entertaining and fun, something kids would look forward to each week. I wanted them to invite their friends, so the program would grow and reach more people. Most of all, I wanted the Bible and prayer time to help enrich their spirits.

I went to the Christian book store and pored over possible topics. How to appeal to both boys and girls? They are so different at that age. What would Jesus do?

As I studied, prayed, took notes, and thought back on the activities I'd found meaningful myself, ideas began to come. The more I thought and scribbled, the faster they came. I began to smile, then grin, then laugh aloud as I put it all down on paper. This was going to be fun.

* * *

As with the BSU, things with the Pleasant Grove youth got off to a rocky start. At our meeting on August 30, the day before I would be taking over the program, I greeted everyone and asked them to show me their Bibles. Not to my surprise, more than half of the kids didn't have one with them.

"You have thirty minutes," I said. "Find one."

"How?" one ninth grade girl asked.

"You'll figure it out."

After some milling around and slitted glares tossed at me, the kids headed off in different directions. For the next half hour, the kids who'd brought their Bibles enjoyed a good time in the pool while they watched their less prepared brethren run around wild-eyed. Some used the Galyons' phone to call their parents and ask them to bring a Bible. A couple of them asked to borrow one from the Galyons. Another enterprising young man walked next door and asked to borrow one. One girl who could drive hopped in her car, drove to her grandmother's house, and came back with an exquisite old family Bible. Within the allotted thirty minutes, everyone was back sitting in a circle in the Galyons' living room, Bibles on their laps. All except Pete. He just sat in the back of the room and watched.

For this, our last co-ed Bible study, I told the kids the rest of

Samuel's story. They gathered in the living room around me, and I directed them to the book of Samuel and waited until everyone found it.

"Remember last week I told you Samuel heard voices, and they weren't inside his head?"

Jimmy nodded. "That sounded interesting."

"Do you think you'd know God's voice if He spoke to you?"

Silence. Finally Angie spoke. "I'm never sure if it's His voice or my imagination."

Several other heads nodded and there were murmurs of agreement.

"You're not the only ones to feel that way. Even God's greatest servants had the same thought. Take Samuel for instance. We read last week that his mother gave him to God even before he was born. He'd lived at the temple with the priest, Eli, for his entire life. At that time God really wasn't talking to people or giving them visions. Israel wasn't doing very well. They had a bad habit of forgetting about God and committing horrible sins—like worshipping other gods—and then begging Him to bail them out when they got into trouble. Then they'd go back to their sinning and get into more trouble and beg Him for help again. This happened over and over again for a number of years so God was understandably annoyed with them.

"One night Samuel was asleep, and he heard a voice call his name. Of course he thought it was Eli. There was no one else around. He jumped up and ran to Eli's room and said, 'Here I am. You called me.' Eli was confused. He hadn't called Samuel and told him to go back to bed.

"Samuel had no sooner gotten back in bed when he heard the voice again. Again he went to Eli's room, and again Eli said he hadn't called him. This happened three times. After the third time, Eli began to get an inkling of what was going on. He told Samuel that if he heard the voice again, he should say, 'Speak, Lord, for your servant is listening.' Samuel obeyed, and this was his first encounter with the Almighty in a lifetime of service to God.

"Now, God doesn't often speak out loud these days, but there are several ways He does communicate with us." I held up my right hand and ticked off my fingers. "First, we have His Word. Everything we need to know about how to live life is in here. God will never tell us to do anything that contradicts His Word. Second, all Christians have the Holy Spirit living inside us. He'll speak to us if we listen. Third, sometimes God sends us messages through people in our lives, people we trust. He's done that to me many times. Sometimes He sends signs, but that's not as common. And sometimes we can hear His still, small voice in our minds and hearts, especially if we are talking to Him.

"He loves us all so much and wants us to talk to Him and know Him. So here's your homework for this week. Spend fifteen minutes a day with God. Ten minutes reading the Bible, and five minutes in prayer. You can do more if you want to, but do at least fifteen minutes. Then we'll talk about it next week."

"I don't know how to read the Bible," said Amber Gillette, one of the younger girls.

"Start with Hezekiah. It's short."

Pete guffawed.

"Problem, Pete?"

"Dude, there's no such book as Hezekiah."

"Right," I said with approval. "Pete passed the test."

He beamed.

"For real, begin with Genesis and read it straight through. Before you begin, ask God to use this time in the Scripture and show Himself to you. Be serious about it. He loves you and wants you to know Him. Now, Mr. and Mrs. Galyon and I have an announcement to make. Would you two please come up here with me?"

They came up, and we stood together and made our announcement about the new boy-girl format. We got blank, *okay-whatever* looks from the boys and wide-eyed, vocal distress from the girls.

"But why?" One of the freshman girls, Jessica Hammond, actually had tears in her eyes. I'd noticed some obvious interest on her part toward tall, blond Jonathan Pearson, although there was no reciprocation from him that I could tell. Freshmen, I was pretty sure, held no interest for him.

"We're not taking away social time," I assured them. "I think social time is really important, and we're going to be doing some new things that I think you'll all like. We're just carving out a little bit of time—about twenty minutes—for some serious Bible study. We'll try it this way and we can always make changes later."

"I may not even come back," she sulked in the classic manner of a teenaged girl who doesn't get her way.

"Let's try it for a month and see what we think."

After all the kids had left, Martha and I were, as usual, cleaning up. Angie came into the kitchen, perched on a barstool, and watched us, thick blond hair pulled back in a ponytail and a troubled look in her beautiful hazel eyes.

"What's up, honey?" Martha asked.

Angie was no dumb blonde. And she was a senior, remarkably mature, headed for UT's communications program. When she spoke, people listened.

"Can I talk to you guys?" she asked.

"Of course." Martha put down her dishtowel and took a stool opposite her daughter. "What's on your mind?"

"Does this thing about separate Bible studies for boys and girls have to apply to everyone?"

Martha and Robert looked at me. I studied Angie. This wasn't, I could tell, a matter of a girl wanting to be around boys.

"Tell me about it," I said. "What's the problem?"

"Well, I think I know why you want to do it this way. And if I'm right, then I'd be a lot better off with the boys than with the girls."

I considered her. She looked back at me, directly into my eyes without wavering. A conviction deep inside told me to take her seriously. "Give me your testimony," I said. She looked startled, then thought about it. It was obvious that no one had ever asked her this before. Robert and Martha listened with keen interest.

"I've been a Christian since I was seven," she said simply. "We were at a revival when I felt God call me to go forward. A man named Arnie Maves was the preacher. I can still remember how it felt, walking down that aisle and praying with him."

"I remember that too," said Martha. "I was so proud of you that night."

Angie smiled, a sheen of tears in her eyes, and continued. "I'm a sinner, but Jesus is my Savior. He died for me and He's Lord of my life. I'm living it for Him. I've got one more year at home, and I know things are going to get a lot tougher when I'm away at college. I'm betting that the boys in this group are going to get more serious Bible teaching, and the girls are going to get the easier stuff because they're not as spiritually mature. I think that's why you're splitting us up, and if I'm right, I belong with the boys." She paused and looked at me. "I knew there was no such book as Hezekiah."

"You're very perceptive," I told her honestly. "Your mother is going to be handling what I call the spiritual milk, and I'll be handling the meat. We split it up by boys and girls because the boys in this group are generally more ready for the meat than the girls. But any girl who can handle the meat should be with us. For now, I think, that would be just you."

Martha nodded in agreement. "I think that's the right decision. Angie is ready, but she's the only one of the bunch who is."

*   *   *

Satisfied with the evening, I helped finish the cleanup and trudged out to my car, rubbing my aching back. It gave me a lot of trouble after long days like this one. I longed to get back to my little room and ease my sore self down onto my firm mattress on the blessedly hard floor. I quickly realized as I drew near to my car, that would have to wait a few more minutes. This was all right because it was Pete who was leaning against my car. He continued to be a bright spot.

"Thought you'd never come out," he said. "Got somethin' for you." He led the way over to his truck, and as we walked he took a closer sideways look at my face. "You okay?"

I straightened up with difficulty. "Just a little sore. I'm glad you waited. I've been missing our fishing trips. Nice job on the Hezekiah trick, by the way. Most people would have fallen for it. Good for you."

"That was an easy one—Ina Gambrell is my mom. I miss fishing too. It's a lot more fun with a buddy."

This was the best compliment Pete could have given me. We were indeed buddies now, and I was glad he felt that way too. "Maybe we can go next week."

"I'd like that."

We reached his truck and he reached in and pulled out a piece of fur. "That's a nice pelt," I said admiringly, remembering my Nome roommate Jack, who was a trapper. He would have loved this. "Did you do that?"

"Nope. You did."

I took a closer look, and comprehension dawned. "Is that what I think it is?"

"Yep. It's old Mister Coyote, who was eating my mama's chickens until you stopped him. You took him down and I thought you should have him."

I examined the glossy fur. Nearly four feet long, counting the tail, the pelt was grayish brown on the top and buff on the belly. Its muzzle and paws were reddish-brown. From living with a trapper, I had some appreciation for the work that had gone into this gift. Pete had to skin this animal soon after it was killed, so he must have sneaked away during supper that night and brought it home. It took a sharp knife, a steady hand, and lots of patience. Then the hide had to be stretched and dried. The features of the coyote's face were intact, which is really difficult to do. When a face is kept intact like this, that part of the pelt can be worn like a hood. All of this must have taken weeks for him to do.

I looked up at Pete, understanding the literal and figurative value of this gift. This hide was worth easily a hundred dollars on the market. His doing this for me was a cementing of our friendship, a gesture beyond words.

"This is incredible work," I said sincerely. "'Thanks, man."

"No problem. You earned it."

With a sting in my eyes and a singing heart, I took the exquisite pelt to my car and drove back to the BSU.

17

Brandon and Kenny had a grand time with the coyote pelt. They put it on and ran around scaring everybody. It worked until people got used to the idea that there was a coyote in our midst—and he wasn't alive anymore.

With the freedom from the responsibility of the entire BSU, Wanda began to blossom. Bob was right—she was a doer, not a manager. The noonday program had always been her baby, and now she was able to give it her whole focus. I made a few suggestions, like getting local churches involved, and then stood back and watched.

After racking her brain to identify her first speaker, one who would set the tone for the year and make people want to come, she found him under her nose. She, Vernon, and I were in the kitchen, fixing some lunch, when Kenny and a tall, dark young man clattered in. He wore a University of Tennessee football jersey, baggy gray athletic shorts, and football cleats. He was covered in sweat and left a trail of finely cut green grass in his wake.

"Hey, you guys!" Kenny said. "I've got someone I want you to meet. This is my brother, Alan."

Alan crossed the kitchen to Wanda and politely shook her hand first, then greeted Vernon and me. "Nice to meet y'all. Kenny's told me all about this place."

"Nice to meet you too," Wanda said with a blue gleam in her eye. I could almost see her mind working, putting two and two together. September. Orange jersey. Cleats. Cut grass. And he wanted to get involved!

To understand her budding excitement, you'd have to understand college football in the South. People plan their schedules around it, down to weddings and funerals. Thousands of people hover and wait until the college football schedule comes out in the spring. Then, and only then, do they plan their special events for the fall. The day the football schedule comes out, event locations are flooded with calls. Weddings, baby showers, and birthday parties get planned for Saturdays when their beloved team has a bye week when they don't play. People count down the days until the first game, beginning at the end of the final game of the previous year. They take their infants to games in the scorching sun and the freezing rain.

And here in East Tennessee, all the focus was on the Vols. The Tennessee Titans literally didn't exist in 1980. The University of Memphis was eight hours away, and at that time—with apologies to current Vandy fans, but you know it's true—Vanderbilt didn't really count as a football school. UT was all there was, and people bled that particular shade of light orange.

This whole town was football crazy these last days before the first game, which was against the Georgia Bulldogs here in Knoxville on September 6. That Georgia team featured a young running back named Herschel Walker who would go on to win the Heisman trophy and lead his team to the 1980 national championship. Of course, we couldn't know that at the time. But it was Tennessee football, and that was reason enough to be excited.

Now, here in the BSU's homey kitchen, was a student who looked very much like a UT football player.

"Didn't I tell you about my older brother?" Kenny asked innocently. "He's UT's starting kicker."

"It seems like forever since the last game," Alan said. "We're ready to get back on the field. I've been wanting to come by here and get involved, and Kenny and I ran into each other after practice outside the stadium. I thought it might be a good time."

Alan Duncan. Every UT fan knew who Alan Duncan was; we just hadn't known that Kenny was his brother. He was entering his third year as the starting placekicker and would end his career in the UT record books tied for longest field goal of 55 yards, and first for most points by a placekicker in a single game with 17, including five field goals.

I decided to help Wanda get to the point. I knew exactly what she was thinking. And the timing was perfect. If he could just show up at the first noonday meeting on September 4, kids would flock here. "You said you wanted to get involved. What did you have in mind?"

"Whatever I can do."

"Alan is a great speaker," Kenny put in. "He speaks at churches around here most weekends. He has some cool stories to tell from our time growing up in Kenya."

Wanda needed no further convincing. "Are you free Thursday at noon?"

Alan didn't hesitate. "Absolutely. What can I do?"

"It's no coincidence that you showed up here today. Have a seat."

*   *   *

Everything fell into place. With the speaker lined up, we just had to plan the details and logistics. Everyone pitched in to help Wanda produce and post flyers, contact the Knoxville and campus newspapers, and get the word out. There was no internet or social media then, so we had to do it the old-fashioned way. As we'd discussed at the first EC meeting, everyone was accountable. And just a few days later, hundreds of screaming, orange-clad students descended upon the BSU. Many probably showed up to see Alan and get his autograph, but just as many actually listened. And to everyone's delight, Alan wasn't the only football player who showed up—half of the team was in attendance. The crowd was standing room only. Kids filled up the big old house and spilled over in the yard, straining to see and hear. Smokers and barbecue pits worked overtime on the front lawn. We turned up the microphone as far as it would go, and someone put a speaker in the front window. The guys in the frat house across the street hung off their balconies. People walking by outside stopped to see what all the commotion was about. It was fantastic.

Kenny began the program by proudly introducing Alan and giving a preview glimpse of how they'd grown up as missionaries' kids. Then Alan captured everyone's attention with edge-of-their-seat stories about life in Africa, including encounters with wild animals, his parents' mission work, and his own story of salvation.

As he wrapped up his presentation, he said, "When I was in Kenya playing with the native kids, I had no idea what the plan for my life was. I've kicked a lot of field goals since when, but the most essential score I've ever made was when I accepted Jesus. You may think your life is full, but I can tell you that if you don't have Jesus, it's not. Now here's Mark Smith, the president of the BSU."

I closed the program by outlining the plan of salvation—believe in Jesus, repent of your sin, accept His plan, and then follow Him unconditionally and unabashedly. I mentioned that we would be there after the program for anyone who wanted to talk. Dozens of people stayed, lining the halls of the old house to talk to one of us.

That wildly successful noonday program was all it took to kick start the BSU, and Wanda's job was suddenly very easy. Singers, magicians, speakers, and other wholesome entertainers lined up to get on our schedule. Local churches, all denominations, clamored to provide free food. Shuttles arrived on Sunday mornings to provide transportation for UT students to church services. It was all working out even better than I could have envisioned.

18

I began to concentrate on my first love—discipleship and Bible study for the BSU and Pleasant Grove. We assigned greeters to be on call, so no one came through the BSU door without feeling welcome. We emphasized mission work and began the process of identifying missionaries to go to Nome next summer. And I began to meet with Corey Bennett, my Campus Crusade for Christ mentor. He had taught and discipled me throughout the year before I left for Alaska and continued to do so now. And I was able to turn around and use the same information to help the young people I was working with. Corey used a small booklet called "Five Steps to Spiritual Maturity" and taught me how to teach it to others. I threw myself into teaching the freshmen and the new Christians.

Time became more and more scarce, and the pain in my back continued to be a constant agony. A full load of pre-med classes, two jobs, the full responsibility of the BSU and its promising ministries—all on about three hours of fitful sleep a night. Everything took a hit, including the time I spent in prayer and in Bible study.

It all came to a culmination one Thursday afternoon in October. Susan answered the ringing phone in the downstairs hallway and called up the stairs. "Mark! Telephone!"

I emerged from my room. "Did they say who it is?"

She covered the mouthpiece and whispered, "It's your dad."

This couldn't be good. My dad never called me. I took the receiver from her and acted innocent. "This is Mark."

"It's Dad."

"Hi, Dad, how's it going?"

"Just fine. You're going to be in Maryville tomorrow?"

"Saturday. I have to work at the lumber company tomorrow."

"Be in town in time to come by the house first thing Saturday morning. Your mother and I need to talk to you."

"What's up?"

"We'll talk when you get here."

Having no idea why I was being summoned, I pondered and fretted for the rest of the day and all day Friday. I had good reason to be apprehensive. When I was younger, my dad took the proverb about sparing the rod and spoiling the child very literally, and he was creative. And in my case, being a preacher's kid was unfortunate because everyone knew us. If I got in trouble at school, he knew before I got home.

Whenever I did anything outside of school, someone in town told him about it. Often I arrived home to find him ready with some sort of rod, belt, or switch. Sometimes he made me cut my own switch, and if it wasn't big or nasty enough, he cut a better one. Time after time when I was growing up, I had to hide welts on my back and legs until they healed, and many times I took Lisa's punishment for her because she couldn't handle the pain. Mellie never got a whipping because all Dad had to do was look at her to make her cry.

On the rare occasions when Lisa was whipped, I advised her to go ahead and cry because he wouldn't stop until she did. I had it timed down to the second. Cry too soon, and he wouldn't believe me. Cry too late, and he'd get angrier and hit harder. People today get arrested for far less, but at that time it was just the way it was. My mom stood up for us when she knew about it, but often she did not. No one else dared interfere with the discipline of a dad.

Even now, the familiar dread settled in my gut. It was ridiculous, really. I had been living on my own and supporting myself for three years. I was paying my own way through college. I'd been to Alaska. I had two jobs and a leadership position at UT. I knew I wasn't going to get switched. But he was still my dad, and I had to honor him. The Bible says so.

Bright and early Saturday morning, I eased into the driveway at my parents' home on Mountain View and trudged to the front door on leaden feet. The closer I got to the house, the slower my steps became. My back ached. I sent up a quick, heartfelt prayer. *Please, God.* And rang the bell. When I first left home, my dad had made it very clear that I was never to come home unannounced. So, even though they were expecting me, I would never dream of just walking in.

"Come in," came my dad's deep voice.

I opened the door to a dark foyer and made my way down the hall to a small den at the back of the house. This, I knew, would be where any meeting would take place. Sure enough, both my parents were there. My dad had a stern look on his face. My mother looked resigned and sympathetic. Mellie was conspicuous in her absence, and I guessed she'd slept over at someone's house. Worse and worse.

"Sit down, Mark," my dad said.

I gingerly sat and waited, eyes never leaving his face. Silence. Finally I could stand no more. "What's this about?" More silence.

"Your mid-term grades came," my mother finally said. "You have a D in French and a C in organic chemistry."

"D in French? Seriously?" My dad exploded, incredulous.

"Dad," I said imploringly, "my French professor is from France. I can't understand anything she says. And she doesn't like me anyway. She says I don't speak French right. I'm from the South! Of course I don't speak French right, and I can't help it."

French was bad enough, but organic chemistry had been the bane of my academic life since I'd been at UT. I'd failed the same class right before I went to Alaska because the final exam was the only grade, and there was only one question. Miss that question, and you failed the class. The class I was in now was a retake by a different professor, and C didn't sound so bad. "How are my ecology and religion classes?"

"You have As in both, but that isn't the point," my dad cut in. "You know Cs and Ds aren't acceptable."

"Dad, my GPA is still three-point-three, even if I end up with those grades in those classes."

He erupted again. "Do you think you're going to succeed in seminary if this is the best you can do in undergraduate school?"

"I have two paying jobs and another non-paying one. People are pulling at me at the BSU all the time. And my back is killing me."

"You have to get your priorities in order, son. Grades are number one. You think organic chemistry is hard? Wait until you get to Greek and Hebrew and have to read a book a day. If you can't maintain your grades, then you're going to have to either give something up or do a better job of delegating."

Delegating? I thought I was doing a fine job of delegating. Hadn't I asked Martha Galyon to help with the girls at Pleasant Grove? And hadn't I given the other residents at the BSU jobs to do? I told my dad as much.

"Have you?" he asked. "Have you really? Have you turned those things over to those people, or have you kept control for yourself? Be honest. Remember Jethro?"

"Who?" I drew a mental blank. The only Jethro I could think of at the moment was on the *Beverly Hillbillies*, and I didn't think that's who my dad was talking about.

"Moses' father-in-law." He opened his Bible, paged through until he found what he wanted and handed it to me. It was turned to Exodus, chapter 18. I read silently and comprehension dawned.

When the people of Israel left Egypt on their way to the Promised Land, there were millions of them. Whenever they had a dispute—and that happened a lot—Moses handled each and every one himself. His rationale was that God had given him, and only him, the Law, and he was responsible for applying it to the people and their issues.

Then his father-in-law, Jethro, came to the Israelites' camp to bring Moses' wife, Zipporah, and two sons. I read this part aloud. "It came about the next day that Moses sat to judge the people, and

105

the people stood about Moses from the morning until the evening. Now when Moses' father-in-law saw all that he was doing for the people, he said, 'What is this thing that you are doing for the people? Why do you alone sit as judge and all the people stand about you from morning until evening?' Moses said to his father-in-law, 'Because the people come to me to inquire of God. When they have a dispute, it comes to me, and I judge between a man and his neighbor and make known the statutes of God and His laws.'"

In essence, Jethro told Moses he was crazy, that he was going to burn himself out and be no good to anyone if he continued at this pace. Jethro suggested that Moses handpick men from among the tribes of Israel to handle the small disputes and only handle the big ones himself. He suggested that men be picked as leaders of thousands, of hundreds, of fifties, and of tens. Then the workload would be manageable for everyone and the people of Israel wouldn't grumble so much. So Moses did, and it worked out for everyone.

My dad had a point. Even though I'd appointed people to manage certain aspects of things, I still hadn't really let go of them. I still planned the Bible studies for the Pleasant Grove girls and all aspects of each youth gathering. I still looked over the shoulders of my committee members and did exactly what I'd told Wanda she was doing—failed to hold them completely accountable for doing their jobs. And I was holding my new discipleship program close, like a newborn baby, not letting anyone else touch it.

No wonder I was exhausted. I was trying to be all things to all people—and all in the name of serving God. Worse, I hadn't even talked to Him about it all that much. I'd just been going full steam ahead. I resolved to fix that immediately.

But I still saw a problem. "Dad, I can't even find a place to concentrate. And I can't sleep because of my back."

"As to the first, UT is a big campus. It shouldn't be too hard to find a private place. And as to the second, we'll just go back to the doctor and tell him what's going on. There may be something else he can do. But the bottom line is, those grades will come up, one way or another.

"God expects your best. This isn't it and you know it. Pray about it. Ask Him to help. People say He won't give you more than you can handle, but that's not true. He won't give you more than you can handle *with His help*."

Silence fell, and I looked at my parents a bit shamefully. They were right and I knew it. It was supposed to be all about Him, and yet I had been so busy trying to do His work that I'd gone lax in consulting Him. Even with the lessons about pride He had been trying to teach me, I was still being prideful and believing that only I knew what He wanted. Now, He'd used my parents to get through to me. My mother knew me well, and she could see on my face when my whirling mind reached this conclusion.

"I'll call Monday morning to make an appointment with the doctor," she finally said. "Then we'll go from there."

19

Knowing I needed some time alone with God, I made a side trip to Look Rock before going to our youth group meeting. The road winds out of Maryville along Montvale Road, then steeply up and up in switchback curves to the Foothills Parkway, which straddles the ridge all the way to the edge of the Great Smoky Mountains National Park.

Serious cyclers, some of whom I'd seen on television in the Tour de France, use the mountainous road for training. Motorcycle engines can be heard for miles. Too often, the local news carries stories about a motorcycle wreck claiming another life. It's easy to understand since there's nothing but treetops between the road and the bottom of the mountain.

I traveled along the Parkway until I came to the parking area for Look Rock, where I got out of my car. I locked up, pulled my jacket up to my ears, and climbed up a well-worn path toward the tower at the top of the mountain. The tower is a popular destination for locals and tourists alike, but I knew a place where I could be alone.

Just before the tower ramp, I veered off on a not-so-well-traveled path, which led to a rock formation overlooking the Tennessee Valley on one side and the Great Smoky Mountains on the other. The wind whipped around me, and I pulled my jacket up higher and settled with my back against a knobby tree, feet braced on the rocks before me.

On the Tennessee Valley side, the landscape below was flat for about fifty miles all the way to the other side of the valley where it began to rise again at the edge of the Cumberland Plateau. Houses, ponds and farmland dotted the land. Maryville was clearly visible to the right, and beyond that, the lights of Knoxville's McGhee-Tyson airport and the city itself.

The mountain side was pure natural splendor. The soft, undulating blue-green of the Great Smoky Mountains stretched on and on and on. Not far away was Chilhowee Lake, where I knew bass lurked in the cold depths year round. Peaks gave way to other, higher peaks—Gregory's Bald, Spence Field, Thunder Head, and Rocky Top. At the far end of the range was Mt. LeConte, the highest peak in the Smokies. All stood in silent and powerful tribute to the Creator. My starving soul soaked it in.

"Lord," I prayed, "please forgive me. I know I need Your help. I can't do any of it without You. Forgive me for thinking I could. These people deserve better, and You certainly do. It's all in Your hands. It always was; I was just too prideful to see it. Please help me get some relief from my back pain, or teach me to live with it better than I have been. Please give me the help I need to do Your work the way You want it done. Show me the things You want me to do. Please use me as You will."

I sat for a long time, keeping the communication line open with my Father, heeding God's instructions in the apostle Paul's writings to "pray without ceasing." I drank in the silence, broken only by the occasional bay of a farm hound, caws of hawks soaring on the breeze overhead, and distant motorcycle engines. Finally, the angle of the sun told me it was time to be on my way. I needed to talk to Robert and Martha before the kids arrived.

Rejuvenated, spiritual thirst quenched, I made my way down the mountain and back to my car.

*   *   *

When you ask the Lord for help, stand back and watch Him work. One of my hardest tasks had been scheduling places to hold our

Saturday youth meetings. I wanted to meet at the kids' homes, but the logistics were time-consuming and my lack of experience in this community made it harder. That effort had seriously lagged, and we'd been meeting at the church.

While sitting on that mountaintop, I suddenly realized I had a tool I wasn't using. Martha Galyon knew everyone in the church, where they lived, the names of their hound dogs, and who had swimming pools or tractors for hayrides. I arrived an hour early that night and leveled with her. "I can't handle all this," I told her, "and you're better at it than I am, anyway."

By the time the last kid arrived that night, she had it all done. Every Saturday meeting for the rest of the school year was scheduled at a variety of places, including farm houses, mountain cabins, barns, city homes with pools and recreation rooms, even campsites in the woods. It was something that would have taken me weeks and wouldn't have been done nearly as well. This would give me the opportunity I'd been looking for to get a glimpse inside the kids' lives and understand what made them tick.

When I got back to the BSU Sunday night, I had a similar talk with the EC members. Basically, I told them I'd been trying to do too much and needed their help. No more looking over their shoulders, I promised. Their jobs were their jobs.

"If you have problems you can't handle, come to me or Bob, but I am formally delegating this work to you. And remember what Paul says in Colossians: 'Whatever you do, do heartily, as unto the Lord. It's the Lord Christ whom you serve,'" I said.

The result was electric. Evidently they'd been leaning on me as much as they had Wanda. Now that they knew it was really, truly all theirs, there was a fire in their eyes that hadn't been there before. When they seriously owned their jobs, and knew I felt the same way, it made all the difference.

20

My mother called the BSU first thing Monday morning with the news that my orthopedist had had a cancellation so he could see me immediately. She met me at his office, and I told him the situation. He did more x-rays, then came in and gave me an update.

"Your x-rays make me even more convinced that Dr. Reed is right, and you have a partially severed disc. I can't see anything else that could be wrong," he said. "Describe your pain."

"Horrible. Burning, stabbing, constant. I can't find a comfortable position, and I can't sleep. Sometimes sciatic pain kicks in, and then I'm completely out of commission."

He sat back and considered me. "You already have some pretty strong pain medication. Is it helping?"

"Barely." I suddenly had a thought. "Dr. Reed said that my athletic days are over. What would happen if I ran or did the other things he told me not to do? Could I hurt myself more?"

"You could split the disc completely."

"But that's a good thing, right? He said if I split the disc completely, then it could be fixed."

"You won't be able to bear the pain. What you're feeling now is nothing compared to what you'll feel if you aggravate that disc."

"But if I can bear it? If I can find a way? This could be over quicker?"

"Theoretically. Do you normally have a pretty high pain threshold?"

"Yes," my mother interrupted. "You should see some of the accidents he's had. He went through the windshield of a van and it took the doctor three hours to pick the pieces of glass out of his hands. He never even whimpered."

"Then let's try it. I'll up your medication as much as I can, but you have to come back and see me every thirty days to get refills. We'll see how it goes."

Armed with new, stronger, pain medication, I amped my athletic life back to nearly where it had been before. The pain was excruciating, but my body drank in the exercise and I saw even more clearly that God can and does use our "thorns in the flesh" for His glory.

We had pickup games of football in the street in front of the BSU. The frat boys saw what was going on and came running. I had big hands and fast feet, so I played receiver. Vernon, the high school quarterback, winged balls as hard as he could, and I ran underneath them, dodging trees and flagpoles.

One day Brandon, Kenny, and I were sitting on the front porch and saw the UT cross country team running down the street in front us. After one look, we grinned at each other and fell in behind them. Several startled glances later, one of them asked, "What you guys doing?"

"Just getting in a little exercise," said Brandon, running loosely and effortlessly.

"If you can keep up with us, go for it," another remarked, and the entire team put on a burst of speed. Across the UT campus we went, down hills, into small ravines, and along a creek near Kingston Pike. We kept our position at the rear of the group, not saying anything. The same guy who'd first spoken dropped back to us.

"Where you guys from?" he asked.

"I grew up in Kenya, but now I'm at the BSU," Kenny said.

"What's that?"

"Baptist Student Union."

"Some religious thing."

"It's a lot more than that."

"Like what?"

"You should come and see."

"Tell you what. If you guys can keep up with us for the whole course, we'll come check it out."

"How far's that?"

"5K. A little over three miles."

Brandon flashed a grin. "Deal."

Cross country running is all about endurance and getting in a groove. Kenny and Brandon had no trouble at all. And I was stubborn. Then, toward the end, with just a few hundred yards to go, I began to lag. Kenny slapped me on the rear and said, "Go!"

With an unnatural burst of speed and energy, like Elijah had when he outran Ahab's chariots for more than twenty miles in 1 Kings, we accelerated and went to the front of the pack, and stayed there until the end. The weird part—I wasn't even winded.

The team promised to come to the noonday program the next day. After that, the twenty-person team became regulars at our events. And our mission and outreach continued to grow.

Intramural teams began to start up at the BSU. We had tennis, basketball, volleyball, and any other sport anyone was interested in. Daniel Bowman and Bert Gibson attended those intramurals. They were like Jimmy and Jonathan at Pleasant Grove—best friends, inseparable. Almost immediately, I began to see the fire in their eyes that I'd seen in my own at that Charles Stanley retreat. They came to see me, much as I'd gone to see Bob Hall in the spring of 1978, and told me they wanted to do something.

"Seriously?" I asked them.

"Absolutely," Daniel said. "Give us jobs."

I sat back and looked at them. "How do you feel about being a missionary?"

"Like, with savages and jungles and stuff? Like Alan Duncan's parents?"

"I was thinking more like Eskimos and tundras."

"What do you have in mind?" Bert asked.

"We're going to send two missionaries to Nome next summer. Several people have already applied, so you'd have to move quickly. We'll be choosing by the end of the year."

"Nome? Like, Alaska?"

"Like, almost to Siberia. Twenty hours of daylight a day during the summer. Natives that haven't heard the Gospel and still believe in the spirit world."

I told them an abridged version of the year I'd spent in Nome. Their eyes began to snap and light up. It made my heart sing. The other young men and women who'd applied for the trip were good people, but I hadn't seen the enthusiasm that I'd hoped for. But first, Daniel and Bert had to prove they were serious and that they could witness and teach—and have fun, which was a key part of dealing with the natives.

I fished around in my desk and came up with two thick application packets. They were two-fold, one for the BSU and one for the North American Mission Board. They were stiff for a reason. We didn't want anyone who wasn't serious and willing to make the sacrifices that would be necessary to spend a summer in Nome. I slid the packets across the desk to Daniel and Bert.

"Fill these out," I told them. "You'll need two letters of recommendation, a résumé, an essay, and personal references. The Mission Board and the BSU will pay for part of the trip, but we can't pay for it all. You'll need to give us a financial plan and tell us how you plan to pay for your part."

"How did you do it?" Daniel wanted to know.

"I worked and earned as much as I could, and appealed to my home church for the rest. They came through for me."

"How much are we talking about?"

"At least a couple thousand dollars. Maybe more." I eyed the two young men, then went with my gut. "I'd like you two to come to our next EC meeting. No matter how this mission trip turns out, I'd like you both to help with the BSU's evangelism program here at UT. If you can evangelize here, you can do it anywhere. It will help beef up your résumé, too."

"We'll be there," said Bert. And the two of them took their application packets and headed out the door.

21

Now that we had varying locations for our Bible studies, the Pleasant Grove youth group gatherings became more and more popular. As it grew, so did my work load. The pastor asked me to preach on the fifth Sunday, which turned out to be about once every three months, and also do children's sermons every Sunday morning.

The concept of separate Bible studies for the boys and the girls was successful once the kids got used to it and the girls understood that there would still be social time, and they could graduate to the serious study when they were ready. Martha and I taught similar concepts, with varying degrees of difficulty. As time went on, some of the younger boys were sent to Martha, and one or two of the girls moved on to my group. As long as they could see it was fair, the kids were fine.

We met in farmhouses, in town homes, at pools and in the woods. Everywhere we went, there was a special lesson. One Saturday afternoon in early October, we were in a field at a farm, holding a cookout. The kids divided into teams and went on a scavenger hunt to find twelve different leaves. The lesson was the intricacy and beauty of the nature around us.

One week we discussed the importance of good input, and how most books, movies, music, and television shows were not focused on things that honor God. Or, at least, on things that don't offend Him.

I flipped in Exodus to the classic scene where Moses receives the Ten Commandments.

"It's clear here," I said. "Right here, God spells out the things He hates. One and two, don't put anything else above Him and don't worship images. If you do, that's your god and He's not. Three, don't dishonor your parents. Four, don't take His name in vain, and that means using it in any way not directly referring to Him in reverence. Five, six, and seven—don't lie, steal, or kill. Eight, don't have sex outside of marriage. Nine, don't look at something that belongs to someone else and want it for yourself. And ten, respect the Sabbath. Worship God and rest. Don't do hard labor, and especially not where people can see it and it can damage your witness.

"Most of us look at these commandments and think we're doing pretty good. But when we listen to today's music and watch today's movies and television shows, aren't we glorifying, or at least accepting, all the things God says He hates? Give me your thoughts here."

Angie raised her hand. "I think a lot of young people think it's okay to have sex because they see it all the time on TV and in the movies, like you said."

"And I don't think I've seen a movie or heard a song on some radio stations that doesn't take the Lord's name in vain," Jonathan put in.

"What do you think it says about us when we put all this stuff into our brains?" I asked them. "Do we risk letting it into our hearts and spirits?"

"I think I'm stronger than that," said Jimmy.

I looked around at them. "Maybe. But listen to these verses from Ephesians. The apostle Paul was in prison in Rome when he wrote this letter to the people of Ephesus, and he's telling them how to lead lives worthy of Christ. 'In reference to your former manner of life, you lay aside the old self, which is being corrupted in accordance with the lusts of deceit.'

"'Speak truth each one of you with his neighbor.' 'Be angry, and yet do not sin; do not let the sun go down on your anger, and do not give the devil an opportunity.' 'Let no unwholesome word proceed from your mouth . . . so that it will give grace to those who hear.' 'Let all bitterness and wrath and anger and clamor and slander be put away from you, along with all malice.'

"And here's one of my favorites, because it seems to speak directly to us today. 'There must be no filthiness and silly talk, or coarse jesting, which are not fitting, but rather giving of thanks.'"

I paused and looked around the circle. "This is how we're told to behave—worthy of Christ. Now think about our input, and the things we spend our time on. What do you think people think about us when they see us singing along with some nasty lyrics that maybe you don't even think about? You're supposed to be Christians. How do you think this reflects on Christ?"

There was silence as the kids digested this.

"What does this tell your friends and family? Does it damage your testimony? More important, is God happy with us? Or would He be a lot happier if we concentrated on things that we know honor Him?"

"I think we get rid of it all," said Angie abruptly.

I looked at her. This girl always managed to surprise me. "What do you mean, get rid of it?"

"Just what I said. At the next youth meeting, we bring any books or movies or tapes that we think wouldn't honor God and make Him proud of us. Anything that would damage our testimony. We'll have a big bonfire and burn it all."

"I think that's a great way to set an example and show your commitment," I said. "Is everybody on board with this?"

Heads nodded around the campfire.

"Let's do it," said Jimmy.

"Let's do it," I said.

The next week, at a meeting in the woods, the kids and I built a huge bonfire out of sticks of all sizes that they gathered themselves. We watched solemnly as all their bad input literally went up in smoke. Movies, cassette tapes, and even a few girlie magazines. As the fire died down and the night grew darker, the stars twinkled brightly in the clear October sky. We held hands and looked up at those bright stars, and thanked our Creator.

*   *   *

I also used my Alaska experiences to teach the kids. At Jonathan Pearson's very nice home, I told them about Matthew Hawkins, the millionaire who saved the church construction project in Nome. We'd been discussing Jesus' parable of the rich young ruler, who wanted to follow Him but didn't want to give up any of his money.

"Some people say money is the root of all evil, but that's not right," I told them. "It's not money—it's the love of money. There's nothing wrong with having money. When God blesses you with financial success, He expects you to be responsible with it. Mr. Hawkins heard and listened to the Lord's voice and helped us. Without him, that church might not be standing today."

As I taught them, I thought fondly of Paul and Prissy and Darren and Atka, and figured they'd be happy that their experiences were now being used to help others. Little Thomas, who was abused by his dad but came to trust and believe in Jesus, was the object of a lesson one Saturday.

Our lessons were also focused on real Bible teaching. I discovered, not to my surprise, that these kids had very little real knowledge of the Scriptures. They seemed to think that it wasn't necessary to study God's Word, that simply believing in Him and praying once in a while was enough. The research I'd done at the Christian bookstore was paying off, and my prayers to be able to help the kids were being answered.

Stories from the Bible proved to be useful history lessons, and I had my ways of getting them to listen. One Saturday I sat with a bag of miniature Three Musketeers candy bars on my lap, the kids—six boys plus Angie and one other older girl—all seated around me. They eyed the candy curiously and waited. I told them to open their Bibles.

"Who can tell me the names of Abraham's two sons?"

Blank looks.

"A Three Musketeers to whoever can give me the answer."

The kids started fumbling around in their Bibles, and after a few minutes I took pity on them.

"Look in Genesis, the sixteenth chapter."

Samson painstakingly found the correct chapter and raised his hand just ahead of Lucas, the son of one of the committee members who'd hired me back in June. "One of them was Ishmael. But he was Abram's son. I thought you said Abraham."

I threw him a candy bar and said, "Read the first twelve verses out loud."

Samson read aloud the story of Hagar, who'd been servant to Abram's wife, Sarai. In the previous chapter, the Lord had promised Abram that he would have many descendants, too many to count. The problem was, Abram and Sarai were both getting pretty old. Abram was in his mid-eighties at the time. Sarai knew about God's promise, but she had her own idea as to how this promise could be fulfilled, and she took the matter into her own hands. She gave Hagar to Abram so children would be possible.

Angie raised her hand when Samson got to this part.

"I've always thought that was pretty strange," she said. "How does a woman just give her husband another woman?"

"The culture was pretty different," I said. "It's something we can't really understand today, but Sarai was within her rights to give Abram her maidservant for the purposes of having children. The problem was, the Lord had already said He would take care of this, and Sarai just didn't want to wait for Him. There are always consequences when you don't wait for God. Samson, go on."

He finished the story. The kids listened wide-eyed as a jealous Sarai treated Hagar horribly during her pregnancy, so horribly that Hagar ran away. The Lord sent an angel to her beside a spring of water in the wilderness and told her to go back and do as Sarai said. Further, the angel made Hagar a promise. I had Samson pause here.

"What the angel said to Hagar would change history for Israel. Pay close attention. Go on, Samson."

He read the last four verses. "Moreover, the Angel of the Lord said to her, 'I will greatly multiply your descendants so that they will be too many to count.' The Angel of the Lord said to her further, 'Behold, you are with child, and you will bear a son: And you shall call his name Ishmael, because the Lord has given heed to your affliction. He will be a wild donkey of a man. His hand will be against everyone, and everyone's hand will be against him. And he will live to the east of his brothers.'"

"Anyone have any idea what this means?" I asked.

Jonathan, the golden boy bound for Vanderbilt, raised his hand slowly. "That sounds an awful lot like war."

"It is like war. Exactly like war," I said and tossed him a candy bar. "Who knows who Israel's enemies are today?"

"Pretty much the entire Middle East," Jonathan responded.

"Look at the passage again. Where would Ishmael's descendants live?"

"To the east."

I sat back. "Afghanistan, Iraq, Iran, and others. Here's the rest of the story. Ishmael's descendants are what is now known as the Arab nation, who worship Islam. They have been a thorn in Israel's flesh throughout history. It actually says later in Genesis that Ishmael 'settled in defiance of all his relatives.' Anybody know the point of all this?"

Jimmy raised his hand. "Wait."

"For what?"

"The point is to wait. For God. Sarai could have avoided everything that happened if she hadn't given Hagar to her husband."

"Exactly." A candy bar landed in his lap. "A few years later, when Abram was one hundred years old, God changed Sarai's and Abram's names to Sarah and Abraham and gave them a son, Isaac. One of Isaac's sons, Jacob, would have twelve sons, who would be the fathers of the twelve tribes of Israel. God's chosen people."

I paused and waited for all the kids' eyes to light on mine. "Here's the point. 'Wait for the Lord. Be strong and let your heart take courage. Yes, wait for the Lord.' That's Psalm 27:14, but we see it all through the Bible. Waiting is sometimes the hardest thing we have to do. We want to take over and do it ourselves. But God always keeps His promises. He will do what's best for us. We have to trust Him and wait."

22

Throughout my work with the youth, Pete was my helper. Too old to be in the youth group, and of course unpaid, he volunteered his time and did the work that I still couldn't do, painkillers or no. Preparing for a Bible study involved lots of manual labor, lifting and straining. Pete literally took that load off of me.

Our friendship grew closer, but I never forgot what Miss Ina had asked of me that first time I visited their home. I'd promised to pray for him and help him find answers. He was in my prayers every day, and I was trying to teach him without preaching at him. Something told me Pete had had enough preaching in his life, and this would turn him off. I prayed that God would use something in our Bible studies to reach into Pete's heart. But as yet, I could see no spark or conviction in his eyes. He came and helped because he enjoyed being with his friend and knew I needed help. Nothing more.

Miss Ina had never mentioned it again, but I could see the questioning look in her eyes every time we saw each other. When word came that she had fallen in her garden and hurt herself, I went to the hospital to see her. It was my first hospital visit in a ministry role, so I was a little nervous. Besides being one of her ministers and feeling somehow responsible for her spiritual well-being, deep inside I knew she was going to ask a question I didn't want to answer. As I walked down the hall I prayed for wisdom to give her a good answer.

Her door was shut so I tapped on it.

"Come in," came a thin, slightly impatient voice. I eased the door open.

"Hi, Miss Ina," I greeted her and entered the dim room. Her tired eyes lit when they saw me.

"Well, if it isn't one of the few people I actually want to see," she said. "I thought you was one of those nurses coming to poke at me again. Feel like a pincushion. Can't get any sleep in this place because they keep waking me up. Nothing wrong with me but a bum knee, and I can take care of that at home." She gestured at her leg, which hung in traction over her bed.

"You seem pretty spry to me." I took her small, plump hand in one of mine and squeezed it. Evidently I was a little too eager and tense, because she winced in pain. I was horrified.

"Oh, Miss Ina, I'm so sorry." I eased back and gently rubbed her cold hand in my warm ones. "What happened to you?"

"Stupidest thing. Got tangled up with a hoe and a hose pipe in my garden and took a spill down the hillside. Must have knocked me out, because the next thing I know I'm in an ambulance with Pete Senior beside me looking scared to death. Dirt on my face and mud in my hair. I was so embarrassed. Liz finally brought me a comb and some hairpins."

I choked back laughter at the mental picture of her accident and noticed for the first time that while Miss Ina wore the ubiquitous hospital gown, her hair was clean and neatly done in its usual bun at the nape of her neck. "Liz's a good daughter."

"That she is."

"When are they letting you out of here?"

"In a couple days. Soon as I convince them I'll be fine at home."

"Everybody at church is all spun up about you. I'll tell them you're just fine."

"You do that." I saw the subject I was dreading come into her eyes and knew there was no avoiding it. I waited. After a moment, she spoke again. "Pete's been spending a lot of time with you."

"He has. He's a good friend and a godsend. I don't know what I'd do without him."

"You remember what I asked you? Back in June?"

"Of course I do."

Those hazel eyes searched my face anxiously. "And?"

"Sometimes it just takes time, Miss Ina."

"He's not coming around, is he?"

"Not yet." Despair clouded her eyes, and I could see that she was questioning whether Pete was reachable. "But you need to remember something."

"What?"

"We don't understand His will. His ways are not our ways. His timing is His timing. Remember what you told me when I asked you to pray for my back to be healed?"

"I remember," she said wryly.

"God does what He wants. It could be that you and I are just planting and watering the seeds in Pete, and they'll sprout somewhere down the road. Maybe everything that's happening now is so that Pete will have a great witness to share with others when the time is right. Maybe not. You and I just have to do our jobs and keep praying. God will do what He wants, when He wants."

"You think you're telling me something new, young man? Solomon said in Ecclesiastes, 'Sow your seed in the morning and do not be idle in the evening, for you do not know whether morning or evening sowing will succeed, or whether both of them alike will be good.' On the other hand, I'm tormented by a passage in John that says, 'No one can come to Me unless it has been granted him from the Father.' What if Pete isn't one of those? I can't stand the thought of my son going to hell."

Her hands were getting warm now, but I kept rubbing them gently and looked into her eyes. A prayer warrior was asking me a question like this? "I think entire denominations have been divided about that for years. Are we predestined, or do we truly have free will? Somehow it's both, and that's something we can't understand. I certainly don't have the answer. We just have to keep praying for Pete."

She sighed, a sheen of tears in her eyes. "It's just really hard. You'll understand some day, when you have children."

"Yes, ma'am."

We visited for a few more minutes, and I could see that Miss Ina was tiring. I again took her hands gently in mine, and we shared a prayer before I left. I hoped that what I'd told her was true, and that Pete wasn't a lost cause like Robert Wallace.

PART 2:
WATERING

23

I took my dad's advice and prowled around campus, looking for a private place to study. The BSU was out. There was never a quiet moment in the big house, even in the areas where you were supposed to be able to study. The library was out. Everybody, his brother, and his second cousin could be found at the library. Benches, clearings, secluded places, picnic tables on campus—all too open and full of distractions. I needed quiet.

One day, searching for an organic chemistry book that wasn't available in the main library, I was directed to the alumni library. I missed it the first two times I walked past it because it didn't look like a library. It looked like any other old building, nestled in a grove of gnarled magnolia trees.

When I went in, the musty quiet enveloped me. On the bottom level, deep underground, I found the sanctuary I'd been looking for. One single desk was tucked away in the corner, at the end of the last row. The only way out was by one ancient elevator, and it was shut down when the staff left. I found that out the hard way when I tried to leave late one night and found myself sleeping in the library.

Classical music was piped through the building all the time, and I developed a love for it that continues today. I could concentrate here, and my grades crept upward. I was confident I'd have nothing lower than a B by the end of the semester.

*   *   *

I'd learned my lesson. I didn't again make the mistake of taking too much on myself, and I seldom again neglected my own prayer time and Bible study. It was one thing to prepare to lead a Bible study, but quite another to keep my personal life under His leadership. I improved at both, and God's blessings poured down.

The BSU continued to grow. The attendance at our weekly noonday programs exploded, expanding from a handful each week to well over two hundred and counting. We held the program in the cafeteria area but were quickly outgrowing it. Wanda blossomed under this singular responsibility.

My discipleship program was more than what I'd hoped and prayed it would be. I continued to meet regularly with Corey Bennett and poured everything I learned from him back into the kids I worked with. Studying the Bible, I realized, doesn't come naturally to most people. Thinking back to when I was a freshman in college, I understood. It takes commitment, discipline, and someone to hold you accountable.

Susan Bryant and I started a Bible study in the dorms. She taught the girls and I taught the boys. The lessons Martha Galyon and I used with the Pleasant Grove kids served well for teaching these freshmen. Susan and I made a list of all the freshman dorms on campus and scheduled one per week for each of us. When word got around, we began to see regulars. One of those was a young man named Randy Barnette, who drank in everything he heard and came back again and again. He reminded me of myself as a freshman.

We made things fun for the BSU regulars and everyone else who came by. Often one of us stood on the porch at lunchtime and greeted those passing by with an invitation to come in for a cold soft drink and a snack. Free grilled hot dogs, iced Cokes, and crisp potato chips were a cheap, surefire way to the heart of a college kid. Add in a couple of ping pong tables, and those students felt welcome and came back again and again.

We kept the place clean and inviting, adhering to Susan's strict schedule. Cleaning the downstairs bathroom was a hated chore, but we all shared it. And we shared meal duties, with each of us cooking one night a week. On Saturdays, we ate up the leftovers.

You could tell who was cooking by the aromas that wafted from the kitchen. For me, it was usually fried fish. Pete and I had racked up a good bit of meat and there was still plenty in the freezer. Vernon usually grilled burgers. Kenny and Brandon cooked Hamburger Helper or Tuna Surprise. The girls prepared more elaborate meals like lasagna and spaghetti, complete with garlic bread and crisp salad. Sometimes we'd chip in together and get some juicy steaks. Brandon was the master griller.

At ten o'clock every night, we locked the doors and had game time for just the residents and anyone else who happened to be sleeping under our roof that night. The girls quickly disappeared to their apartment and left us boys alone. We played ping pong, foosball, Nerf darts, and whatever else struck our fancy. One weekend my best friend, Doug Taylor, came to visit from Georgia Tech. We treated him to a particularly brutal game of Nerf sniper, played in the pitch darkness. Brandon always won this game. He was unpredictable, off the grid. He would hang silently from the sturdy chandelier in the foyer, or hide behind a door, or balance on a rafter, and pick people off one by one. When you were hit, you had to surrender your arms and go to the POW room. The last man standing was the winner.

This time, Doug Taylor and I hatched an idea. Maybe it bent the rules a little, but all's fair in love and war, right? Nerf gun tucked securely at the small of my back, I stealthily sneaked to the POW room and sat with the people who'd been shot. Brandon waited for an hour and finally figured everyone had been killed, and entered the POW room waiting for his usual accolades. I smoothly pulled out my gun and shot him between the eyes.

"You're dead," I said. Everyone cracked up.

"No fair," he said, rubbing at the welt on his forehead. "What were you doing in the POW camp?"

"Just visiting the prisoners. No rule against that." After that, though, we made a rule. No fraternizing in the POW camp.

For the first time since my accident, I got back onto the tennis court with Doug, my former doubles partner. The pain in my back was excruciating, even with my strong painkillers. I continued to hope and pray that athletic activity would cause that disc to sever completely, and this agony would end with a surgery.

*   *   *

One night Daniel, Bert, and I got a firsthand look at how other houses had their fun. I decided it was time to see these two in action. From observing them, I knew that they worked together naturally and seamlessly. Bert was outgoing; Daniel was more reserved and thoughtful. They took cues from each other without words. They reminded me of my relationship with Doug Taylor.

I thought I was fearless spiritually, but I'd never really seen Bert in action. The three of us walked right in the front door of the bawdiest fraternity on campus. This night, as every night, an alcohol-saturated party was in full swing. At that time the legal drinking age for beer and wine was eighteen, and these kids took full advantage of it. Beer bottles and cans carpeted the floor. Potato chips spilled out of bags that had been discarded on rickety tables. On every flat surface, frat boys snuggled and groped with eager coeds. From a turntable record player, Lynyrd Skynyrd's "Sweet Home Alabama" blared. A few couples gyrated and weaved drunkenly.

We knew many of these kids from the pickup football games in the street and the shared pranks over the past weeks. I recognized one girl from the rat-throwing incident back in August. She'd screamed particularly loudly.

Bert, Daniel, and I stood in the middle of the room and watched. Then Bert reached over to the record player and switched the music off. All eyes swiveled to his face. He held his silence for a long moment and made eye contact with every person in the room.

"Jesus loves you," he finally said. "All of you. Just like you are."

"Dude, what you doin'?" one drunken boy said in a slurred voice.

"Just telling you. It's true. We can show you. Come see us at the BSU."

Then Bert turned the music back on and we left as quietly as we'd come.

Nothing more was ever said about that incident, but over the next few weeks we began to see some of those faces at our noonday programs or for a free hot dog. We swamped those kids with love and kindness, and some of them began to develop spiritually.

24

Little children had never been my forte. Prissy had been an exception. She and I had bonded instantly and completely. Generally, though, I had found that I was better with older kids. So, when Pastor Dunkel asked me to give children's sermons on Sunday mornings, I was at a loss. What in the world could I say to kids who hadn't even started school yet? I'd be sitting at the front of the church with a microphone, and the entire congregation would know if I messed up. What if I froze? What if every word that came out of my mouth was met with blank stares?

I gave the situation to God and quickly found that I had nothing to worry about. The children's sermon was already a highlight of the service, and the attraction was not with the sermon itself—it was with the kids. When Pastor Dunkel called the children up front, about two dozen of them filed down the aisle in their lacy dresses, starched shirts, and shiny black shoes. The girls wore their hair curled into fat ringlets and adorned with homemade bows, while the boys' short hair was neatly greased and combed back. And they sat Indian-style at my feet and looked up at me with completely innocent eyes.

I only had five minutes, but I made the most of them. I used a microphone and passed it around to children so the whole congregation could hear their questions and comments. Object lessons seemed to catch their interest and spark conversations. One Sunday I wore my prized coyote pelt on my head while I told the children about wolves masquerading in sheep's clothing to deceive others. Another Sunday I showed them an Eskimo yo-yo, which is completely unlike traditional yo-yos, and another Sunday I demonstrated a bullroarer, a device used to scare off wolves in the wild. Bullroarers are made completely from native objects such as seal intestines and baleen, from whales. As it swung in a circle and made its whooping noise, the kids erupted into applause.

The kids participated by asking and answering questions, and giving examples from their own lives. Their comments sometimes illustrated the points I was trying to make. They talked about their chickens and their dogs and their pigs, and everyone enjoyed the interplay. Then, one particular Sunday, we were discussing vegetables—beans, in particular. I shared with them that some of the best meals I'd ever eaten had come from the gardens of the people here in this church, and how God provides for His children.

An adorable little girl named Hannah raised her hand. She had fat blond curls and huge blue eyes and wore a pink ruffled dress, lacy white socks, and black patent leather shoes. Kermit the Frog and Miss Piggy sat primly on her lap. I passed her the microphone.

"I like beans," she whispered. Her little voice reverberated through the sanctuary.

"You do?" I asked.

She nodded. "We have them a lot at my house, but starting about seven o'clock we'd better watch out."

I swallowed the bait just like a large-mouthed bass. "Why?"

"Because that's when my mom starts passing gas, and it's really smelly."

The church exploded into titters. Hannah's mom, as always sitting on the second row, pressed her hand to her mouth, her face red and her eyes huge. Her husband, sitting next to her, fell over sideways, guffawing uncontrollably. She glared at him. "Hal! It's not funny," she hissed.

"Aw, yes it is. And it's so true," he whispered back and laughed harder.

This sent a message to the kids that if they embarrassed their parents, they could make everyone laugh, and they wouldn't get into trouble. A few other instances followed, and I finally took pity on the red-faced moms and stopped handing the microphone around. I kept it in my hand and repeated the kids' questions for the benefit of the audience.

*　　*　　*

Every week, I prayed for inspiration on what the Lord wanted me to teach these kids. It was always an adventure; things seldom went completely as planned. It was far better to simply leave it in the Lord's hands than to try to plan every moment. I just did my part and watched Him work.

I found simple Bible stories that could be told in five minutes, using something tangible that seemed to work so well with these small children. When I could find something that the bigger kids could be involved in, so much the better.

One week I happened upon the familiar story in the Gospel of John where Jesus gave sight to a blind man. Jesus had just had an encounter with the Jewish leaders that almost ended in Him getting stoned. He somehow walked right through their midst and left the temple. In the next chapter, He passed by a man in Judea who had been blind from birth.

I imagined the scene, and suddenly knew how the older kids and I could teach this lesson in a memorable way. At the youth meeting the day before, we planned, prepared, and practiced.

Pastor Dunkel called the kids up front as usual, and they came down the aisle and settled into their places at my feet.

"Hi everybody, what a beautiful day!" I greeted them.

They nodded their heads, their eyes never leaving mine.

"The sun is shining, and the leaves are turning beautiful colors."

They nodded again. I pointed to a young boy. "Tony, what color is the sky?"

He looked startled. "Blue."

"What color blue?"

He considered. "Light blue."

"Light blue. That's right. But what if you didn't know what that meant? Y'all up for a little experiment?"

"What's a 'speriment?" asked a young boy named Sammy.

"It just means a way of showing you something. Want to try something new?"

"Sure!" they chorused.

I gestured to the older kids, who all came forward with strips of cloth and tied them across the younger kids' eyes. When everyone was blindfolded, I said, "Now stand up."

They all gingerly stood.

"Now walk around."

They staggered around, bumping into each other and holding their hands out in front of them to feel their way. The older kids stayed close, to be sure no one got hurt. The congregation watched intently.

After a minute I told them to sit back down, but leave their blindfolds on.

"This is fun for a minute, but what if you couldn't see? What if you'd never been able to see? What if you didn't even know what colors looked like? Someone could talk about the beautiful blue sky, and you wouldn't even know what that meant because you'd never seen the color blue."

"That would stink," said a girl named Lucy, who was about ten years old. Everyone nodded somberly.

"At the time Jesus lived, people had a difficult life if they couldn't see. They had to beg on the streets for money from other people. They were considered worthless. No one even noticed them.

"One time Jesus was passing through this town and saw a man like that. This man had been blind since he was born. He'd never been able to see anything at all. Anyone have any idea what Jesus did?"

"He made the man be able to see," Tony chimed in.

"Yes, but how?"

No one knew.

"He made some mud pies. Who here has ever made a mud pie?"
Most of the kids raised their hands.

"What did you make it with?"

"Dirt and water," little Sammy blurted.

"Jesus made it with His own spit," I told them. "He spit on the ground and made some dirt into clay. Then He put the clay on the blind man's eyes."

"Ewwwww," said Hannah. "That's gross. That's like when my mom spits on a Kleenex and uses it to wash my face. I hate that."

"My mom used to do that too," I agreed with her. "I didn't like it either. But here's what happened next. Jesus told the man to go wash in a pool, and all of a sudden the man could see. All of his life everything had been dark, just like you see now with your blindfolds on. This man couldn't see anything. Then, after he washed the clay off, he could see perfectly. Like taking a blindfold off. By the time he came back Jesus was gone, so he didn't even know what Jesus looked like. But he knew His name.

"Now, no one even recognized this man. They were used to seeing him begging on the streets, and now he was walking around like everyone else. He told everyone what happened, and who had healed him."

I paused. "You can take your blindfolds off now."

They took off the blindfolds and looked up at me with big eyes.

"How did Jesus do that?" Sammy whispered.

"It was a miracle," I said. "It proved that He was the Son of God. Everyone thought of this man as trash, but Jesus loved him and healed him."

I hesitated, and it came to me in an unplanned flash. This was the whole point that God wanted me to make. "Jesus healed a lot of people. He helped everyone who came to Him. In a few cases, family members asked Him to heal their sons or daughters, and He always did it. He cured skin diseases, and made deaf people hear, and helped people who couldn't walk or had demons inside them.

"But this man . . . he was special because he didn't ask to be healed. This man didn't even know Jesus was there. Jesus was busy just like all of us. He could have just walked on by, but He did it because He cared and He could. The man was so happy that Jesus had healed him.

"That's what I want you to remember from today. Jesus loves everyone, no matter who you are. And He will do amazing things, when you least expect it."

*   *   *

I sat in my church office on a Saturday afternoon in late November preparing for a youth group meeting, thinking back at that children's sermon when Hannah had so embarrassed her mother. Something was dancing around the edges of my mind, something that had escaped me at the time. What was it? I closed my eyes and thought back, bringing Hannah into my head as she was that day—so cute, with her frilly dress and blonde ringlets. It was hard to remember that day without laughing, but I resisted, concentrating instead on how she looked.

Whatever it was that I was supposed to remember continued to elude me, so I went to the next thing on my to-do list, which was clearing off my desk. The mail pile was getting tall, so I attacked it. On top was a letter with an impressive logo, announcing that Knoxville would be hosting the World's Fair for six months. Or, as it was officially known, the Knoxville International Energy Exposition.

The fact that the World's Fair was coming was not news, but the information in this letter was. Massive construction work was going on in Knoxville to be ready for the opening date, which was May 1, 1982—about eighteen months from now. One of the projects was a Sunsphere, which still dominates the Knoxville skyline. Another was an amphitheater in the United States pavilion, which was the point of the letter in my hands. Christian entertainment had to be booked for this amphitheater. They were looking for actors, singers, musicians, and any other entertainers they could get to fill the time. This letter, obviously a form letter, had been sent to the Pleasant

Grove Youth Director from the amphitheater's scheduling coordinator, a woman named Nancy Mahoney. Scanning down the letter, I realized that this was a ministry of the North American Mission Board, who'd sent me to Alaska.

I sat back and thought. What a golden opportunity for ministry. People from dozens of countries around the globe would be in Knoxville for six months. The BSU would be a natural fit to help with some of this. But I sensed there was more, and that it involved Pleasant Grove and the amphitheater. It was no coincidence that the letter had come across my desk at this moment. God wanted something of me and of my youth group. What in the world could a group of country kids do that would interest a crowd like that?

The mental picture of Hannah that I'd been struggling to bring to mind suddenly crystallized. Not only was she adorable in her Sunday finery, but she'd been holding something on her lap. Not just stuffed animals, but Kermit the Frog and Miss Piggy. And then I knew.

I did some research over the next couple of hours and by six o'clock that night, when the kids congregated at the Pearsons' house, I was ready. "God is calling you."

The boys and girls sitting around me looked startled. "He is?" asked Jonathan.

"He is."

"What's He want us to do?"

"You know the Muppets, right?"

"Yeah. My kid sister watches *Sesame Street* all the time. I love Oscar the Grouch," said a new girl named Leanne. She'd just moved to town with her parents and younger sister and positively sparkled with personality.

"Me, I like the Cookie Monster," Samson put in.

"You would." Jimmy punched his massive bicep.

"What do you have in mind, Mark?" Angie asked in her quiet, deliberate and thoughtful way.

I pulled the letter out of my pocket and read it aloud to them, then folded it and put it aside. "Anybody know how many countries

Sesame Street and *The Muppet Show* are seen in?"

"A lot?" Jimmy ventured.

"I think it's safe to say that most every kid in the world who has a TV in their house knows who the Muppets are."

"What does that mean to us?"

"It's an opportunity," I said. "Millions of people, including lots of kids, from all over the world will be in Knoxville next summer. They need to be entertained. The North American Mission Board is handling some of that at the new amphitheater. This lady—" I looked at the letter again because I couldn't remember her name, "Nancy Mahoney, is inviting us to participate. So I started thinking, what can we do?"

"What *can* we do?" Jonathan asked.

"We can do puppets. Muppets, to be more exact." I sat down in the chair at the head of the circle of kids. "Think about it. I'll buy the puppets if I have to, but I bet the church will help. You guys can help build a stage. We'll write scripts and practice. By the time the World's Fair gets here, we'll all be ready. The kids will love it. And we'll get the Gospel out to who knows how many people."

The more I talked, the more excited I got, and I could see the excitement growing in the eyes of the kids. Here was something tangible they could do. I wasn't nervous about it. I'd done puppets in my youth groups in Athens and Maryville. How much harder could Muppets be? It just took some dedication, practice and character, and we had plenty of that.

"I'm in," Angie said. "I'll be at UT, so I can help a lot."

"You'd be a great Miss Piggy," her younger brother interjected. She whacked him lightly on the head with her Bible.

"So I should buy the Muppets?"

"Yes," they chorused.

So I did. After a few phone calls on Monday, ten real Muppets were on their way to us from Jim Henson Productions. We'd have real tryouts and casting for the roles of Miss Piggy, Fozzie Bear, Kermit the Frog, Gonzo, Oscar the Grouch, Bert, Ernie, the Cookie Monster, Grover, and the Count.

The Muppets would be here within a few weeks, and we'd start practicing. I couldn't wait.

*   *   *

How to make a lasting impression on young kids about Christmas? The children at Pleasant Grove were more grounded than most, but Santa was still very much in evidence. Such a difference from last year in Nome, when there was absolutely no commercialization. The group home kids hadn't even known that people give each other presents for Christmas. There were no ads, no trees, no turkey dinners. I'd told them the story of Jesus' birth, and their eyes lit with wonder.

Kids here in the Lower Forty Eight were harder to impress. All they wanted to do was write out their Christmas lists and see Santa ride the fire engine at the parade.

I shared my dilemma with Susan Bryant. She was vivacious but so sweet, and excellent with children.

"How would you do it?" I asked her one night as we cleaned the kitchen after supper at the BSU. I had cooked that night, so the stove area was completely covered with spattered grease from where I'd fried fish. She wiped the counter with a soapy rag and thought.

"Let's think birthdays," she said. "The whole point of Christmas is that we're celebrating Jesus' birth. Isn't that the point you want to make?"

"Absolutely. Let's forget all about all the other stuff. Kids get more than enough of that."

"That means no presents."

"Right. These kids can't afford presents anyway. And I only have about five minutes."

"So what do they do for their birthdays, other than presents?"

I put away the fryer and shut the cabinet door, then leaned against the counter and rubbed my back. It ached, as usual. I was still praying, but the silence from the Lord on this subject was deafening. I'd tried physical therapy, faith healers, and had hands laid on me in several churches. Some told me that since I was still hurting, I just didn't have enough faith.

I didn't think it was a lack of faith. I had plenty of faith. The apostle Paul had had his "thorn in the flesh," and the Lord never took away his suffering. But he'd managed to provide a good witness for the Lord. I was determined to do the same, with or without back pain.

So I was carefully managing my pain medication, taking enough to keep the edge off, but not so much that I would fall into the dangerous trap of addiction. I had been dutifully seeing my doctor every thirty days and getting refills of the strong medicine, and he seemed content that I was handling it okay. Now, it had been hours since I'd had a pain pill, and I was feeling it.

I mentally turned my back on the pain and thought back to my childhood birthdays. We hadn't had much money, but my mother had always made sure I had a party of some kind. She made me a cake, my friends came and sang "Happy Birthday" to me, and we swam in the lake. My birthday was August 4, and Lisa's was August 22. Things were chaotic, and even more so after my younger sister, Mellie, was born on July 25 when I was nearly seven years old.

But we each had our own special, unique birthday celebration. I smiled, remembering. "Eat cake and sing."

She looked at me. "I think you have your answer."

25

Three weeks went by. I planned and practiced my Christmas children's sermon, worked on year-end paperwork at my bookkeeping job, finished my final exams, and did preliminary planning for the next semester. While I waited for the puppets to come, I wrote a letter to Nancy Mahoney. There were no computers or even self-correcting typewriters in 1980, so I drafted the letter longhand and then laboriously typed and retyped it until it was error-free without any whiteout. Finally, I pulled it off the typewriter.

Dear Miss Mahoney:

I am writing you on behalf of both the youth at Pleasant Grove Baptist Church in Maryville, Tennessee, and the Baptist Student Union at the University of Tennessee in Knoxville.

Thank you for the invitation to participate in the World's Fair. The whole Knoxville area is already looking forward to it and getting ready for it. It is an immense opportunity for ministry to people around the world.

I would like to offer you the performances of our Muppet ministry at Pleasant Grove and whatever services you need from the BSU for the duration of the Fair. We look forward to helping you however you need.

Sincerely,
Mark R. Smith
Youth Director, Pleasant Grove Baptist Church
President, Baptist Student Union,
University of Tennessee Knoxville

Satisfied, I typed her address on an envelope and neatly folded the letter. As I slid it into the envelope and added it to our outgoing mail, I had no idea that this letter was going to change my life.

*   *   *

The evening of December 20, I sat in my parents' kitchen and painstakingly put the final touches on the first birthday cake I'd ever made in my life. My mother had repeatedly volunteered to do this for me and had hovered anxiously around the kitchen while I performed this love task in at least triple the amount of time it would have taken her. But I wanted to do this myself.

The cake was yellow with chocolate icing. I'd followed her recipe to the letter, but it hadn't turned out like hers. The layers didn't quite line up, and the frosting seemed determined not to stay where it belonged. As I started to write "Happy Birthday Jesus" on the top with a decorating tube, the cake suddenly threatened to fall apart. Alarmed, I glopped more frosting on the cracks and stuck a whole box of toothpicks in the cake to hold it together, then held my breath and hoped. Then I finished the words.

What about the candles? A birthday cake wasn't a birthday cake without candles. Jesus' birth was nearly two thousand years ago. Obviously that many candles wouldn't fit on a cake. I rummaged through my mother's kitchen cabinet and pulled out as many birthday candles as I could find. With all the cakes she made for her three kids, she had a lot. I counted nine boxes of twenty-four candles, plus a few extra. One candle for every decade? That seemed like a good idea. Into the cake went 198 candles. They wouldn't all fit on the top, so I stuck them in the sides too. The result looked like a rather odd porcupine.

I covered the cake lightly with foil, practiced my sermon one more time, and went to bed knowing I'd done my best.

*   *   *

The next day when Pastor Dunkel called the kids up front for the children's sermon, I was ready.

"Anybody know what Thursday is?" I asked the group.

Tony's hand shot up. "Christmas!" he shouted before I could even call on him.

"That's right, Christmas," I agreed. "What are you guys doing for Christmas?"

"Eating," Hannah said. "My mom's mom and her sisters and their whole families are coming to our house. There's going to be like thirty people there. My dad says he can't wait for it to be over."

One by one, the kids shared their families' holiday plans. Cookies and milk for Santa, hay and oats for the reindeer, gifts, food, and family traditions. I waited for the opening I wanted, and finally little Sammy gave it to me.

"I have to go to bed early Wednesday so Santa can come, but we're coming to church first," he said.

"That's right! All the food and gifts are nice, but why do we celebrate Christmas to begin with?" I asked them.

"It's the day Jesus was born," Hannah said.

"Right! Christmas is special because it's Jesus' birthday. He was God's Son, but He came down to earth from heaven as a tiny baby. It's the most special birthday ever, so I think we should celebrate it, don't you?"

I motioned for Pete and Angie, who were standing at the back of the church. They came to the front, Pete carrying the rather lopsided cake and Angie with her arms full of birthday hats and horns.

As Angie put a hat on the children and handed them their birthday horns, Pete and I lit the candles on the cake.

"Probably everyone here was born somewhere clean and safe, but not Jesus," I told them as the candles flickered to life, one by one. "He was born in a filthy place where they kept animals, with no one there except His mother and Joseph.

"Mary was only about fifteen, younger than Angie here, really just a child herself, and Joseph wasn't much older. We hear songs like 'Silent Night' and 'Away in a Manger' that make it sound so wonderful and beautiful. But actually, the ground was hard, the night was cold, and Mary and Joseph had to be scared. They were responsible for God's Son, even though they couldn't have any idea what that really meant, not yet."

By the time Pete and I finished lighting the candles, the first ones that had been lit were almost melted down to their nubs and the cake was ablaze on all sides. It was like a small bonfire, and some of the kids backed away from the heat. "Let's sing 'Happy Birthday' to Jesus," I encouraged them quickly.

Their young, sweet voices rose to the rafters as they sang the old birthday song. Greg Wilson, the music minister, quickly joined in and upped the tempo because the cake was already covered in wax from the melting candles. The kids alternately sang and blew their noisemakers, and then everyone leaned in close and helped blow out the candles.

Until this moment, I was thinking that all in all, this sermon had been a great way to recognize the true meaning of Christmas in a way a little child could understand. What I didn't reckon on was what happens when you blow that many candles out.

Smoke. Lots of smoke.

The front of the church billowed with it. Kids began to cough, choke, and run to their parents. Then, as the smoke wafted toward the ceiling, fire alarms began to wail. People ran to open all the doors and windows, which didn't help all that much.

Within a few minutes the entire congregation had evacuated into the yard and fire engines screamed into the parking lot. Fortunately it was a beautiful, sunny December day. Kids bounced around their parents excitedly. "Mom, did you see that cake?! That was awesome!" The children hadn't been scared at all. They'd had a front row seat and knew exactly what was going on.

I, on the other hand, had taken the whole thing seriously and was now mortified. Pastor Dunkel, Greg, and I stood there and watched the melee.

"Sorry, Pastor," I said sheepishly as firemen charged into the sanctuary.

Greg couldn't hold it in another minute. He bent over double, laughing. Before long Pastor Dunkel joined him, heaving and holding his sides. I stared for a minute before I sighed in relief and let the absurdity of the situation take over. *God does have a sense of humor,* I thought, and started laughing along with them. We howled hysterically and leaned on each other in hilarity.

"Next time," Greg said when he finally caught his breath, "let me handle the birthday celebrations."

26

My final grades arrived from the fall semester, and I breathed a sigh of both frustration and relief. I'd pulled out a B in organic chemistry, which I considered a triumph. My French grade had come up to a C, but no further. I had As in both my religion and ecology classes, and my cumulative GPA had actually risen from 3.22 to 3.33. I knew my dad would be unhappy with the C in French, but I was just glad to have this one over with.

I enjoyed spending time with my family, but too much was too much. The house seemed very full now, with all three of us kids there plus Lisa's fiancé in and out all the time. My mother's brother and sister came with their families. Her parents were unable to make the trip from Oklahoma because of their health. My grandfather was still doing poorly, and my grandmother was almost blind.

The busier and more hectic things got, the more time I needed to spend by myself and with God. The latter was especially important because I could sense that something was coming. Good or bad, I didn't know. Where it was coming from or what it would bring, I had no idea. One thing was pretty sure—whatever God had in mind, the devil and his minions would try to fight it. It would be fruitless, of course, but the battle had to be fought. I'd had some brushes with dark forces, and I knew they had to be respected. Scripture was the best preparation.

I escaped to my nook on top of Look Rock and soaked in the peace with my Bible. I took solace in several specific Scripture passages as I prepared for whatever was coming.

Psalm 138:8 says, "The Lord will accomplish what concerns me; Your lovingkindness, O Lord, is everlasting; Do not forsake the work of Your hands." This told me that no matter what mistakes I made, as long as I was striving to do God's will, He would accomplish in me whatever it was that I was put here to do. That brought me immeasurable comfort. Sometimes I considered myself a complete screw-up, but the Lord would still get His work done through me.

In Jeremiah: "Behold, I am the Lord, the God of all flesh; is anything too difficult for Me?"

And also in Jeremiah, my favorite verse, "'For I know the plans I have for you,' declares the Lord, 'plans for welfare and not for calamity to give you a future and a hope.'" The Lord was specifically addressing the Israelites in this passage, but the broader application is for all of His people. Including us. The words soothed my soul. I closed my eyes, stilled my churning thoughts, lifted my face toward heaven, and opened myself up to my Father.

"Father," I prayed, "something is about to happen. Everything seems to be on the verge of something. My family, the church, the BSU, the World's Fair, even my job at the lumber company.

"Please grant me strength, wisdom, and discernment, Father. Please help me to know and do Your will. Help me reach people in Your name. I depend on Your help in whatever it is You want me to do."

I paused and flipped through my Bible until the parable of the soils caught my eye. I read it in Matthew, then slowly paged to the Gospel of Mark and read it there, and finally to Luke and read that account.

As always, it amazed me that anyone could read the Bible and doubt that an omniscient One had been behind it. Three very different men had told this story in almost the exact same way. There were no tape recorders, no way to quickly take notes to ensure accuracy. These men were traveling with Jesus, learning from Him night and day. It was much, much later—probably about thirty years—

when they wrote their accounts of His life and teachings. And they were not together at the time they wrote. The only Person who helped them was the Holy Spirit Himself.

This particular parable reminded me of my conversation in the hospital with Miss Ina.

Seeds have to be thrown onto the ground before they can possibly take root. That's the first step. But that doesn't guarantee anything. The wind can blow the seeds away immediately. The seeds might fall in the middle of weeds and thorns and be choked out. They might fall on rocks and seem to thrive at first, but they have no sustenance and eventually die. Then there are the seeds that fall on fertile ground. They grow and thrive and multiply.

This is the end of Jesus' parable, but I kept thinking down the road. We also see plants that have somehow, miraculously, pushed impudently and bravely through rocks and trees, even through cracks in city sidewalks. My heart had always gone out to these brave sprouts. They are determined to grow, thrive, and bear fruit despite all odds.

Our job on earth is to plant the seeds and take care of them. If one looks weak, we take care of it and help it grow. We weed and we water. Some plants will bear fruit and others will not. Some will die. We might take care of a plant and then have to move on to another field, never seeing or knowing that the plant eventually bears a big harvest after we're gone.

Since Alaska, I'd felt that my strength was in the nurturing. I could throw seeds out, but I was much better at taking care of them and helping them grow. I could spot a blade of grass or a flower in a sidewalk crack. If it had food, sunshine, and water, it had a chance. But only God knew. My job was simply to do my best. Then, leave the rest to God.

I bowed my head again. "Thank You for this day, Father, and for this time with You. Help me to find those sprouts and to know what to do for them. In your Son's name I pray, amen."

27

Suddenly 1981 arrived, and the spring semester began with barely a minute to take a breath. Classes began on January 12, and I had a slightly more reasonable course load—my last French class, child psychology with an accompanying lab, comparative invertebrate anatomy, and weight training. This last course was Vernon Douglas's suggestion.

The BSU Executive Committee's first meeting of the semester was scheduled for Wednesday, January 14, and it was an important one because we would select the missionaries who would go to Alaska this summer. Besides being the BSU president, I'd also kept my position as mission chair, so I had a significant responsibility. My feelings were even stronger when I pictured the church and the children, and I knew that this decision was important for their future.

I wanted to make the right choice, the one that was God's will, so I fasted that day and spent longer than usual in prayer and meditation the night before. I knelt in my little bedroom beside my mattress. My back ached. I ignored it.

"How, God?" I asked. "How do I make sure the people we choose are the ones you want?" I relaxed, blanked my mind and let my spirit drift. I wanted a scriptural answer to my question, so I'd know this was right. There'd been times in the Bible when someone had to choose people to do a job for the Lord. The choice was usually made obvious.

There was the time my dad and I had discussed recently, when Moses listened to his father-in-law's advice and chose leaders from the tribes of Israel to help resolve issues. There was the time when a twelfth apostle had to be chosen to replace Judas, who'd betrayed Jesus. In that case, they drew lots and trusted the Lord to ensure the result was His will. It was the last time lots were drawn; after that the Holy Spirit came and dealt directly with God's people.

My wandering thoughts lit on Gideon, the young son of the tribe of Manasseh who'd been directly instructed by an angel. He questioned his selection and dared ask the Lord for proof. Not once, not twice, but three times.

Here's the thing, I thought to myself. *The Lord uses ordinary people.*

Immediately, I knew I'd hit on the key. This is a common theme in the Bible. He uses people who are unsure, who would not be able to do these things on their own. Then there's no doubt that the Lord is responsible. Moses thought he couldn't speak. David was a child watching sheep when Samuel came and anointed him. And in Gideon's case, his people had been overrun and overtaken by the enemy Midianites. The people of Israel thought God had forgotten them.

Gideon was going about his business, doing his usual job, beating out wheat in wine presses so his family would have something to eat, when an angel came to him and told him God wanted him to deliver Israel from the Midianites.

I laughed to myself. I could imagine Gideon's first response. One minute he was laboring through a horrible life, and the next he was being commissioned by the Lord for an impossible task. Save the people of Israel? By himself? He must have looked behind him to make sure the angel wasn't talking to someone else.

When God finally sent him enough signs that Gideon was convinced, he then had the job of carrying out his mission. He gathered men for the coming battle. God told him he had too many men. In the book of Judges, the Lord told Gideon, "The people who are with you are too many for Me to give Midian into their hands, for Israel would become boastful, saying, 'My own power has delivered me.'"

What followed was what spoke to me now, as I contemplated choosing two missionaries to go to Alaska. Gideon performed a winnowing out process. First, he told his men that if they were afraid, they could go home. Of thirty-two thousand people, twenty-two thousand left. Ten thousand remained.

God told Gideon that was still too many and gave him specific instructions to further narrow it down. Gideon was to bring the men down to the water and separate them into two groups: those who lapped their water from their hands like a dog, and those who knelt to drink. Only three hundred lapped their water, and those were the ones God wanted.

So Gideon's army was narrowed from more than thirty thousand down to three hundred. All the rest were sent home. And those three hundred men—using even more specific instructions from the Lord—took Israel back from Midian, where the army was "as numerous as locusts." More than 130,000.

I was onto something. I could feel it. I took out the application packets that the thirty aspiring missionaries had submitted and found what I was looking for.

All of the applicants were qualified. All had professional looking resumes. All had financial plans. All had sterling references. No one seemed to have an edge until I got to the personal questionnaire section. This part had been written especially for this mission trip because the North American Mission Board standard application hadn't included it, and I wanted some personal insights into the applicants' characters.

Question 1: Why do you want to be a missionary?

Question 2: Why do you want to go to Alaska?

Question 3: What do you hope to get out of this trip?

Question 4: If you were to get there and find that the situation had changed, and your funding had been cancelled, what would you do?

From there it was easy. The application packet had been exhaustive, and the Q&A section was near the end. Most people were tired and ready to finish. Only the most dedicated people put thought and insight into their answers. Into the first discard pile went those who had simply said they wanted to help people. Into the second went those who had said they wanted an adventure away from home. The last two questions were harder, and I deliberated. So far, five applications had survived the winnowing out process. They were all regulars at the BSU, and all would be good missionaries. But we could only take two.

I knew the two the Lord wanted were there in this small stack, but now the decision had to belong to the whole committee. It was too important.

*   *   *

The night arrived. In addition to the six residents, Bert and Daniel had been added to the EC to help with evangelism and outreach, and we had invited Randy Barnette to participate tonight as well. He had started attending freshmen Bible studies in the fall and had quietly caught fire. Shy but extremely inspired and capable, he was quickly becoming the heartbeat of the dorm Bible studies. I had learned to listen to his ideas.

At the end of the meeting, when we had finished our regular agenda, Randy tentatively raised his hand. I gestured toward him. "The chair recognizes Randy Barnette. Yes, Randy?"

"Well," he gulped, "first of all I think it's great that the BSU had the Bible studies in the dorms last semester. I was a Christian before, but those changed me."

"That's great," Vernon said. "It's good to know God's using those studies."

"That is great," I agreed. "You said 'first of all.' What else?"

He took a deep breath. "I think we should expand them."

I sat back and looked at him. Expanding the Bible studies was something I'd considered, but we simply hadn't had the manpower. "Tell us your ideas," I said.

"There are so many dorms that when we do it like we're doing it now, one per week, it just isn't enough," he said. "When kids start getting it, they want more. They need more, and freshman year is the best time to reach them."

"I totally agree," I said. "Go on."

"I'd like to see us double our schedule this semester. You and Susan keep doing what you're doing. I'll learn from your lessons and do another one later in the week for the boys."

"How about the girls?" Susan wanted to know.

"I have a friend who wants to help out the same way with the girls. Joanne Knightley. Susan, I think you know her."

"I do. I think she'd be excellent."

"When do you want to start?" I asked.

"Right away."

We debated Randy's idea for a few more minutes, but there was really no down side, as long as he and Joanne were committed to doing this the right way. We were convinced that they were. And when young people started growing like this, I wanted to see God work in their lives.

The committee approved Randy's idea unanimously, and we moved to a private session for just the six residents and Bob Hall to make a decision on the missionaries.

As Bert, Daniel, and Randy exited the room, I led the group in prayer.

"Father," I said, "please be with us as we make this important decision. It's going to affect the lives of a lot of people, and we want to make the right choice. Thy will be done, amen."

I passed around a concise list of all thirty applicants and the necessary information. As I'd already observed, everything seemed in order on the surface.

"How do we choose?" Wanda said. "Everyone looks fine."

"Well," I said, "I've prayed about that and I have an idea."

Everyone knew the story of Gideon, but I reminded them and watched comprehension dawn on their faces.

"You're going to find a way to narrow them down," said Kenny. "Seeing as how we can't take them down to the creek and watch them drink the water."

"Actually, I already have." I told them about the questions, and how I'd narrowed the applications down to a final five for their review.

"Excellent," said Vernon. "Show us the finalists."

"It's too close to call from the Q&As. The next step is yours. Here's your assignment." I passed around a plate with five names on it, one for each of them. They each drew a name. "You'll know these names. They're all here a lot. I want you to watch them for the next week. Like Kenny said, we're not going to watch them drink water from the creek but look for things that strike you as unusual or beyond the expected.

"Two rules—don't let them know you're watching them, and don't talk to each other about it. We'll have a special meeting one week from now to report on what you've seen and make a final decision together. Understood?"

"Got it," Brandon said. Everyone nodded, and we adjourned.

*   *   *

The next week was a comedy. Every EC member took this assignment personally. The applicants, unknowing and unaware, went about their business with BSU work. Giving Brandon and Kenny license to spy was like a gift from heaven. Kenny nicknamed himself 007. Expert at Nerf sniper, they crept around on cat feet and watched their prey from around corners, the balconies, and the roof. Wanda and Vernon did their assignments in more businesslike ways, using the noonday event and our welcome program as excuses to be present everywhere. And Susan kept watch from the kitchen and the study area in the front room, where everyone came and went at some point. Bob Hall and I observed in amusement. He quickly figured out who the finalists were by watching the surveillance efforts.

In the end, our five finalists never knew they were under a microscope. And like a jury, we didn't discuss it until the end of the week, when we were safely gathered for our special meeting.

I convened the meeting, began with a prayer for the Lord's guidance, and called for reports. "Who wants to go first?"

Kenny's hand shot up.

"The chair recognizes Kenny Duncan. Who were you assigned to this week, Kenny?"

"Daniel Bowman." He bounced in his seat with excitement. "You told us to be looking out for anything above and beyond, and I'm telling you, this guy is for real. He thought he was alone in the kitchen, and he saw the trash was full and took it out."

I liked Daniel, but taking out the trash didn't seem to be an adequate qualification for being a missionary. "Anything else?"

"Oh, I'm just getting started. Take a look at this." He passed around copies of his neatly typed report. We scanned them. "He sits and prays before every meal, even when he's alone. He greets people at the front door and makes them feel at home." He shuffled his papers. "I saw him out front helping a younger kid who dropped his book bag and everything spilled out on the sidewalk. He participates in Bible studies and helps people who don't understand the passages. Bottom line, he lives his faith, and he does it because it's in his heart."

Susan went next, followed by Brandon and Vernon. They all had watched kids who seemed to be good, committed Christians but hadn't done anything over and above what was expected. My heart was beginning to sink. Daniel looked like an obvious choice, but the second missionary seemed fuzzy. Then Wanda took the floor.

"I know what you're all thinking, and I think I can help clear this up," she said. "I watched Bert Gibson. That boy is a spark plug. I noticed that Bert interacts well with everyone, but when he's with Daniel it's like a well-oiled machine. They're like partners. One picks up where the other leaves off."

I nodded and shared my own observation from the past week. One night I couldn't sleep because of my back pain and got up to go to the kitchen for a snack and fell smack over Bert, who'd fallen asleep on the floor in the living room. That, to me, signified his commitment to us and our work. "It was like God literally put Bert in front of me for me to trip over," I told the EC members. "Go on, Wanda."

"At the noonday program last week, he and Daniel took over and led a small group after the program. It wasn't even planned. They just saw a bunch of kids hanging around and pulled them together. The next thing I knew, they were all pulling out their Bibles and turning them to Romans. They finished up with a group prayer." She glanced at her notes. "There's more, but it's along the same lines. I don't have any doubt in my mind. Bert and Daniel are the team we want. They'll make a difference up there."

I felt the same and, looking around the room, knew everyone else did too. This process had worked, just like it had with Gideon. We had narrowed down the field, and God had done the rest. We cast a final vote, but the decision had been made. We had our missionaries.

"Who wants to tell them?" I asked.

"Let me," said Bob. "I have a special prayer I want to share with them. Is that okay?"

"More than okay," I asserted. "I'll work with them over the next few months to get them ready. You can tell them right away."

"Consider it done," he said.

28

Girls. The thought crossed my mind more and more often as I watched couples at UT stroll the campus together. My schedule was jam packed, but surely I could make room for a date. She had to be the right one, though. I had no interest in dating anyone that I couldn't see a future with. Of all the girls I saw at UT, there just didn't seem to be one that caught my interest.

I'd had girlfriends before but never a serious one. One I'd dated in high school was now a student at Carson Newman, a couple of hours north on Interstate 81. Before I left for Alaska I tried seeing her, but the distance was too great and the chemistry not strong enough. I saw no reason to pursue that avenue again.

Sandy was a friend, a girl I'd always liked, but the timing had never been right. I gave her a call now and discovered that she was seeing someone. Oh well.

When I could finagle a weekend off, I went to Georgia Tech to visit Doug Taylor and found myself double dating with him, his girlfriend, and her sister—who happened to be twice as pretty as Doug's girlfriend. Their parents wouldn't let either of them date unless they were together, so I did Doug a favor by allowing him some time with his girl. Still, no chemistry, no matter how pretty she was.

Maybe I'm being too picky, I thought one weekend as I settled at my desk at Pleasant Grove. I definitely didn't lack for things to fill my time. The right girl would come along when God was ready, and not before.

I scanned through my mail and found a letter from Nancy Mahoney, the lady I'd written to about supporting the World's Fair with the youth and the BSU. *That was quick,* I thought as I tore open the letter and read it. I'd only sent her my offer about a month before. I checked the date—this letter was dated about a week before, so it probably been sitting here for a few days.

Dear Mr. Smith:

I gratefully accept your offer to have your youth group perform at the World's Fair next summer, and also your offer for the UT Baptist Student Union to support us in other ways.

I am scheduling your youth group for two performances each week for the duration of the Fair: Wednesday evenings and Saturday mornings. Hopefully this will work with your and their schedules. As for the BSU, I will be in contact with you over the coming months about specific ways they can support the Fair. With your close proximity, I am sure we will find plenty for them to do.

Again, thank you for your offer and I look forward to working with you. Together, with the Lord's help, we can reach numerous people from around the globe in His name.

> Sincerely,
> Nancy Mahoney, event coordinator
> Knoxville World's Fair

I let out a whoop and punched a fist into the air. Two performances a week, including Saturday mornings! This was more than I'd hoped for, more than I'd bargained for or even prayed for.

A verse came to mind from Ephesians. "Now to Him who is able to do far more abundantly beyond all that we ask or think, according to the power that works within us." This was an example of that, no doubt.

And when the mail came that day I was even more confident. The mailman came puffing up to the church lugging a huge box with my name on it. Snuggled in packing peanuts and bubble wrap were the Muppets I'd ordered from Jim Henson Productions. I carefully lifted them out and looked on the faces of Miss Piggy and Kermit the Frog, among all the others. And an idea was born.

*   *   *

I was smiling secretively when I pulled up to the house where the youth meeting was being held that night, deliberately a couple of minutes late. Pete was waiting outside for me, my helper as usual.

"What in tarnation is that?" he asked.

"You're going to like it," I answered. "Just wait until you see those kids' faces."

We heaved the huge box out of my car and put it down at the doorstep, then rang the bell. When the mom answered and saw the enormous box, her eyes grew round. I put a finger to my lips for her to be quiet, and we slid the box into the foyer.

I walked into the living room where the kids were already gathered, Pete behind me with the box. As we went, I whistled the iconic tune to *Sesame Street*.

"No way!" Samson was the first to pick up on it. He pounced on the box as soon as Pete set it down. I stood back and grinned as they tore in. Samson quickly found the Cookie Monster and paraded around, shouting, "COOKIES!"

Leanne pulled out Oscar the Grouch and experimented with the controls inside the intricate puppet. Before long she had Oscar growling.

Angie, grinning from ear to ear, pulled out Miss Piggy from her packing. The famous Muppet wore a sequined evening gown and a jeweled scarf in her long, blonde hair, which looked a lot like Angie's.

After a few minutes all the kids had a Muppet on their laps and a glow in their eyes. Kermit sat on Jonathan's knee. Jimmy had Grover. Angie's younger brother, Travis, who would be in my youth program when the school year was over, had Fozzie Bear. Two girls who were best friends had Bert and Ernie. Two Muppets had yet to be claimed, but I knew that Gonzo and the Count would have operators as soon as the word got out.

"So what do you think?" I asked, beaming, when the hullabaloo had died down.

"Awesome," said Travis. He almost never spoke in the midst of all the bigger kids, but this was a different day and he had a purpose. His mom, who still led the elementary group on Saturday nights, stood in the back. Her eyes glistened.

"Incredible," said Angie. She clutched Miss Piggy tight.

"I have some more news," I said. "Hang onto your hats."

"Shoot," Jimmy said.

"Remember the letter I told you about? The one from the lady with the World's Fair?" They nodded and gawked, eyes round. I grinned and rushed on. "She answered me this week. Ladies and gentlemen, you are going to be taking the stage at the World's Fair twice a week, for six months. Wednesday evenings and Saturday mornings, May through October of next year."

"Oh!" Leanne exclaimed. "Oh, oh!"

"Man!" Samson said. "It's really real."

"It doesn't get any realer than this. We wanted to make a difference, and you're going to get that chance. People will be coming from all over the world."

"How can we be ready in time?" Angie asked with a worried look on her face.

"We have sixteen months. We practice during our meetings and every chance we get for outside groups. In fact—I was thinking, what do you say we give these little guys a test drive tomorrow?"

"Tomorrow?" The young girl who'd claimed Bert, Jessica Hammond, gulped hard. A few short months before, she'd been starry-eyed toward Jonathan. Now, she'd grown up a lot. I was considering moving her to the advanced group.

"Tomorrow. We need help with costumes, sets, transportation, and probably a lot of other stuff that we don't even know yet. No time like the present to start signing people up."

"But how can we be ready tomorrow?"

I smiled. "We have a group that doesn't care if we're ready or not."

* * *

We worked later than usual that night, and well before the worship service the next morning we were staged and ready. Pastor Dunkel called the children to come forward for the children's sermon, and as usual they filed forward and settled at my feet.

I opened my mouth to speak, and was immediately interrupted by the Cookie Monster leaping up. "COOKIES!" he screamed and scurried back and forth. "COOKIES!"

Pandemonium ensued. Everyone's eyes grew huge and the children leaped as one to their feet to see better.

"It's the Cookie Monster!" Hannah squealed.

"Wait!" I interrupted. "What are you doing here, fella? This is a children's sermon. I don't see any cookies."

"ME WANT COOKIES!"

"And I need some water!" Kermit the Frog popped up from the baptismal. "I am a frog, after all."

"You're always wanting something." Miss Piggy leaped up from behind two pews near the front of the room. "You have moi. Gorgeous moi. Who could ask for anything more?"

By now the children were screaming. Anyone who had a television in their homes knew these Muppets. With difficulty, I restrained my hilarity and kept a stern look on my face as Oscar the Grouch, Grover, Bert, Ernie, and Fozzie Bear popped up from the choir loft and joined the pandemonium.

"What do you guys think you're doing?" I demanded. "I'm trying to talk here. These kids want to listen to me, not you. Don't you, kids?"

"No!" the children chorused.

"What are you saying? You'd rather listen to them?"

"Yes!" they yelled.

I heaved a deep sigh. "All right, then. They're listening. There must be some reason you guys are here interrupting my children's sermon. What do you want to tell them?"

Kermit cleared his throat and gave a froggy smile. "Ahem, we have an announcement to make."

"Go ahead."

"We're not visitors. We have a job to do."

"You do? Tell us about it."

Miss Piggy took over. "We're going to be performing at the World's Fair next summer! Two days a week. We're going to be the stars of the show."

"Well, not really the stars," Kermit objected. "Jesus gave us this chance, so He's the star. This is a huge chance to tell thousands and thousands of people about Him. We can tell everyone how much He loves them."

"WILL THERE BE COOKIES?" the Cookie Monster bellowed.

"I think we can arrange that. What do you think?" I asked the kids. "Do you think all those people will listen to these Muppets about Jesus?"

"Yes!" the kids screamed.

"Good job making the announcement, guys. I couldn't have said it better myself. It's a big responsibility, and we have a lot to do before next summer. We'll need a lot of help. Kids, can we practice on you?"

"Yes!"

"Parents, there's a lot to do, and we need all the help we can get. If you're willing to help us, please see me after the service." As I talked, the youth Muppeteers sneaked out with the Muppets.

The children went back to their seats, still babbling. I joined the youth in the back of the church. They were brimming over with excitement.

"Did you hear them? Did you see them?" Angie's eyes sparkled. "That was so much fun. We can really do this!"

"Yes, we can," I agreed. After some high-fiving and congratulations, the kids dispersed and put their Muppets safely away. We didn't want the children to see them and have the illusion spoiled. And just in time. Within fifteen minutes, Pastor Dunkel finished his sermon and the congregation started filing out.

I expected help, but what happened next was far beyond anything I could dream or imagine. Parents came to me in droves to offer their services. By the time everyone cleared out, a group of men had volunteered their excellent carpentry skills to make a set. Women had committed to make curtains and costumes and provide food. And a bunch of other people had volunteered to provide transportation and do whatever we needed them to do.

Miss Ina waited until everyone had left and pulled me aside. "Well done, Mark."

I looked into her eyes. "Thank you, Miss Ina. But it's all about Him."

"That's why you're succeeding here. In this ministry. You know it's about Him. You just keep throwing out those seeds. Some of them will sprout. You'll see."

"You know Pete's helping us."

"I do. He's one of the seeds I'm talking about. I'm still hoping and praying."

"Me too."

As usual, I had been invited to a church member's house for Sunday lunch, and the Muppets were the sole topic of conversation. People were beyond excited about this ministry opportunity.

But the whole time, I was thinking about what Miss Ina had said. It was, indeed, all about Him. I drove back to the church to get ready for tonight's youth meeting. I went into my office, closed the door, and sank to my knees in front of my chair.

"Lord," I prayed, "thank You for the great opportunity You've given us to spread Your Word and praise Your name. Thank You for the wonderful people here and their offers of support. Help us to keep doing Your will and be worthy of this opportunity. In Jesus' name I pray, amen."

I stayed there a long time, drinking in the silence and the presence of the Spirit. At times like this, I was absolutely certain that I was walking in His will, and it was a wonderful feeling. It was with peace and serenity that I eased into my chair and began preparing for the evening session.

29

January turned into February, and my life was a blur of Muppet practices, Bible studies, BSU life, my bookkeeping job, and—of course—classes and homework. Things were so hectic at the BSU that I stepped up the time I spent in my hideaway at the library. No way did I want my grades to suffer.

I had no idea how to operate puppets on a big stage or do ventriloquism, but I did my research and began helping the Pleasant Grove kids with the difficult skill of throwing their voices. This wasn't as critical with Muppets because the kids themselves were hidden and wouldn't have to talk with their mouths closed. They would, however, have to train their diaphragm muscles to project their voices to a large area. The amphitheater where they would be performing was very large and open to the outdoors. Greg Wilson volunteered to help teach the kids how to use and expand their diaphragms.

As missions chair, I began training Daniel and Bert around the end of February for their upcoming journey. I'd also asked Kenny and Brandon, as missionaries' children, to provide their viewpoints during this three-month training time.

Daniel and Bert had no way of really knowing what they were in for, but I did. I intended to prepare them as best I could, then send them for a week with Charles and Patsy Chandler in Anchorage before they arrived in Nome. The Chandlers were a wonderful couple who had made sure I had the clothing I needed and had also worked with me on spiritual, mental, and emotional preparation for my nine months in northwestern Alaska. Their advice had saved my life on several occasions in the brutal Nome winter. Daniel and Bert wouldn't have to suffer the extreme cold, but they needed training nonetheless. They were about to enter a completely different culture.

The feeling I'd had on Look Rock in December—that something was coming—was stronger than ever. I still didn't know if it was good or bad, but I had a sense that it would be both. God's will was being done in several arenas, and the devil and his minions would do their best to derail whatever good things we were doing in the Lord's name. Our new missionaries needed to be ready for this.

Scriptures, I knew, are essential in being prepared to face dark forces. In preparation for missionary training, I spent even more time than usual in the Word.

In the book of Daniel, I reread a passage in which Daniel, the Lord's prophet to the nation of Israel, had been praying for days for forgiveness, mercy, and deliverance for Israel from her enemies. The people had sinned abominably for generations, and God had forgiven them and rescued them time and time again. Daniel was asking Him to do it again. Day after day—three weeks—he prayed, fasted, and prayed some more.

One day he was by the bank of the Tigris River, and a man appeared to him to tell him what was in store for Israel. The interesting thing about this passage for my purposes today was that this man—an angel of heaven—was sent by God on the first day that Daniel had prayed, with a message in response to his prayers. The angel had been detained by a being described in Scriptures as the prince of Persia, but my concordance told me that this person was actually an evil spirit specifically anointed with Persian power to thwart the work of God.

The angel who appeared to Daniel is believed to be Gabriel. Michael, the chief angel of heaven, came to help Gabriel fight the dark being and continue on his divine mission. More than three weeks after Daniel first began to pray, Gabriel finally came to him with God's answer.

I sat back and thought. *We just never know, do we, what's going on around us?* We might wonder why Gabriel didn't just appear instantaneously in a vision, or arrive in a poof from heaven. The passage says Gabriel touched Daniel and comforted him. Perhaps God just knew that Daniel needed direct, personal confirmation.

Satan and his minions are continually engaging in warfare to keep people from doing good things for the Lord. Our job is to put on the full armor of God and stay in His will. "Tomorrow," as Jesus tells us in the sixth chapter of Matthew, "will care for itself."

It was imperative that Daniel and Bert understand this. I reread and jotted notes from other Scripture references, in Romans, Ephesians, and 1 Peter. One weekday I sat the new missionaries down for their first training session.

I began with prayer as usual, asking God to bless our preparation and Daniel and Bert as missionaries to do His work.

I opened my eyes, took a deep breath, and sat back. I looked both of them in the eye, one at a time.

"Why are you going to Alaska?" I asked them.

Bert, always the fearless, forthright one of the pair, answered first. "To work for the Lord. To do His will. To help and to minister."

I looked at Daniel expectantly. He met my gaze. "To continue the work going on there and spread God's word."

"You're exactly right, and you're a great team. That's the big picture, as we see it. But the picture is really a lot bigger than that. Bigger than we can possibly know, and you have to be prepared in every way—physically, emotionally, mentally, and spiritually. Today we're going to work on getting more spiritually aware."

Daniel looked confused. "What do you mean?"

"Do you believe in demons and angels?"

A long pause. Again, Bert answered first. "In what sense?"

"In the sense that demons are here, active, doing everything they can to keep us from doing God's work. That angels are continually protecting you from them. That there are battles going on all the time, all around us, that we never even know about."

"I know demons were active in the Bible," said Daniel. "Satan himself tempted Jesus, and demons had to be cast out of people. I hadn't thought much about him still being here, now."

I turned to the passage I'd picked in Ephesians, which Bob Hall had used with me so effectively before I left for Nome last fall. "Finally, be strong in the Lord and in the strength of His might. Put on the full armor of God, so that you will be able to stand firm against the schemes of the devil. For our struggle is not against flesh and blood, but against the rulers, against the powers, against the world forces of this darkness, against the spiritual forces of wickedness in the heavenly places. Therefore, take up the full armor of God, so that you will be able to resist in the evil day, and having done everything, to stand firm."

Bert and Daniel were silent, listening. I paged to the passage in 1 Peter. "Be of sober spirit, be on the alert. Your adversary, the devil, prowls about like a roaring lion, seeking someone to devour. But resist him, firm in your faith, knowing that the same experiences of suffering are being accomplished by your brethren who are in the world."

Finally, I turned back to Romans, chapter 8. "I am convinced that neither death, nor life, nor angels, nor principalities, nor things present, nor things to come, nor powers, nor height, nor depth, nor any other created thing, will be able to separate us from the love of God, which is in Christ Jesus our Lord."

I looked up. "What does all this tell you?"

Bert hesitated and spoke. "That the devil is real and here, and we need to guard against him. That God loves us and will protect us if we trust Him."

"This is something you're going to have to believe and reinforce inside yourselves every single day while you're gone," I said. "You're there to do God's work, and you have to keep Him at the front and center of your heart. Dark forces like to stay hidden, subterranean, and anonymous, but they will try to derail you, especially when you start to make an impact. You can count on it. Pray a lot. Study your Bible every day. Then listen and do what the Holy Spirit tells you to do. Don't get distracted from your main mission.

"In the end, this is not our fight. You're there for a purpose. Just be prepared for whatever comes. God's promised to protect you, and He always keeps His promises."

We talked and prayed about this some more, and then our time was up and they left.

After they left, I sank to my knees again and folded my hands. I still had the feeling that something was coming, and my conversation with Bert and Daniel had had little or no impact on that. "Lord, tell me what to do," I begged. "I know there's something You expect of me, but I don't know what it is. Please help me."

Silence. No still small voice. No leading in my heart. Just an assurance of exactly what I'd told Bert and Daniel: As Dr. Charles Stanley teaches as one of his Life Principles—obey God and leave the consequences to Him.

Within the next few days, I understood. The devil and his minions were indeed alive and well. As prepared as I thought I was, I didn't know the half of it.

30

On a Thursday in early March, which was toward mid-term, I sat on the mattress in my room, door shut, and studied invertebrate anatomy. The BSU's noonday program had just concluded, and as usual the house was full of people. I'd let Vernon and the others handle the students who wanted to stay and talk because I had an exam coming up. Usually I retreated to my cubby at the alumni library to study, but today I'd opted to stay in my room and shut the door.

With half of one ear I registered that the steady drone coming from downstairs became more of a roar, with punctuated shouts, but I was too deep in my textbook to pay much attention. That is until Vernon Douglas burst through my door.

"Mark, Bob needs you now." He looked shaken and disheveled.

"What?" I leaped to my feet.

"Just come. Quick."

We sprinted to the bottom of the stone spiral stairs and I took in the scene. A young man I recognized was backed up to the wall in the kitchen, a large knife from the kitchen in his hand, with the sharp edge held to the throat of a female student. She looked terrified and about to faint. Bob caught my appearance with his peripheral vision and said, "Mark, I need you to handle this. I'll take care of all the other students."

The girl looked at me helplessly, eyes huge. I nodded reassuringly.

I did not know the young man's name. He'd been in the BSU before and had always been regarded as quiet, a loner, and slightly awkward. We'd always welcomed him, as we welcomed everyone, but he had never given us reason to feel overly concerned for him.

Now this.

Vernon spoke quietly. "What do we need to do, Mark?"

"You stay with me."

"I'm getting everyone out and I'll call the campus police," Bob said. A crowd of students had gathered, gawking, at the kitchen door. "Come on, ladies and gentlemen. We've got this under control. Police will be here soon. Everybody out."

Slowly they began to shuffle towards the front door, some watching the young man and the terrified girl as they exited. Finally everyone was out, and I heard the lock snick home.

The young man watched me, eyes darting from side to side. The girl stood motionless, breathing fast and hard. I looked back and forth from him to her and spoke to him.

"Come on, man, what's this all about? You don't want to hurt this girl. Let's talk."

What came forth from the young man's mouth was a stream of some language I'd never heard. Distinct words, so he wasn't babbling. I only understood English and a smattering of French, but I at least recognized most languages. This wasn't one of them. And this young man didn't look like a foreigner. He looked like a hometown boy, just like any of the rest of us.

Bible passages began to flash in my head. Not the ones I'd quoted to Bert and Daniel a few days before, but the numerous passages where Jesus, and then His apostles, cast out demons. Jesus could handle any demon because He was, well, the Son of God, with all the authority of His Father through the Holy Spirit. The apostles were given the same power, and they could do similar things if, and only if, they did them in the name of Jesus.

But a demon possessing a person now? In the twentieth century? I'd heard of this happening but had never witnessed it first-hand or really understood it. In my Baptist upbringing, this kind of thing was seldom, if ever, discussed in any details. Then, immediately, the doubt dissipated. Why not? Wasn't this exactly what I'd just told our new missionaries? "The devil prowls about like a roaring lion, seeking someone to devour." The young man I was looking at was obviously not in control of himself. And good things were happening at the BSU. Dark forces did not like it in the least.

"Okay, okay," I said to the young man. "Let's just let this young lady go now. She's scared. I'll stay here with you. We can talk."

"What do I do?" Vernon asked in a low tone, eyes never leaving the young man's face. "Do you want me to take him down?" As an ex-football player, he could. But I knew that wasn't the answer, at least not yet.

"Pray," I said. "In the name of Jesus. Out loud. Keep mentioning His name. Don't stop."

"Okay, but if he gets any weirder, I'm taking him out."

Over the next few minutes I persuaded the young man to let the girl go. After a few staggering steps, Susan intercepted her and led her safely upstairs to the girls' apartment and out of sight. Vernon kept praying.

The young man continued to hold the knife to his own throat, obviously threatening to kill himself. I talked, Vernon kept praying, and every time he mentioned Jesus' name the young man recoiled as if in pain and kept talking in that incomprehensible language.

Slowly, together, we maneuvered the boy to the back of the house, into a conference room. One wall was solid windows, which were open on this warm, spring-like day. Within moments, students crowded into the courtyard at the back of the house and watched through the windows, wide-eyed. Bob kept them at a safe distance.

I took a deep breath. Now was the time. I slowly reached out and laid my hands on the sides of the boy's face and spoke to whatever was in him.

"You aren't going to hurt this boy. In the name of Jesus Christ, the Son of God, leave him now."

The boy bared his teeth and laughed in my face. Vernon fell on his face on the floor and prayed harder, shouting now the name of Jesus.

Heart pounding, sweating, but strangely calm, I looked into the boy's eyes, directly into the face of evil, and spoke louder and with authority.

"I am commanding you, in the Lord Jesus' name and with His authority, to leave this boy NOW! Go wherever He tells you to go, but you must leave NOW. You're not going to hurt or torment this boy anymore."

The boy dropped the knife, collapsed, and began foaming at the mouth, and convulsing. He screamed, eyes rolling in his head, and writhed on the carpeted floor. The kids outside shrieked. After what seemed like an eternity, he went limp and passed out.

"Whoa." Vernon and I went to his side. He slid the knife out of sight. "What was that?"

"Exactly what you think it was," I said. "You did just right. They can't stand the name of Jesus. Go get him a glass of water and put that knife away."

Vernon ran and came back with a glass of water, and after a few minutes the boy's eyelids fluttered. He sat up and looked around, obviously bewildered. We helped him ease into a chair.

"Where am I?" he asked. His voice was completely different, even from the slightly awkward person we'd met in the past few weeks.

"You're in the BSU," I said and gave him the water. "Do you remember what happened?"

"No." He accepted the glass and drank deeply. "The last thing I remember, I was walking down the street and I saw a bunch of people coming out your front door. What happened?"

Vernon and I exchanged glances. "You were acting upset and agitated, but you're fine now," I said.

"Upset? How?"

"Don't worry about it," Vernon interjected. "You're here now, and everybody's okay. We brought you back here to calm down."

At that moment Bob and the campus police strolled into the room. The police were too late for the spectacle but had obviously already been briefed. One of them squatted down beside the still-shaken young man. "What's going on here? You okay, fella?"

"I'm okay, I just don't remember anything," he said.

The police spent a few minutes talking to the three of us. "What happened?" the leader asked me.

"This boy was upset with another student, and wasn't acting like himself, but everything's fine now," I said. "The other student is okay."

They eventually left, evidently satisfied that the boy no longer posed any threat. He took his backpack and Bob led him out. Susan had counseled the girl who'd had a knife to her throat, so she was completely aware of what had happened. She didn't want to pursue the matter any further.

Finally, only the residents of the BSU remained in the building. Shaken, we called Bert and Daniel and gathered for an emergency EC meeting. We prayed, put the pieces together, and discussed strategy. No one had seen the boy come in, so we didn't know exactly what had happened, but we could make a good guess.

The boy had evidently come into the side door while the dozens and dozens of people were leaving through the front door after the noonday program. He must have slipped into the kitchen and taken the knife, then grabbed the girl.

"What did you tell the police?" I asked Bob.

"I just told them that a boy got very upset with another student and we almost had an incident, but it's taken care of now. Then I brought them into the conference room."

"Susan, what happened with the girl? What was her name?"

"Cindy."

"What did she say?"

Susan took a deep breath. She looked drained. "She didn't know any more than what we saw. The boy came up to her and grabbed her, and put the knife to her throat."

"That's all?"

"He was acting weird and talking nonsense."

"Is she okay?"

"She's shaken up but she's fine. She went back to her dorm."

Wanda, Kenny, and Brandon were all for spreading the news that a demon—maybe more than one demon—had been subdued and Jesus had prevailed. Kenny and Brandon had heard about things like this before during their parents' mission years and wanted to spread the word. Susan and Bob were less enthusiastic. The rest of us just sat and listened. Finally Bob spoke again.

"I think we've had enough exposure," he said. "What happened here today was an obvious attempt by dark forces to derail what we're trying to do. Think what would have happened if someone had gotten hurt. We'd have been shut down. What we're trying to do is encourage people to have a closer walk with the Lord. It won't help us to sensationalize this."

"I agree," I said. "A lot of people saw what happened. If God wants to use this for His glory, He will. Let's count it a blessing that the boy didn't get arrested and hauled away. We just go from here and do what we're doing, because obviously it's working."

"I agree," Vernon said, "but I move that we all keep a sharp eye out for this kid. If he comes back, at least one of us stays nearby."

"I also move that we do a prayer walk around this whole house, right now," Kenny said. "All of us."

"A prayer walk?" Daniel asked. "What's that?"

"Exactly what it sounds like." Brandon nodded his head in agreement. "We go as a group around the house, praying. It will keep away whatever came in here with that boy."

We cast a vote, agreed, and adjourned. For the next hour, we moved slowly around the house together, Bibles in hand. In each room we read Scripture and prayed aloud for protection, and for the house to be cleansed. Bert, who couldn't carry a tune in a bucket but never did anything halfway, sang hymns loudly as we went. I supposed it was the motive, not perfect pitch, that counted. The Lord would undoubtedly think the off-key notes coming out of Bert's mouth were beautiful music, coming from a big, pure, beautiful heart.

Everyone across campus hunkered down for exams in those last days before spring break. That young man did come back to the

BSU. More than once. As we'd agreed, one of us was always close by. But now, he seemed normal.

And we could not know it yet, but Bert would have a dramatic impact on this young man's life. The story wasn't over.

PART 3:
REAPING

31

My mother and I had always been like most mothers and sons—we loved each other but quibbled about minor stuff. One of my jobs until I left for college was to take out the trash every day. My independent streak blossomed into a misplaced anger as I grew older and older. Mom could look at the trash can, and then look at me, and my temper boiled over. It was a constant battle until my dad put an end to it and told me that she was my mother and I would respect her and do what she said. He had enough firepower behind him—spiritually, and as my dad—that I stifled my sulky attitude and obeyed.

My mom had always been there for me, though, in her consistent love and unswerving support. Now, to my complete surprise, I found in her a companion in a whole new way.

She had been a Christian my entire life, but now she had taken a spiritual leap. Her growth and relationship with the Lord were blossoming. I saw in her the same things I was feeling in myself, and over spring break we had unprecedented Bible study and prayer times together. We sat on the screened porch at Mountain View and shared new ideas and insights. It was with renewed mental and spiritual fortitude that I went back to UT after spring break.

And, as it turned out, I very much needed the respite.

When the campus refilled after spring break, the change at the BSU was dramatic. In 1981 we had no internet or Facebook or Twitter, or even cell phones, but word of mouth proved to be just as effective. The BSU ministry exploded. The crowds at noonday programs tripled. Kids overflowed the rooms in our dorm Bible studies. Students crowded our comfortable sitting rooms and began to take turns helping with food. Kids chipped in for groceries. Several well-known local churches began to take notice and put their collective weight behind our ministry. The blessings rained down, and we worked harder and harder.

One day I was sitting in my room studying French, which was still the bane of my existence but was, thankfully, nearly over. Vernon knocked lightly and poked his head in.

"Dude," he said with a flabbergasted smile, "did you know there are six people lined up out here, waiting to talk to you?"

I stared at him. "Me?"

"That's what they said."

"Why?"

"Guess you have to find that out for yourself." With that, he stepped out and closed the door behind him. I stared at the smooth wooden panel. Why in the world would kids be lined up to talk to me? I could think of only one reason, and I would have to be very careful with this.

"Lord," I prayed, "give me the words and the wisdom to deal with these young people as You would have me deal with them. It's all about You. In Your Son's name I pray, amen."

Then I stuck my head out the door and saw, as Vernon had described, six people about my age sitting near the door, backs against the wall, patiently waiting, textbooks open. They all looked up when I opened the door. I looked at the one nearest to me. "Hi. Did you want to talk to me about something?

"Yeah, man." He stood and offered his hand. I shook it. "My name's Adam."

"I'm Mark."

"Can we go somewhere private?"

"Sure." We went into my room and shut the door.

For the next hour, and for at least a couple of hours every day for the rest of the semester, I met with students who had various problems in their lives. Adam was having issues with his parents. Another was having academic problems and was being tempted to cheat. Others had "friends" who had problems associated with drugs and alcohol. Others were being tempted and corrupted by pornography. Some had roommate issues. A few just wanted to know if what they'd heard about the demon-possessed boy was true. In all cases, I sat, listened, and waited for the Holy Spirit's prompting. Many times I asked them for their testimony.

"How's your walk with the Lord?" I asked.

"What do you mean?"

"Are you saved? Do you know Jesus as your Lord?"

"I went to church growing up and walked down the aisle when I was little," was a common answer.

"Do you have a church?"

"Not here. I have the one I grew up in at home."

"Do you pray?"

"Sometimes . . . usually when things are bad."

"Do you read the Bible?"

"I don't really have time to read the Bible and I don't understand it anyway."

"Are you interested in giving your life to Jesus? Or rededicating it?"

Sometimes the answer to this was yes, in which case we prayed together and I helped the students understand how they could grow and be stronger in the Lord. More often, they either said they were already saved, or they had to think about it.

Every time someone came in, though, I prayed with them about their specific problem, and that the Lord would work in their lives and show them the answer. Often a Scripture verse came to mind, dealing directly with their specific problem, and I shared it with them. Otherwise I shared verses that God had used in my life the past few years, verses that had always brought me strength and comfort.

Always . . . always . . . I looked for the Lord to lead and simply let Him speak through me. When they wanted to know my opinion,

I gently steered the conversation back to things I could back up with Scripture.

When girls came in, I left the door wide open and sat well across the room to avoid any question of impropriety. The line of kids outside was pushed back so they were all out of earshot, and we kept our voices low enough to ensure privacy.

One, a girl named Allison Bedford, had a boyfriend who wanted to go farther physically than she was willing to go. The pressure was growing, and she was uncomfortable but didn't want to lose him. I listened as she described the mental and emotional anguish she was feeling.

"He says it's okay because we love each other and we're going to get married," she said, twisting her fingers together and dabbing at the tears on her face.

"Are you married now?" I asked.

She looked confused. "Of course not."

"Then you have your answer."

"But nobody waits until they get married to have sex. If you love someone, it's okay. That's what all the books and movies say. I'm just trying to decide if this is the right person and the right time."

"Back up," I said. "The Bible tells us that sex is between a husband and wife. Period."

"But my boyfriend says he can't wait. He says we've been together for six months and it's time to take the next step. He says if I love him, I'll want it too."

Good grief. I couldn't say I completely understood the fellow, because I'd been a Christian since way before desire was an issue. I'd always known that I was going to wait for my wife, and I'd deliberately not put myself in the path of temptation that might sway my resolve. No being completely alone with a girl I was attracted to. No hands in any area that would be covered by a swimsuit. Just avoid the situation to begin with. In my opinion, that was the key to sexual chastity—be committed and stick to it. And trust God to help with temptations, as He promises He will. Now, I looked at her and tried to communicate this concept through Scriptures, in a way that would soothe her and help her.

"Allison, I know that physical desire can be strong. That's the way God made us. But here's the thing . . . if you are a Christian and living for Jesus, then He will give you the strength to withstand any temptation." I flipped to 1 Corinthians and read aloud. "No temptation has overtaken you but such as is common to man; and God is faithful, who will not allow you to be tempted beyond what you are able, but with the temptation will provide the way of escape also, so that you will be able to endure it."

"What does that mean?"

"It means that if you want to do what God wants you to do, He will help you. He will give you a way out of any temptation you face."

"How do I get Him to help me?"

"Just ask."

"Will you help me do that?"

So I knelt with Allison and we prayed together, asking God for strength and guidance, and the discernment to handle her situation. And we prayed for His will to be done in her life.

It became a pattern, and my instinct not to voice my own opinion put me in good stead every time. Soon, a sign appeared on my door and spread throughout the BSU.

OPINIONS ARE LIKE ARMPITS.
WE ALL HAVE THEM AND THEY ALL STINK.

32

One day in early April I sat in my room, tailbone carefully positioned on my mattress, back braced against the wall, studying child psychology. Bert burst in without knocking, breathless.

"Hey, man," I greeted him.

"You'll never guess who I saw in the cafeteria."

"Billy Graham?"

He gave me an exasperated look. "For real, man. Guess. Never mind. It was that guy."

"Which guy?" Sometimes Bert raced ahead of me in his conversation, and I had to struggle to keep up. "Who?"

"That guy. The demon guy. Turns out his name is Joe. Joe Barton."

"Oh." Now he had my interest. "How did he look?"

"That's the thing. He looked fine, but the timing was so weird. I had just been reading in Matthew, and this passage jumped out at me." He opened his Bible and paged to the twelfth chapter of Matthew.

"Now when the unclean spirit goes out of a man, it passes through waterless places seeking rest, and does not find it. Then it says, 'I will return to my house from which I came'; and when it comes, it finds it unoccupied, swept, and put in order. Then it goes and takes along with it seven other spirits more wicked than itself, and they go in and live there; and the last state of that man becomes worse than the first. That is the way it will also be with this evil generation."

He looked up at me. "Do you read this like I do?"

I saw where he was going. "That guy came in here that day and got cleansed of his demon, but unless he gets Jesus in his heart, he runs the risk of that demon coming back and bringing seven of his evil buddies."

"That's exactly what I thought when I read it. And then I saw Joe in the cafeteria."

"What did you do?"

"What do you think I did? I went up and talked to him."

"Tell me."

He sat down on the floor near my mattress and began his story. He had raced into the cafeteria, intent on grabbing a quick lunch between classes, and skidded to a stop when he saw Joe sitting by himself near the back of the room.

"Dude, it was weird," he said. "I had just read that Matthew passage, and it was on my mind, and here the kid was."

"You obeyed." I nodded with understanding. "It was a clear example of the Spirit leading and you following."

He hopped to his feet, unable to sit still. "So I just went up to him and said hi. He didn't know who I was. I guess you and Vernon were the only ones he really saw that day."

"That would make sense."

"So I told him I was there that day and asked him how he was doing. And Mark—the guy just started bawling, right there in the cafeteria."

"Bawling?"

"Yeah, like crying his head off. Loud. People were looking and everything."

"What did you do?"

"Sat down next to him and put my hand on his shoulder, and just waited. Finally he calmed down and told me he'd been so scared and confused, like about what he should do next. He doesn't remember anything, but he'd heard details from other people who saw it."

Bert was starting to grin, so I knew he was leading up to something big.

"Then what?"

"I shared that Scripture in Matthew with him and told him that he needed Jesus to come live in that empty space inside him. Then nothing evil could ever hurt him again."

I stared, agog. "And?"

"And we knelt together right there in the cafeteria and he accepted Jesus."

"Just like that."

"Yep. Then he wanted to know what was next. Like, where he goes from here."

"We can help him with that."

"I know, but he's embarrassed to come back here. He appreciates what you and Vernon did for him, but he's embarrassed."

"To begin with, Vernon and I didn't do anything," I said. "God did it. It's all about Him. Second, there are other choices. Other places he can go. He needs to nurture that seed inside him. Help it grow."

"That's exactly what I said. I told him about Calvary Baptist, which is where I go to church."

I nodded in complete endorsement. Calvary was where I'd attended church my sophomore year at UT, during the year when I was preparing for the mission field. Corey Bennett, the Campus Crusade for Christ worker who still helped me stay on track and grow, had walked up to me in Sunday school class and formed a permanent bond. Calvary had an excellent collegiate program and would be a wonderful nurturing ground for this new Christian. Maybe, in time, he would grow enough confidence to share his amazing testimony.

"Excellent," I said. "Sounds like you did everything exactly right. Exactly as the Spirit led you."

"It feels good to obey," he said with a glow in his eyes. "It's amazing to see things happen right before your eyes."

"Bert," I said with conviction, "I know exactly what you mean. And you're just getting started."

33

Work continued at Pleasant Grove, with weekly children's sermons and monthly Sunday evening sermons. The youth met on Wednesday evenings, Saturday evenings, and Sunday evenings. Greg Wilson worked with the kids on using their diaphragms and projecting their voices. This would be critical in the outdoor amphitheater where our Muppets would be performing.

Day by day, week by week, the older kids became more knowledgeable about the Scriptures and, before long, were able to find passages without fumbling through their Bibles. As the weeks went on, fruit began to show. One Sunday morning, a boy who had visited the youth group the previous week walked down the aisle during the invitation and spoke quietly to Pastor Dunkel. I didn't know until later that something from that meeting had taken root in his heart, and he dedicated his life to Christ.

We worked hard to come up with ideas to practice with the Muppets. And, as it turned out, we didn't have a year to get ready. We performed in another children's sermon, and Pastor Dunkel was so impressed that he spread the word. Within days, my phone rang as I sat at my desk putting the finishing touches on a sermon for the next night. I put my pen down and stretched.

"Pleasant Grove, this is Mark."

"Is this Mark Smith, the youth minister?"

"It is."

"This is Brad Abbott, the pastor at Rocky Branch in Walland."

Rocky Branch was smaller than Pleasant Grove, but just down the road from us. I'd seen the church but had never been to a service. The pastor was reputed to be a good leader with solid biblical teachings.

"Hi there, Rev. Abbott. What can I do for you?"

"Brad. You're making quite the name for yourself with your Muppets."

"We are?"

"Yes indeed. Your pastor can't stop talking about you, and some of our kids want to visit your services to see for themselves."

"Well, that's excellent to know. We'd love to have your kids visit. Whatever we can do for the Lord. It's all about Him."

"I have a better idea. You can help us out a lot if you're willing."

He went on to explain that Rocky Branch wanted to do a Vacation Bible School but didn't have the money or manpower. Many companies offer prepackaged, themed programs for churches to use for VBS programs. But they were expensive. Too expensive for most smaller churches.

"I'm following you—but how can we help?" I asked, tipping up my water bottle for a drink.

He paused. "Bring your kids and your Muppets and lead our Bible School for us."

I sat up, water forgotten. "Can you elaborate a little?"

"From what I hear, you're doing a great job leading both your youth group and the children's sermons. Pick five of the sermons you've already done for the younger kids, and five of the lessons you've already taught for the older kids. Have the Muppets perform once a day."

"You've really thought this out."

"I have. I want our children to have a Bible School, and this is the only way it's going to happen. Will you pray about it and get back to me?"

"Absolutely. I'll talk to the kids about it tonight and get back to you early next week."

I hung up the phone and stared at it. Lead a Vacation Bible School? What an opportunity to help make a difference in many kids' lives. But just because the pastor asked me didn't mean the Lord wanted me to say yes. The decision had to be His, not mine. I sank to my knees and closed my eyes.

"Father, I'm listening." I said. "Is this what You want? If so, I'm completely on board."

I fell silent and soaked in the stillness. I was the only one in the church, which was common on Saturday afternoons. The building creaked. The trees rustled in a slight wind outside. The building was close enough to a nearby creek that I could hear frogs making bird-like sounds.

And suddenly pictures began flashing across my brain. Pictures from Alaska, where I'd taught so many children at the church and at the Lighthouse, and pastored a church for seven weeks. In New Mexico, where I'd gone on a mission trip with my mom and dad as a teenager and helped with the Native American children. The huge horned toad I found in the desert wasn't thrilled, but the kids loved him. Scenes from here in East Tennessee, where God had blessed me with opportunities to work for Him and make a difference, both here at Pleasant Grove and at the BSU. Picture after picture flashed across my mind, proof that God could and would use me. It didn't have to be seven thousand miles away. Suddenly I was very excited about the opportunity and knew it was right.

I let out a thankful breath. "Thank you, Father. We'll do our best and trust You with the details. It's all Yours. Amen."

*   *   *

It was with a bounce in my step and a sly look in my eye that I nonchalantly pulled up to the old barn where we were having our youth meeting that night. The older boys were already there, putting together what would be our bonfire later that evening.

The kids weren't fooled. They had learned to recognize that look.

"Uh-oh." Jimmy elbowed Jonathan in the ribs. "Something's up." Everyone nodded.

"What's going on, Mark?" Pete called out.

"We'll talk later," I said.

We still did a double Bible study, with Martha handling the less mature members and me teaching the others. The system was working well, with both boys and girls graduating from her group to mine and younger or new members rotating in. The two groups stayed about even in number. Currently her son, Travis, who was about to become an official member, was in her group. I still had Angie, who was about to graduate.

When the last regular member arrived, before social time began, I got everyone's attention.

"I guess I'm not too good at hiding things," I began sheepishly. "You guys were onto me from the minute I drove up."

"Now 'fess up," said Samson. "What's up?"

"We have an opportunity," I said and paused dramatically. "The pastor at Rocky Branch called me and wants us and our Muppets to lead their Vacation Bible School."

"Why?" asked Travis.

"How?" Angie wanted to know.

"Cool!" said Leanne, always open to anything new and exciting.

"Dude," said Jimmy, stunned.

I waited until they calmed down.

"When would this happen, Mark?" Martha Galyon asked.

"In the middle of June." More pandemonium. "I know that's just a couple of months away, but I've already been praying about this and I'm convinced God wants us to do it."

Doubtful looks dominated the circle of kids around me. I focused on them, face by face.

"We thought we couldn't do Muppets, and we have. We thought we couldn't minister at the World's Fair, but we're booked for it. We thought we couldn't make a difference in lives, but we're doing it." I let the silence hang. "Without us, these kids don't get a Bible School."

"You said you're convinced this is God's will," Samson said. "How do you know? How can you know for sure?"

All around the circle kids' heads nodded, and I knew this was a serious question that many people struggle with. They'd do God's will, they say, if they just knew what it was. They look for signs, and they test the Lord for their own reassurance.

For me, the answer was simple, but I chose my words carefully. "Psalm 37:4 says if we delight in the Lord, He will give us the desire of our heart. He'll put the desire there. Follow the desire He gives you, then start moving." I paused. "I know it's God's will because I asked Him, and now I really, really want to do it."

"But that verse makes it seem like we can have anything we want," Angie said, confused.

"No, it doesn't." I held up my right hand and ticked off my points. "One, you have to be saved. Two, you have to let the Holy Spirit take control. That means time in His Word and prayer to stay close to Him. Three, you have to work hard to keep yourself pure. No drinking, pornography, or sex outside of marriage. Our bodies are temples of the Holy Spirit and we have to treat them like temples and be living representatives of Jesus. Four, you have to honestly and constantly submit your will to His. For most people, this is the hardest thing. It includes obeying the authorities He's given you on this earth—like the government and law enforcement and your parents, even if the rules and laws don't seem like they make sense. Five, you have to stand up for Him. Suffer for Him if necessary. And finally, give thanks to Him for everything. Everything. Turn to 1 Thessalonians 5:18." I waited until everyone had arrived at the correct verse, then read aloud. 'In everything give thanks, for this is God's will for you in Christ Jesus.'

I looked around the circle of faces. "It doesn't get any clearer than that. This is all His will, spelled out very clearly in the Scriptures. If you do all the things that you know are His will, then the desires of your heart will be from Him." I paused.

More silence, then Jessica Hammond spoke up. "How would we do it?" she asked.

"One step at a time," I said. "Make the commitment and then watch God work. But you each have to make your own choice. Let's pray together. Everyone kneel."

The kids, along with Robert and Martha, all knelt and closed their eyes.

"Lord," I said, "we come to You eager to do Your will and minister to Your people. We ask You now to give everyone in this room guidance, discernment, and peace about what You want them to do. If You want them to take part in this Vacation Bible School, please give them the desire and the peace in their heart to do it. In Jesus' name I pray, amen."

Everyone looked up. Moments ticked by.

"Who's in?" I asked softly.

One by one, hands silently went up. Some kids had to check with their parents, but by the time everyone left that night, the commitment was complete. One hundred percent.

Pete helped me pack up when the last person had left. "Dude, this is big," he said as he folded a tarp and tucked it into my trunk.

"I know," I said. "It's a big opportunity and a big responsibility."

"How in the world are you going to fit it in with everything else you've got going on? This is going to cut into our fishing time."

"I prayed about that," I said. "All of a sudden I knew it's not an obstacle, but an opportunity. There's a verse in Jeremiah … 'Behold, I am the Lord, the God of all flesh. Is anything too difficult for me?' Nothing is impossible, Pete. I hope it's not going to cut into our fishing time, but I do need your help."

He still looked doubtful. I shut the trunk and looked him in the eye.

"Think of it this way. God created this world, and He's going to get His way, with or without you. You might as well get on board, because He's got it rigged."

34

Everything fell together in a way that only God could have done. The dads finished the Muppet stage months before they'd planned to, and these mountain craftsmen did a masterful job. The final product was a contraption made of PVC pipe, lightweight and strong, which was important because we would be carting it around from place to place. Setup had to be quick. The moms finished the stage curtains and costumes well ahead of time. The costumes looked just like the ones on TV.

Greg Wilson worked for hours and hours with the young Muppeteers, and the result was dramatic. Before long all of them, even the ones with the softest, most timid voices, could use their diaphragms and project across a large room. Anonymity helped. Shy people became bold when they were speaking through a Muppet. It was then we discovered that Jimmy was actually a natural singer, which no one knew until then.

Jessica and her best friend, Tiffany, had loads of fun with Bert and Ernie. Their natural camaraderie spilled forth when the two Muppets were interacting, and it seemed flawless and seamless, just like it was supposed to be.

We planned our lessons and activities, and we were ready for our first VBS much quicker than I could have ever imagined. Other churches got wind of what we were doing, and by the time school was out in May, we were lined up to host six VBS programs at various small churches in June and July. Because of the sheer magnitude of the work, the youth group kids agreed that this would take the place of a trip to Myrtle Beach this year. I was secretly grateful for this for selfish reasons. Last year's beach trip was among the worst experiences of my life, and I was still paying for it. I knew it wasn't Myrtle Beach's fault, but still . . . if I never went back there again, it would be just fine.

We practiced our Muppet shows by going to Townsend, where people rode tubes—which people in East Tennessee pronounce "toob"—down the rushing river. We chose a spot along the water and set up our stage, and did intermittent performances as people came floating by. Most families stopped their tubes and let their children watch, wide-eyed, as Kermit and Miss Piggy argued, the Cookie Monster screamed for cookies, and the Count counted. We also practiced nearly every week during children's sermons at Pleasant Grove, and the crowd of children doubled as more and more visitors came to see the Muppets' antics. As support grew, and the youth group members could see the Lord working in this ministry, their confidence blossomed and they began to coach and encourage each other.

May was a bittersweet time. We all watched with teary eyes as Angie graduated from high school and completed her plans to attend UT. She would be continuing on with the youth group as a graduate assistant, like Pete, and she would continue to be Miss Piggy through the World's Fair.

I finished my spring classes and kept my overall GPA above 3.2. Thankfully, French was now over. Wanda Wells graduated with honors and moved on to a full-time job. Bob decided to squeeze in one more resident by renovating an area we had been using to access the roof. Daniel Bowman would be moving in when he returned from Alaska. And a girl named Kelsey Rhodes, who none of us had met yet, would be taking Wanda's place in the girls' apartment.

Missionary training ramped up until mid-May, right before Daniel and Bert left for Alaska. At our last session, we sat and looked at each other with peace in our eyes, knowing these two new missionaries were ready. I was envious because they would be working all summer with people I loved.

"You'll be busy, so don't worry about staying in touch here," I told them. "You just do your best by Will and Denise and those kids, and bring back a full report. Spend lots of time on your knees and in the Word. You can't afford not to. And give Prissy and Atka and Darren and Paul big hugs for me and tell them I love them." I paused. "I wish I could go with you."

"You're going to be plenty busy here," Bert said. Everyone knew about the challenge of the upcoming VBS programs and the World's Fair.

"That I will." I stretched my aching back. In my heart, I knew that my time in Alaska had been only for a season and I had moved on. Plenty of challenges and opportunities lay ahead.

*   *   *

The day arrived quickly, and the youth and I gathered in a staging room just off the sanctuary where our first Vacation Bible School would begin in just a few minutes. Rocky Branch was a small church, so there was only a thin wall between us and the sanctuary, and we could clearly hear the excited squeals of the kids. Brad had told us that this was the first actual VBS the church had ever been able to have. Some of the kids had attended VBS at other churches, but this was a first for them here.

I knew my mom was in the congregation too, excitedly waiting to see our first service. She and her prayer warrior sister, Sandra, had been ceaselessly praying for our success and blessing ever since they'd learned of this opportunity.

My youth group gathered in a circle and looked at me, waiting and eager. Only ten of them could be Muppeteers at one time, but many others worked behind the scenes and were more than capable of operating the Muppets if needed. I looked back at them, amazed at what had been accomplished in a few short weeks. Obviously the Lord was at work here. In no other way could we have done everything we'd done and actually be ready to give these kids an entire week's worth of something substantial and important, something that might just be life-changing. The electricity was in the air already.

There really wasn't much to say at this point. We'd all worked too hard and come too far to put it into words now. So I just looked each of my youth in the eye and said, "We're ready. Let's get out there and do what God brought us here to do. Everybody take a knee."

With a rustle, everyone in the room went down on one knee and bowed their heads.

"Lord," I prayed, "we're here because You brought us here and allowed everything to fall into place so this could happen. You have Your plans for us and for everyone here, and we know that. Please be with us today and for this whole week. Help us say the things we need to say and act the way we need to act, to get Your purpose accomplished. To You be all the glory. In Jesus' name I pray, amen."

Everyone looked up. Angie broke the silence first. "Let's do it," she said. Everyone picked up their Muppets and moved en masse to the door.

Just before we eased into the sanctuary, the room went dark as planned. From each side of the church, Pete and I began to whistle the iconic *Sesame Street* theme song. The children in the church squealed. By the time we got through one chorus, the Muppeteers had moved silently to their positions and Kermit and his friends were staged and ready.

On cue, when Pete and I finished whistling, there were a few seconds of silence and then the lights came on full, showing ten Muppets scattered about the front of the church, waving madly at the audience. The squeals turned into shrieks as the kids recognized their favorites. The pandemonium continued until Kermit raised his webbed hand to calm the kids down. He looked around as if amazed at the crowd.

"Boy, there are a lot of you!" he said. "Did y'all come here just to see us?"

"Yes!" yelled the children.

"We're really happy to be here, and it's going to be a great week!"

More screams.

"But you know why we really came, right?"

A young girl in the second row raised her hand. This was tricky, because Kermit—being a puppet with a hidden handler—couldn't see the people. Strategically positioned spotters had to cue him at times like this. He pointed to the little girl.

"You came to tell us about Jesus," she said loudly.

"You're exactly right!" Fozzie Bear took over. "We're here to tell you about Jesus and how much He loves you."

Miss Piggy, who'd been standing regally but silently up to this point, interjected. "We all love Jesus here," she said. "I know I'm beautiful, but I also know He's the one who made me that way. He made us all beautiful and gave us all gifts. We're going to spend this week learning all about that and thanking Him for everything He's done for us."

"We're going to count the blessings we have," growled the Count. "And I'm not sure I can count that high. Maybe you can all help me. One blessing is …"

"COOKIES!" screamed the Cookie Monster, and ran back and forth. "The number one blessing is cookies!"

Over the next five minutes, all the other Muppets gave their two cents' worth on gifts and blessings, and the kids in the audience listened with rapt, wide-eyed looks. Some, like the little girl who'd first raised her hand, were bold enough to participate.

When the Muppets had everyone whipped into a frenzy, I stepped up to the front of the church.

"Great job, guys," I told the Muppets. "We've got a big job this week, sharing the love of Jesus and talking about what He did for us. That's why He sent us here. Now we're going to break up into smaller groups and get started."

Over the next three hours, we split the kids into age groups, led by the most capable members of the youth group, and alternated short lessons, snacks, crafts, and singing. I floated from group to group and supervised the teaching. As I went, I marveled at how naturally and beautifully my youth were interacting with these children. Bonds were already starting to form. It was going to be a wonderful week.

At the end of the day, we gathered back into the big room. I took my place at the front of the room. The Muppets were there, but they were "seated" in their spots.

"Who can tell me what you learned today?"

A little boy about seven years old raised his hand. I pointed at him. "God gave all of us things we're good at."

"Good. The Bible tells us that we're all good at something. Some people are good at lots of things. We all are part of God's plan. Who here knows what you want to be when you grow up?"

One boy piped up. "I want to be a fireman."

"I want to be a nurse," said a girl.

"I want to be a teacher," said another.

"I want to drive a dump truck," a little boy said.

"A dump truck?" I asked with interest. This had been one of my "side" jobs in Alaska.

"Yeah, I like trucks and I want to have fun at my job."

"Those are all good things," I said. "But there's a point to all this. Who can tell me what it is?"

Silence.

Kermit spoke up. "It means that whatever we're good at, whatever we do, we're supposed to use it for God."

"That's exactly right, Kermit. If you're a good teacher, then your job is to work with people and help them understand more about the Lord. If you're a good speaker, then tell everyone you can about Jesus. There are all kinds of gifts and blessings, and every single one can be used for the Lord. Sometimes it's your actual job, and sometimes it's something you do for the church or some other ministry. But we can always serve the Lord."

We closed the day by singing "Jesus Loves Me," and then the parents herded the kids out and I was alone with my youth group.

Angie's eyes were shining with tears. "That was so much fun!" she said excitedly. "We can really do this."

"You all did an awesome job," I told them. "You kept the focus right where it needed to be . . . on the Lord. You kept Him at the forefront and you let Him speak through you. You keep that up, and by the end of the week we'll have little kids coming to Jesus."

"I can't even imagine," Jessica said. "Being the one God uses to bring someone to Him."

"I have a feeling you're about to find out," I said honestly.

*   *   *

My feeling was right. At the end of that week, eight children came forward to dedicate their lives to Christ and be baptized. Over the next few weeks, our programs became cleaner, slicker, and more professional, and our effectiveness and ability to work together grew. These youth were now my partners in this ministry, and they handled the responsibility with maturity, humility, and grace. They grew to love these little children, and the children formed strong bonds with them. On the last day of each session, children were throwing themselves into the arms of my youth helpers, sad because the week was over.

And, more importantly, we saw more and more kids—nearly a hundred in all by the end of July—come to Christ. Every time it felt like a miracle, and we gave thanks that God used us in this way.

After each session, one member of the youth group gave a testimony and a report to the Pleasant Grove congregation on the previous week's VBS program. Angie, as the only graduating senior in the group, went first and told about our experience at Rocky Branch. At first she couldn't even speak. She stood there, tears rolling down her cheeks, trying to get control of herself enough to be able to talk. Finally she began.

"I've been a Christian since I was just a little kid," she said. "I've known I belonged to Jesus, but until the past year I didn't know what it was like to grow and really have a relationship with

Him. And now, this past week, working with those kids at Rocky Branch, for the first time I really feel like He's using me. Looking at those kids' faces, sharing Jesus' love with them, it was the most amazing feeling ever."

Her voice quavered and she paused, visibly gaining control again. "There was this one little girl. Her name is Anne. She was in my small group. All week, I could see the love of Jesus working in her little heart. On that last day, right before the end, she came up to me and said she loved Jesus and wanted to give her life to Him." Fresh tears rolled down her face. "I can't tell you what it means, to have God use me like that. Anne was just one of eight kids who came to Christ this week. We can't wait to see what happens for the rest of this summer."

Jimmy was chosen to give the report after the second VBS program. He related the story of a little boy, Joel, who'd attached himself to Jimmy from the beginning of the first day. Joel was there because school was out and his parents wanted to get rid of him for a few hours a day. Joel and Jimmy bonded instantly. Joel hungered for love and Jimmy had ample love to give. By the end of the week, they were inseparable.

"That little boy—" his voice broke. "He needs whatever love and help anyone can give him. He needed to know Jesus loves him, no matter what. He knows that now. And he knows I love him too."

Week after week, the stories were the same. Children bonded with our youth, and the group had the experience of their lives. Finally, toward the end of July, we led our last VBS program of the year. It was bittersweet because we'd all grown to love this. An opportunity that had at first terrified this youth group had become an incredible blessing to them. And we knew it wasn't over. Most of the churches where we'd served had asked us to come back next year, and we'd immediately said yes.

Sitting in my office on a Saturday afternoon, after the final VBS had been completed the day before, I was overcome with gratitude and emotion. Who was I, that God would use me like this? I was just a vessel, a bruised and broken one at that. God could use anyone. Why me? I bowed my head to thank Him, and before long found myself prostrate on the floor, face down, tears flowing into the carpet, despite the fact that this position caused my always present back pain to become unbearable.

"Father, thank You," I wept. "Thank You for using me and the kids You've entrusted to me. I have one more year in this ministry, and I pray that You'll continue to use me and guide me. Thy will be done. Amen."

I rose and eased slowly into my chair. This experience had been incredible. The entire past two years had been amazing. But I had the feeling that more huge things were about to happen, right around the corner. I had no idea how big, or how impactful they would be. Sooner than I could possibly know, I would begin to find out.

35

On the last Monday in July, I sat on the mattress in my room at the BSU. The building was deserted except for Bob, who I could distantly hear clattering away on his typewriter. It was summer in Knoxville, so it was sweltering hot. A small electric fan whirred valiantly in my room, but it did little good. My t-shirt and gym shorts clung damply to my body.

All the other residents were home for the summer. Even Kenny and Brandon had traveled to Kenya and Indonesia to spend time with their parents. I found that I could work better here in this quiet house, so I'd opted to stay. Besides, there were always kids here at UT for summer school. You never knew when the Lord might give you an opportunity to do something for Him.

I was making a list of things to talk with Bob about for the upcoming school year. My senior year. I was full of ideas, but I needed Bob's take on everything. Wanda had graduated, so someone had to take over the noonday program. We wanted to further expand the freshman Bible studies. Evangelism needed a boost. Daniel and Bert were doing a phenomenal, gutsy job, but they were only two people and college campuses like ours were home to more than thirty thousand students. Kids were free and on their own for perhaps the first time in their lives, dealing with temptations they'd likely never had to face before. They needed a place to go, someone to turn to, to keep them on the right track. We wanted to give them that, but that meant more volunteers had to step up and be trained.

The steps we'd taken last year were huge and important, but now I wanted to do more. And there would be an election for this year's EC members. I had some thoughts on that too.

I couldn't wait for Daniel and Bert to come back from Alaska in about two weeks. We'd heard nothing from them, but then I hadn't expected to. I was, with difficulty, keeping my mind off of that. I hungered for news of Prissy, Darren, Atka, the guys at the jail, and the others. And even Snickers, Will West's lead dog.

I distantly heard and registered the sound of the front door opening and closing, and the clattering of Bob's typewriter ceasing, but paid no real attention. I had started a detailed list and was pondering, tapping my pencil with one hand and shoving my sweat-damp hair off my forehead with the other, when a knock came at the door.

"Come in," I called absently, not looking up.

Bob poked his head in. "Mark, you got a minute?"

"Sure."

"There's somebody here you should meet."

I scribbled one more thing on my list, not wanting to lose the idea while it was in my head. "I'll be there in just a second."

"Take your time."

I finished what I was doing, then stood and stretched, first one way then the other. My spine popped. I sighed in momentary relief. Who in the world could be here in July that Bob thought I should meet? There was only one way to find out.

I jogged down the stone spiral steps and down the short hall to Bob's office. The door was open, so I stuck my head in to see Bob sitting at his desk with a young woman in the opposite chair.

"Sorry it took so long," I said. "Is this who you wanted me to meet?"

"It is," he said. Both he and the girl stood. "I think you already know this young lady, but it's time you met face to face. This is Nancy Mahoney."

Surprised, I turned to face Nancy. We'd only communicated via mail, and only twice. This was definitely not how I'd pictured her. I thought she'd be older, kind of short, and maybe a little overweight. This young woman was tall—taller than me—and looked to be about my age. She wore khaki shorts just above her knees, a dark blue polo shirt, and sturdy sandals. She had a slender but very curvaceous build to go with long, slightly curling dark hair and velvet brown eyes. Her face was interesting —not beautiful but definitely not unattractive. Arching brows and high cheekbones accentuated her eyes. Full lips curved in a confident smile. She had a gregarious light in her eyes as she stuck out her hand.

"So you're Mark," she said. "Nice to meet you at last."

I took her hand and shook it, careful not to squeeze too hard. The incident in the hospital with Miss Ina had taught me a permanent lesson. But there was no need to worry about that in this case. Nancy gave me a firm, confident handshake. "Nice to meet you too. We're all really looking forward to the World's Fair."

"Which is—" she checked her watch, "nine months and four days away. We've got a lot of work to do."

"Nancy is with the North American Mission Board," Bob put in. "She graduated from Florida State last year and has been working full-time on this for several months."

"I'll try not to hold it against you that you went to Florida State," I joked. "You're in SEC country now."

She laughed. "At least Florida State and Tennessee don't play each other. So I won't be doing any war chants or tomahawk chops in Neyland Stadium."

"That wouldn't be smart," I said.

"Yours was one of the first letters I got after I took this job," she said. "Tell me more about your ministry."

We sat in the comfortable chairs in Bob's office and I told her all about the incredible summer we'd just had. "We started the ministry specifically for the World's Fair, but God had other plans." I shook my head. "Well beyond anything I could have ever imagined."

"Ephesians, chapter three," she said.

"Exactly," I said, impressed.

"He has a way of doing that," she said. "When you let Him lead, you never know where He's going to take you."

I told her a little about my experience in Alaska and how I'd found out suddenly and definitively that I'd been living my life according to my own plan, not the Lord's. He'd pulled me back, and the results had been miraculous. "It's been an amazing two years," I said. "I can't wait to see what comes next."

"Mark's got one more year here and then he's headed to seminary," Bob told Nancy with an odd gleam in his eye.

"Really? Where?" she asked.

"I haven't decided yet, but my dad went to Southern in Louisville," I said. "I'll probably look around, but that will definitely be one of the top places I consider. I want to go somewhere that will make me ask and answer hard questions. If it's a place that just rubber-stamps its students with its own theology, then I'm not interested."

"Nancy will be living here until the World's Fair is over next October," Bob said. "She's already found an apartment and is looking for a church."

"You should come visit us at Pleasant Grove," I told her. "Our pastor is really good, and you can see our Muppet ministry for yourself."

"That sounds great. I'll check it out." She looked at her watch. "Gotta go. I have an appointment to sign the lease on my apartment."

We shook hands again. "See you later," I said. "It was really nice to meet you."

"Same here. It's going to be a fun year."

"We can't wait," I told her sincerely.

She left the room with a long, gliding gait, and we soon heard the front door open and close.

"So, what do you think?" Bob asked.

"About what?" I looked at him innocently.

He gave me an exasperated, *you're-not-fooling-me* look. "Nancy, of course. I saw that look on your face. You're going to be working with her a lot over the next year, so it would be good if you hit it off."

The light dawned. "I was just surprised, Bob. Really. She wasn't like I pictured her, that's all. I've got too much to do over the next year to think about girls, if that's what you're getting at."

"I'm just saying. She is pretty, don't you think?"

"I guess." That curvaceous brunette look had never been my type. My ideal woman stemmed from a blonde, willowy, small-chested girl who'd worked as a lifeguard in Athens when I was about eleven. She was about seventeen and was also my next-door neighbor. When my sisters and I were younger, she sometimes babysat for us.

One day my best friend, Eric, and I were climbing around in a huge magnolia tree that sat at the edge of our yard. Its limbs were sturdy, flat, and plentiful—perfect for a treehouse. As Eric and I clambered around, plotting where to put our treehouse, the girl came outside in a beach cover-up and sat down on a lawn chair. I motioned Eric to be quiet; I didn't want to startle or embarrass her. And so we sat stock-still and silent as she shed her cover-up, rubbed oil on her glistening skin, spritzed herself with cooling mist, and stretched out in the sun in her tiny bikini. It was then that I felt my first real male urges and formed my ideal of femininity.

Later I felt really bad about that, like I'd invaded on the girl's privacy, and I never climbed that tree again. We didn't build that treehouse. But the mental picture was still etched on my brain, and that picture was completely opposite from Nancy.

The long-ago memory was still so powerful that I had to mentally shake myself now to tune back in to what Bob was saying.

"Just keep your options open, that's all I'm saying," he said.

I went back to my room and thought about it, then dismissed it for the moment. Time would tell, and God would lead. If this was something He wanted me to pursue, then He would let me know.

I fell back into my plans for the next year at UT, and forgot all about Nancy Mahoney.

36

With just two weeks before school started back, Doug Taylor and I wanted to make them count. He'd been my best friend since ninth grade and had, pretty much singlehandedly, assured that I would succeed at Maryville High. I had moved to Maryville from the poorest part of Athens, Tennessee, when I was twelve years old. My friends were, to say the least, unsavory. Doug and I had met soon after I arrived in Maryville, and he'd convinced me to try out for the high school tennis team. We became undefeated doubles partners and lifelong friends. His consistency and my aggression made us unbeatable.

During my first two years at UT, I'd spent some weekends with him in Atlanta and attended First Baptist Atlanta with him. That was how I'd become inspired by Dr. Charles Stanley and ended up being called into the mission field for a year.

Doug had come to spend a week with me in Alaska right before Christmas last year. He was on his way to spend the holiday with his parents in Perth, Australia, and decided to detour to Alaska to see his best friend. It was a pretty big detour, not to mention a temperature swing of nearly two hundred degrees between Alaska and Australia, and it was something I would never forget. His friendship and continued support were—and are—one of God's greatest gifts in my life.

He was about to begin his senior year at Georgia Tech and, as he liked to say, he would be a heck of an engineer when he graduated. After that, who knew where our paths would take us? We decided to take these last two weeks and do something fun together. Next week we planned to go to Myrtle Beach on a family errand. Doug's sister, Dianne, was there and needed her car so we'd agreed to take it to her. And Doug's family was picking up the cost of our food, gas, and hotel room because we were doing a favor for Dianne. I mentally groaned over the idea of going back to Myrtle Beach but figured it would be fun with Doug. And a free beach vacation was hard to turn down.

This week, though, was about adventure. My dad's lumber company owned a small cabin in Wears Valley, which lies between Maryville and Pigeon Forge at the base of the Great Smoky Mountains. I'd been there before, and it was remote and rustic— perfect for two Eagle Scouts looking to get away from reality for a bit. I had checked with my dad, and the cabin was available for three days and two nights in the middle of the first week in August.

Doug and I plotted, planned, and packed. Early one morning we loaded up some light backpacks with the essentials of survival for three days and hopped on our bikes. Lighthearted, with the breeze in our hair, we headed through Townsend and turned left toward Pigeon Forge. The road snakes back and forth between the mountains, in nearly hairpin turns. Far below, a river about forty yards wide rushes over huge, mossy rocks and plunges over small waterfalls and eddies into pools where hungry mountain trout lie in wait. In my pack was a compact fly fishing kit, and I knew I had to toss a fly into one of those pools before this day was over. Maybe I could catch our supper.

As we rode, a peace came over my spirit and I knew that whatever waited for me over the next year, this time would be an oasis where I could just enjoy being in God's creation with my best friend.

The turnoff to the cabin was easy to miss, and Doug had never been here, so after we passed through Wears Valley I began to watch closely. I knew it was near a very wide waterfall, and finally I spotted a faint trail of a dirt road, which took a sharp right and descended steeply toward the river. We cautiously edged our bikes onto the dirt tracks and made our way slowly down. After several hundred yards, the cabin came into view on our left. Built solidly of logs, it squatted at the very edge of the river, water swirling at its wooden legs, just upstream from the wide waterfall.

But the best thing about this place was not the house itself, or even the river. The owner had built a concrete-walled pool, filled with a sluice by the cold mountain water. The river rushed into the pool, filled it to the brim, then eventually flowed through other sluices back into the river. The result was an icy cold, moss-covered swimming hole, perfect for two boys looking for adventure.

We stopped our bikes at the pool, just short of the cabin. Doug stared.

"Dude," he said. "This is awesome."

"Isn't it?" We were hot and grubby after our long bike ride, and the water looked cold and inviting. We exchanged looks, grinned, and did what any boys our age would do. We stripped down to our underpants and leaped into the pool.

The cold was literally breathtaking. I emerged first, sputtering. "Holy cow."

"I'm definitely not hot now," Doug announced, teeth already chattering.

I eyed him. "Race you," I said. "Five laps." Then I took off for the far end of the pool. Doug, never one to turn down a challenge, plunged after me. We were both good swimmers, but I had a little more endurance and beat him by a knuckle.

We dragged ourselves out of the pool and sprawled on the ground, panting. I turned my head sideways and beamed at him. "Beat you," I said.

"Yeah, well, I pinned you when we wrestled in Alaska."

"That was so not fair. You ambushed me."

"I still pinned you."

"Yeah, okay." I had to give him that. "I'll give you a rematch anytime."

We dressed and got back on our bikes. We rolled up to the cabin and leaned our bikes against the rail. Up close, this cabin reminded me a lot of Miss Ina's house up in the mountains. It was hand built in the 1930s and hewn out of solid wood. It had to be strong to withstand the river that always swirled around its foundations. Even when the water was down, as it was today, there was still a rushing torrent.

I fished the key out of my pack, and we unlocked the door and lugged our stuff in.

"Rustic" was an understatement. "Primitive" was a better word. This cabin looked like no one had done anything to improve it in the fifty years it had been standing here. No electricity. No phone. Just a wood stove in the corner that we could use to heat up a can of stew or bake anything we managed to pull out of the river. And plenty of forest stood nearby for firewood.

We wandered toward the front side of the house, the side that faced the river, and understood why people still liked to come here. The entire front side was windows or doors, providing a constant view of the rushing river. We could see no other houses back here, so we were completely on our own—just us, the critters, and the crickets.

We still had plenty of daylight, but we had to get ourselves set for the night. We had lightweight hammocks that we planned to hang on the front porch, so sleeping wasn't an issue. But food was. Our stomachs were grumbling and my thoughts kept going back to those pools in the river where fat trout just had to be hanging, waiting for something delectable to drop down. We could heat up a can of stew, but I hankered for fresh trout.

Doug was an Eagle Scout too and could do most anything out-doors, but he was not a fisherman. We decided that I would try some fly fishing while he gathered firewood. With luck, I'd catch us a tasty supper.

I put the rod together, tied a fly on the end, made my way down-stream and waded against the current toward the deep-looking pools near the cabin. Fly fishing, as I'd discovered in Alaska, is different from any other kind of fishing. You don't just cast your line, like you do if you're fishing for bass. And you don't drop a minnow or a cricket on a specific spot, like you would if you were fishing for crappie or bluegill. With fly fishing, you aim at a spot and try to toss your line upstream from it, so it will run downstream across the eddying pools. Then, hopefully, a waiting trout will see the tasty-looking fly, or the flash of the hook, and pounce.

Fly fishing is difficult, but my experience on the Nome River helped and I got the hang of it pretty quickly. Mountain trout aren't as big as Alaskan salmon, but they fight just as hard. Within an hour I had two rainbow trout, plenty of meat for our supper, and I felt I'd earned every bite.

I arrived back at the cabin to see Doug dragging a huge dead tree into the yard. "This," he puffed, "will be perfect firewood. It's already been there for a while, you can tell. It will burn easy. It should last us all weekend." He dropped the end of the tree onto a pile of kindling wood that he'd already gathered.

"Good job." I nodded and held up my two fish. "Hope you're hungry."

"Starved."

"Let's get these guys on the spit."

I cleaned the trout and packaged them into foil with salt and pepper, much like Jack Barker and I had done with the fish I caught in the frozen Bering Sea. Then they were ready to cook. All we needed was a fire.

To build a good fire, you have to have several kinds of wood— small shavings to get the fire started, bigger sticks to build it up, and bigger logs to keep it hot. This dead tree would give us everything we needed, but we had to split some of it to make it the right size.

As with the mechanical bull a year ago, this was one of the moments that would be a vivid memory for the rest of my life. But there's a big difference. Looking back on the mechanical bull, I can see the dark forces looming and plotting. When I look back on the day when Doug and I were perusing that tree, I don't see any of that. I just see a kid who was too preoccupied to take safety precautions. Doug and I both paid for it.

We found two hatchets and began to split the dead tree into the sizes we wanted. I positioned two other trees so that they were parallel, then placed the dead wood horizontally across the others. Then I stood, one foot on each of the two parallel logs, and chopped downward, between my feet. The logs fell into nice even chunks, ready for the fire.

The system worked as long as I paid attention to what I was doing. But for one instant, my attention wandered and the hatchet went just a little too far off center, hit a knot in the tree and bounced to the right. Through my shoe and into my foot.

There was one quick *surely-I-didn't-just-do-that* moment, and then the blood began to flow and the pain set in.

Doug realized I wasn't chopping anymore and turned to look.

"You okay, man?"

"I don't think so." I eased down off the logs and onto the ground. "This may not be good."

"Let's see." He hunkered down beside me and eased the shoe off my foot. As we looked at the wound, we realized it was bad but it could have been much worse. The hatchet had gone into my foot just below my ankle bone and had taken out a huge hunk of meat, which now hung wetly, pouring fresh blood. Somehow, I'd managed to miss bones and major blood vessels. And the hunk of meat wasn't completely severed. It was just hanging there by a small piece of skin.

We surveyed the damage. "So what do you think?" Doug asked.

"I think we should put my foot back together, then build a fire and cook these fish. Maybe it will stop bleeding and be okay."

He eyed me doubtfully. "I don't think so. That looks to me like it might need stitches."

"The worst part is going to be getting it clean. We can do that while the fish are cooking. Then after we eat we can decide what to do."

He lifted my foot and looked closer. The doubtful look turned into a stern glare, and his eyes lifted to mine. "Mark, you know, just like I know, you're definitely going to have to have stitches."

I was in denial. Surely a moment of extreme stupidity wasn't going to cost us our much-anticipated three days in the woods together. "Maybe. But we have to eat, so let's do that first."

We built up the fire and tossed the trout packets in, then went down to the river to clean my wound. I've always had a pretty high pain threshold, but I had to grit my teeth as Doug gently washed out the grit from my mangled foot. By the time we were finished and the wound was bandaged, the food was ready.

And thunder clouds were menacing. We barely got our meal into the house before a storm hit, complete with torrential rain, crashing thunder and cracking lightning. The "road" leading to the cabin quickly became a muddy, mucky morass. It would be impossible for a car, or even a bike, to get in or out. We watched the melee from the shelter of the front porch.

"Well," Doug said as he picked fish off the bones, "this complicates things." A bolt of lightning flashed close by, so close that the hairs on my arms stood on end. The crack of thunder was deafening and instant. The wind kicked up, and small hail began to fall.

"I'm sorry, Doug." I still couldn't believe this had happened.

"Stop it, dude. Let's just talk this through." He swallowed his last bite of fish, balled up his foil, and leaned forward, elbows on his knees. "One, you need help. That foot needs stitches and we both know it."

I sighed. "Agreed."

"Second, you're in no shape to walk or get on a bike—even if we could get on our bikes, which we can't, at least not between here and the main road."

"Right."

"Which means that I need to get to a phone and get us some help."

I knew from experience with the Pleasant Grove people that mountain folk were reluctant to open the door to strangers. And if they did, they would likely have a shotgun in their hands. "Doug, did you see any houses anywhere near here? We passed some a few miles back, but they didn't look very inviting."

"Aren't you a bright ray of sunshine? No, I didn't, which means I have to go back to the main road and keep going toward Pigeon Forge until I find one. And I need to go now, before it gets completely dark."

I struggled for something to say but could find no fault with any of his logic, so he donned his rain gear, headed into the storm, and slogged down the muddy track, carrying his bike. I watched him until he was out of sight, which wasn't long with the blasting rain.

I made my painful way into the cabin and plopped heavily beside the fire. I checked my watch. Eight o'clock. The sun sets fast in these mountains, and I figured it would be a while before Doug came back. First, he had to get to the main road. Second, he had to find an inhabited house in these rough mountains where people had a phone and would actually open the door. Third, he had to contact someone—probably my parents, if he could get them. And fourth, he had to get back here to me. In the best possible scenario, that would all take at least an hour, maybe two. True friends, I realized, were hard to find. Doug was one.

I settled in and waited, watching the crackling flames. Maybe I was being punished. Maybe it was a test. Or maybe it was just something that had happened. As the Bible teaches us, I examined my heart and spirit and asked God to show me anything in my heart that shouldn't be there. All I felt was His strong presence, and a peace that all would be fine. I kept praying, this time for Doug's safety and success. This was my brother, my best friend, and I prayed that my foolhardiness wouldn't put him in danger.

The seconds turned into minutes, and the minutes into hours. The pain had ebbed, but the blood still seeped out of the bandage. Finally, when my watch told me it was ten o'clock, I heard steps on the front porch and Doug staggered through the door.

I sprang up and hobbled to his side, weak with relief that he was back and in one piece. "You okay, man?"

"Yeah, I'm fine. Your parents are on their way."

"You look awful."

He gave me a disgusted look. "Thanks a lot, bro. We got any food?"

I opened a can of stew and set it to heat over the fire, and Doug was soon wolfing it down.

"Dude, you weren't kidding about the people around here," he said between bites.

"Tell me."

"First of all, I had to carry my bike all the way to the main road. That's a long way, man. Then, when I finally got to a house, I could tell people were home, but they wouldn't come to the door."

"Doesn't surprise me at all."

"At the second one, a big mean dog chased me away. And I could see a guy at the window watching the whole thing. I tried to yell that I had a medical emergency, but it's pretty hard to communicate when a big dog is snapping and snarling at you, and you can tell he's serious."

"That could have been bad."

"Yeah, it could. I just barely got away with my skin. Then at the next house, they opened the door but they didn't have a phone."

"So how many houses did you have to go to?"

He scraped the bottom of his bowl. "Six."

"Six?"

"Yep, six. Finally a lady answered the door. I stood way back so she wouldn't think she was in danger or anything and explained what was going on. Then her husband came up beside her. Man, he was a mountain of a guy with a big shotgun."

"Everybody out here has shotguns."

"His looked really big."

"You must have been very convincing."

"They were good people. When they found out what was going on, they led me straight to the phone. That was another ordeal."

"What?"

"Getting somebody to answer the phone at your parents' house. I kept getting a busy signal."

"Yeah, Lisa's always on the phone."

"Those nice people gave me a place to sit beside their fire while I kept trying to get through. After about seven times, your mom finally picked up. I barely had a chance to tell her what happened before they were out the door. It took me a while to get back, so they should be here pretty soon."

Just as those words came out of Doug's mouth, I heard the squealing of tires on the road above us and knew it had to be my parents. They were taking those curves way too fast because they knew I was in trouble. I also knew they were in for an ordeal when they tried to come down to the house. No way would our station wagon make it through the mud. They'd have to walk, just like Doug had.

Within a few minutes, the door burst open and my mom ran straight to me and squatted at my feet. "Let me see," she said.

Wordlessly I held my foot out. She peered underneath the bandage but didn't disturb it. "Oh, honey."

"I'm sorry, Mom."

My dad came up behind her. "Boy, when you do something, you don't do it halfway," he said to me gruffly.

Doug laughed weakly. "I've always known that."

"How are we going to get him out of here?" Mom fretted. "He can't walk on that foot."

"You're right," Dad said. "If he gets that mud in it, it won't be good." He thought about it and sighed. "Only one way to do it. I'll have to carry him as far as the station wagon. The bikes will fit in the back."

So we started back up the muddy, slippery road, rain still coming down in a steady torrent, with me clinging to Dad's back and Doug carrying the bikes. Mom carried our backpacks. Slipping and sliding for several hundred yards up the steep mountain dirt road, we eventually arrived at the station wagon. Dad went to his knees in the mud several times, but he never let me hit the ground.

I apologized at least a dozen times on the way to the hospital, but no one was angry with me. They were just worried and thankful that it wasn't worse than it was. Dad only said, "You knew better, Mark, but we're just glad you're okay."

We arrived at Blount Memorial Hospital around midnight, and I lost count of the stitches it took to put my foot back together. The doctor said what Doug and I already knew—I had only hacked off a hunk of meat. It could have been bone or major blood vessels.

"You're a very lucky young man," the doctor said as he finished the last stitch.

My mom and I exchanged meaningful looks. We knew it hadn't been luck but divine protection. For the umpteenth time in my life, God had protected me from my own carelessness.

The doctor left the room, and the four of us immediately joined hands. "Father," my dad said, "We thank You for everything You did tonight to protect us all. Mark could have chopped off his foot and bled to death. Doug could have been hurt or worse when he went to get help. Sharon and I could have slid off that mountain road while we were trying to get to them. A hundred things could have easily happened, but they didn't, and we know why. You were there, guarding and protecting us all. We thank You for loving us and stepping in for us, because we surely don't deserve it. We're so grateful to You and we just want to serve You and do Your will. We love you, Lord. In Jesus' name I pray, amen."

Safe in bed that night, I lay there and thought about it. There's a story in 2 Kings about Israel being surrounded, seemingly about to be conquered. All the children of Israel were convinced they were about to die. Then Elisha prayed that his servant be allowed a glimpse of what was really going on. The servant saw, just for an instant, the army of angels around them, protecting them. Israel escaped that day because of God's protection.

That was what had happened to Doug and me today. God had sent angels to protect us, which meant He still had work for us to do. He wasn't finished with any of us yet.

37

Two days later, Doug sat in our living room and looked at me, flabbergasted. "You mean you seriously still want to go to Myrtle Beach tomorrow?"

"Of course. Why wouldn't I? Dianne still needs her car, right?"

"Well, yeah, but . . ." he eyed my foot. "How much fun do you think you're going to have with that?"

"It's got stitches and it's healing just fine. The salt water will do it good. I'll be careful."

He snorted and put his hands out to each side, like a scale. "You and careful." He waggled his hands back and forth and suddenly dropped his right hand down to his knees. "Careful never wins. This is me, your best friend. I know you."

"We're going. I hereby give you permission to tackle me to the ground if I do something stupid."

A light came into his eyes, and I knew I was going to regret those words. "Deal."

We planned to drive down on Sunday in two cars. I would drive mine, and Doug would drive Dianne's. The drive would take about eight hours. We would deliver Dianne's car and then spend three days playing putt-putt and getting some rays. There would be pretty girls in bikinis, which would provide some good scenery. No mechanical bulls allowed. We'd head back on Thursday, suntanned and relaxed and ready to tackle our senior years.

Everything went exactly as planned. We played all the putt-putt courses in the area, walked the beach, and kicked each other's rears at arcade games. As I'd expected, the female flesh on the beaches was abundant, but Doug and I both had a *look-but-don't-touch* mindset.

This was a vacation town with license plates from nearly every state and a few from Canada. We knew we'd never see any of these girls again. Neither of us was interested in anything temporary at this point in our lives or even anything permanent at the moment. It would be nice to have a promising relationship, though.

On Wednesday afternoon, our last day in Myrtle Beach, we meandered up the beach, the ocean lapping at our feet. As always, we carried light backpacks with a towel, a bottle of water, a Frisbee, and a few other essentials. You just never knew what you might need. The sun was hot, the tide was low, and the waves were gentle. I'd been right—my wound was doing fine. It was drying up nicely, and I'd put duct tape over the bandage to keep the water out.

Suddenly, whatever Doug was saying became a distant, tinny voice in my ear. About halfway between us and the strip of hotels, two girls sunned themselves on lounge chairs. One, a nicely built blonde with long, straight hair pulled back in a ponytail, sat engrossed in a book. She had a visor on her head, sunglasses on her nose, and oil covering her skin.

The other girl had laid her lounge chair flat, obviously to get some sun on her back side. Her top half was in the shade of an umbrella, but her bottom half was in the full sun. Thick blonde curls were clipped atop her head. Her bikini top was untied, to eliminate any tan lines. Her bottom covered her assets, but just barely. And her arms flopped down beside her. Even at this distance, it was obvious she was deeply asleep.

And the skin on the back of her legs was already lobster red. Not an everyday sunburn, but a second-degree burn.

The scene was so like the long-ago vision of the girl next door that it took my breath away. I couldn't see this girl's face or even any of her front side, but what I could see was perfect. Long, slim legs with toned muscles. Full, round backside. Perfect curve to her back and hips, leading to lean shoulders and arms. But she was going to be in a great deal of pain when she woke up.

I elbowed Doug in the ribs. "Look."

He looked. "Man, she's hot." I could tell he was looking at the girl who was sitting upright.

"No, dude, the other one."

He shifted his focus. "Ouch," he said. "She's going to feel that tonight. But I like the other one."

I was already veering in the girls' direction. I walked up and stood between them. Up close, the young woman was even more exquisite. She lay securely and modestly on her stomach, nestled in her beach chair, but I could tell that she was slim all over. No big-busted girl here. Neither of them noticed I was there.

"Hey," I said softly, so as not to startle them. The one with the book peered over her sunglasses.

"Hey," she said.

"I promise I'm not a weirdo—but your friend here looks like she's about to need some help."

The girl looked at her friend and gasped. "Oh my gosh. She was under the umbrella when she went to sleep. I made sure."

"I guess the sun moved," Doug supplied. "Hi there. My name's Doug."

"I'm Joy." She leaned over to wake her friend up.

I stopped her. "Unless she wants to flash the whole beach, you might want to wake her up carefully," I said.

Joy reached over and gently tied her friend's bikini top into place, then shook her gently. "Wake up. The sun moved."

The girl shifted and immediately groaned. And as she sat up, her eyes opened and locked onto mine. My whole world tilted. This girl did remind me of my childhood fantasy, but she was so much better. Besides that wonderful body that I'd already noted and responded to, her face was perfect. Small, pert nose. Smooth, perfect skin, glistening with a sheen of sweat. Oval face. Long, blonde lashes that framed eyes of electric blue. Those eyes lasered straight into my gut and heart.

Just for an instant, I saw the same recognition in those eyes that I felt in my own heart. And then the pain of the intense sunburn must have hit. Her eyes filled with pain.

"Don't move," I said. "I have something that can help you."

"I can't be sunburned," she said with a distinct Southern drawl. "I never sunburn. I'm a lifeguard."

"You're Scotch-Irish, right?" I knew that skin because I had the same ancestry, except I had a little Native American thrown in.

"Yes, how'd you know that?"

"You and I have the same skin. Just be still for a minute. I was a lifeguard too, and I'm an Eagle Scout. I know a second-degree burn when I see one."

I pulled my pack off my back and rummaged for a bottle of green aloe goo. I gently squirted some into my palm and smoothed it over the backs of her legs, being careful to cover the burned areas but not to take liberties. Her top half was fine—but her legs would cause her pain for days.

She lay under my ministrations, groaning. "Oh, this is going to be bad. We're supposed to head home tomorrow. How can I ride in a car for five hours like this?"

"It's going to hurt," I told her frankly as I smoothed on the goo.

But by the time I finished her right leg, I had developed a significant problem. I was a red-blooded American male and everything, but this was far different than anything I'd ever seen or felt. I was having a physical reaction that was going to be obvious when I stood up. And the more I touched her, the more intense it got.

As she lay there, with nothing to look at but the ground, she noticed my foot. "What's with the duct tape?"

I sighed and squirted more goo into my palm. "It's a long story."

"I think we've got a minute," she said.

So as I spread the aloe on her left leg, I told her of our recent mishap. Both she and Joy gasped and howled in disbelief and hilarity. The more they laughed, the more we embellished. I stayed crouched down as I worked on her and told her the story.

"And you taped it together with duct tape? Why?" Joy asked

with tears of mirth streaming down her face.

"Duct tape is good for everything," I said matter-of-factly.

As I finished, I caught Doug's eye with a look of panic. He understood immediately and moved between me and the girls.

"So, you're headed home tomorrow," he said, to give me a moment to compose myself. I made myself think about something intensely undesirable, like a dead skunk in the road.

"Yep," Joy said. "Going back to college next week. We're going to be juniors."

"We're about to start our last year," he said. "We're headed back tomorrow too."

"Thanks for stopping when you did," she said. "I was so absorbed in my book I don't know when I would have noticed she was getting burned."

The dead skunk had helped. Finally able to stand up, I handed over the bottle of aloe. "Take this with you and keep putting it on. It'll help."

Those electric blue eyes met mine again. Tousled blonde curls escaped her hair clip and framed her face. Again I felt the click and saw the soul-to-soul recognition that had been there before. "Thank you," she said. "If you hadn't stopped to help I'd have been in much worse shape. I appreciate it."

"No problem. Y'all have a safe trip back tomorrow."

"You too."

Doug and I picked up our packs and walked back the way we'd come. The sun was now getting lower, about to dip behind the tall hotels on the strip. When we were well out of earshot, he looked sideways at me and gave me a punch on the arm.

"Dude, you okay? You've got a weird look in your eye."

I shook my head to jar loose the cobwebs. "I don't have a clue. Something happened back there."

"Like what?"

"Like, something." I waved my arms. "Something. I've never felt what I felt when I looked into her eyes. And then, touching her—it was special."

"Well, that's great. Maybe you just met *the one*."

"Why is that great?"

"Mark, everyone wants to find *the one*. I'm looking for her all the time."

"Doug, I don't know anything about this girl. I don't even know her name. I know she's with a girl named Joy, they have a five-hour ride home, and she's a junior in college. That's all I know. If she's *the one*, then that's really bad news for me because I have no idea how to find her."

"So let's go back and find out."

We wheeled around and went back, but when we got to where the girls' chairs had been, the spot was empty. Obviously the girls had had enough sun and had gone inside. Where, we had no idea. And we could hardly go knocking on nearby hotel room doors. There was nothing more we could do.

We went silently back to our hotel room and looked at each other, bewildered and defeated.

"We could go back to that spot before we leave tomorrow, just in case they decided to go to the beach one more time," Doug offered.

"Let's do that," I agreed, "but I seriously doubt a girl with that kind of sunburn is going to want to go back in the sun tomorrow."

He looked at me wisely. "You're probably right about that. But remember this—if she's *the one*, God will put her back into your path. Sometime, somewhere. You just have to keep your eyes open. And Mark?"

"Yes?"

"Next time, get her phone number."

*   *   *

Just as I'd predicted, Joy and her friend were not on the beach the next morning. As Doug and I drove home, I couldn't get the girl out of my mind. Doug noticed my preoccupation.

"Snap out of it, man. We did all we could," he said. "You know, you're really not very smart about girls, are you? Remember Janice in Alaska?"

I groaned. "Let's not go there, okay? And that was totally opposite. I was clueless that she had thoughts and feelings about me because I had none for her. This time—" I turned to face him, willing him to understand. "This was more than just a physical reaction from rubbing aloe on her sunburn. There was a connection. Something inside me jumped. I saw it in her eyes too, which makes it even worse because even if she felt the same thing, she has no more idea how to get in touch with me than I do with her. But I don't know what to do now."

We rode in silence. Then Doug spoke again. "You do know what to do," he said. "You do what you always do. You pray about it and leave it in the Lord's hands."

We rode back toward Knoxville, mostly silent, and I did just that.

38

We made it back to Maryville, packed up, and went our separate ways for now—Doug back to Atlanta and me back to Knoxville. He had an engineering degree to finish. I had no clue what God had in store for me, but I knew it would be beyond anything I could imagine.

Right now, I was mostly excited because I knew that I would soon see Bert and Daniel, and they would have news of the people I loved in Nome.

I didn't have long to wait. As I lugged my stuff up the stone spiral stairs, I met Daniel coming down, empty-handed, heading back to his car for another load. He was in the middle of moving into the newly-renovated space between Vernon Douglas's room and mine.

"Dude!" We gave each other a quick, one-armed hug. "I've been about to bust, waiting to see you. You have to tell me everything."

"It was the most amazing experience of my life," he said simply. "Let's wait for Bert before we get into the details. He's coming by in a few minutes."

And after a few more laborious loads, Bert showed up. Daniel and I were heaving in exertion from our trips up and down the steps. Bert was literally bouncing around on the balls of his feet, unable to stand still in his excitement.

"We just got back," he said. "Man oh man. If I didn't know before what I want to do with my life, this sealed the deal."

We went into the big drawing room and sat. "Tell me," I said. They exchanged *where-do-I-begin* looks. "To begin with," Daniel said, "everything you told us was spot-on. The Chandlers were amazing. The Wests were amazing. Atka and his family—I could never have imagined how the natives live until I saw it for myself. He's an incredible kid, and I don't know how Missy does it. Raising those three kids all by herself in that little hut. And those children at the group home—" he waved a hand in the air, at a loss for words. "I'm in love with Prissy."

"But she's not at the group home anymore, right?" I asked. "She's with Jack and Connie."

"She is," Bert affirmed. "But she thinks of those other kids as her brothers and sisters, so they visit a lot. In fact," he slanted an amused look at Daniel, "Jack and Connie are about to give her a brother or two."

"Or two?"

"She's pregnant."

"With twins?"

"No, and she's so early in her pregnancy she doesn't know if it's a boy or a girl. The other child is Paul. They're going to adopt him too."

I sat back, aghast. "Jack and Connie just got married a year ago, and they're about to have three kids?"

"Yep," Bert said.

"Well, bless their hearts."

"And she's talking."

"Who?"

"Prissy."

"Prissy? Talking?"

"All the time. They can't shut her up. Not that they'd want to."

This was big news. Prissy had been abandoned at the group home by her alcoholic native parents when she was just an infant. When I first got to Alaska, she was five years old and wouldn't speak at all. By the time I left, she was saying a few words here and there. But talking? Carrying on a conversation? The Lord had used

Jack and Connie in her life, for sure. And Paul. That little boy, who'd lost an eye and his parents in a mining accident when he was just a toddler, had hoped and hoped that he would be adopted. But no one had ever wanted him, and he'd almost given up. The thought that Paul was about to have a family, and how he must have reacted to that news, was so stirring it brought tears to my eyes.

I took a deep breath to compose myself.

"And the Leos? How are they?" The Leos were the houseparents at the group home.

"My hat's off to them, big time." Daniel shook his head. "Being mom and dad to kids that have the problems those kids do. They have eight right now. The youngest is just a baby, and when Paul leaves, the oldest will be seven."

I racked my brain. "Who's that?"

"A kid named Thomas. I don't think he was at the group home at the time you left."

Thomas. No, he hadn't been at the group home, but I knew him well. Like many Nome kids, he was a victim of child abuse—but never bad enough to be taken away from his parents. He was one of several kids who came to the Lighthouse regularly. With his bright eyes and a bubbling curiosity, he'd reminded me a lot of myself at that age. Then, on Easter weekend, just weeks before I left to come home, he'd dedicated his life to Christ and I'd baptized him in our new church. "But why is Thomas at the group home? He has parents," I asked.

"He showed up one day beaten up pretty bad," Bert said. "It happened while we were there. It was so bad that they wouldn't give him back to his parents."

My heart went out to that sweet child and all he'd been through. But now, with the Leos, he'd have a chance to be loved and get back on his feet.

"And Darren? How's he?"

"We didn't see much of him, but we heard he's doing great with the Sanders and is on track for a big scholarship at the college in Nome."

"The University of Alaska Fairbanks. Northwest campus."

"Yep."

"Doesn't surprise me at all. He was always smart, always a leader. Did you get to see the guys at the jail?"

"Every week." Bert's eyes sparkled even brighter. "Our last week there, Will let us do the sermon."

"How many guys did you have?"

"Six."

"Is Hank still there?"

"The big guy with the tattoos?"

"Yep."

"Not only is he still there, but he's leading Bible studies every week," said Daniel. "God's using him in that place, big time. At this point, I don't think he'd want to get out. He's having too much fun."

"And Jasper? The native guy who believes in the ancient ways?"

"He comes to church but doesn't say much," Daniel said. "I don't think he speaks much English, but I picked up a little Siberian Upik."

"Tell me about the church building. How's it holding up?"

"Great." Daniel grinned. "We painted it."

When I left, the church had been plain brown boards, but we'd worked so hard on it that we thought it was beautiful. I couldn't imagine it painted. "What color?"

"White." Daniel produced a small photo. "Check it out."

I snapped up the photo and studied it. Memories flooded back. For three months, taking full advantage of the long hours of daylight near the Arctic Circle, a core team of three had erected this building from the ground up. It was the hardest work I'd ever done. We'd drilled pilings into the permafrost so that it would hold firm. As the Bible says, on the solid rock. We'd worked around problems and, in the end when we'd run out of money, an oil-rich millionaire from Texas had come through with the money and materials we needed to finish the job.

That building had turned into a church home for many, and I'd seen the seeds start to sprout before I'd left. I smiled, remembering. Then I thought of something else.

"What'd you think of Denise's food?"

"That woman can cook," Bert said. "I gained ten pounds in three months. I never thought I'd eat moose and like it."

"And Snickers?"

"Still there, still leading the team," Daniel supplied. Snickers had saved my life a couple of times when I would have lost my way on the Alaskan tundra. And she was the one who'd lost her patience and ripped the throat out of a new wheel dog when he'd stopped to poop one time too many.

"She's a good girl," I said, and paused. "So, what did you take away from this trip?"

"Oh, man," Bert said. "I told you already, this changed me. I know now what I want to do with my life. God's calling me to full-time mission work."

"How about you, Daniel?"

He thought for a minute, then met my eyes. "I'm heading in that same direction. Just seeing those people, and how much they need to know the love of Jesus. I've never been anywhere where people had never even heard about Him. It's an unbelievable feeling and privilege to be the one God allows to share the good news with them." He paused. "In fact, I want to go back next summer. It was great to work with the kids, but I want to reach the adults too. I'm going to work really hard over the next year to learn their language. What do you think?"

"You'll have to apply again, like you did this year, but I think you're a shoe-in," I told him. I knew exactly how he felt. I could still remember the awe and humility I'd felt when telling the Christmas story to the little children. It was the first time they'd ever heard it. The moment had brought tears to my eyes and still had the power to give me goosebumps and a lump in my throat. "So you think we should keep sending missionaries to Nome every summer?"

"Absolutely." Daniel didn't hesitate. "Their mission is expanding, and they can use every pair of hands they can get."

"Do you want the mission job on the EC?"

Daniel opened his mouth and then closed it again.

"What about me?" Bert wanted to know. "What am I, chopped liver?"

"Your gift is evangelism, and that's where I think you need to stay. If you're willing and Bob agrees, and the committee elects you."

"I'd be honored to take that job," Daniel said. "I appreciate your confidence. I know those people are special to you."

"Daniel," I said, "you're just beginning to understand."

39

The new girl, Kelsey Rhodes, moved into Wanda Wells' old room, and the first EC meeting took place not long after. People were surprised, but I'd prayed about it and talked it over with Bob, and I knew it was right that Vernon be elected president this year. I'd move to vice president. The election went smoothly, with Susan remaining as secretary, Brandon as treasurer, and Kenny special projects. Kelsey Rhodes took over the noonday program, while Bert remained in evangelism and Daniel took over as mission chair. And we added a new position—Bible study chair. Randy Barnette became part of the EC and the official leader of all the dorm Bible studies. He'd have to have help, of course, to do it the way we all envisioned, but he already had volunteers.

One of those volunteers was Angie Galyon. She'd appeared at the BSU the first day freshmen moved into the dorms and announced her intent to get involved in our ministry in a big way. The Bible study ministry was a natural fit for her, and she immediately joined the team to help Susan with the girls.

So what if I did a double-take every time I saw a slender girl with blonde hair? Who could blame me? In my heart I knew that my girl was not at UT, but I couldn't get her out of my mind.

I had work to do, though. My major jobs as vice president were to be Vernon's second-in-command and to manage our involvement with the World's Fair, since I was already neck-deep in that event anyway. And part of that was Nancy Mahoney.

She was in and out of the BSU all the time, deciding how we could best help with logistics. The BSU's geographical location, near the center of UT, made us ideal to be a central part, almost a home base, for the Fair. Nancy and I worked smoothly together, bouncing ideas off each other and making each other better. During one of those visits, she told me she'd decided to take me up on my invitation to visit Pleasant Grove and get a first-hand look at the Muppet ministry.

"That's great," I told her. I wanted her to see for herself the passion of my youth group.

She appeared in church the very next Sunday and sat on the front pew, spellbound, as the young Muppeteers wowed the children. They'd become slick, professional, and accomplished during their summer doing Bible schools, and they got better every time they performed. We always prayed before each performance that the Lord would work through them to accomplish His will, and He was blessing this ministry. The number of kids at the children's sermons had exploded when word got out that the Muppets were here. Now they were a regular feature. Kids were disappointed if they didn't see at least one Muppet. I continued to lead this portion of the service with a pre-planned scriptural lesson, but now a Muppet usually helped.

After the service, Nancy stayed back to meet the youth. They were in the back room, packing up and preparing to leave, when I led Nancy in.

"Everybody, I've got someone you need to meet," I said. "This is Nancy Mahoney, from the North American Mission Board. She's the reason you're getting to perform at the World's Fair next summer. She's the one who scheduled you."

Jimmy came forward first. "This ministry has changed my life," he said. "It wouldn't have happened if you hadn't sent Mark that letter. So thank you." He offered his hand, and she took it with her firm handshake.

"I'm glad this work is already making such a difference," she said. "I've been following your progress through Mark. You've done some amazing things over the summer."

"No, the Lord did it," I said. "He just used us. It's what, kids?" I held up my finger to the sky.

"It's all about Him," they said in unison.

All the other kids gathered around Nancy and either hugged her or shook her hand, and we were all smiling by the time we left.

"So what do you do now?" Nancy asked as we walked toward our cars. "You have several hours to fill before tonight's youth meeting. I'm assuming you don't drive all the way back to Knoxville."

"I spend the time with one of the church families," I said, and told her how the people here had lined up to invite me to lunch on Sunday afternoons from the moment I'd arrived at Pleasant Grove. "It's a great way to get to know the church families, especially the ones where my youth group members live. I've had some incredible mountain cooking this past year. The first Sunday it was possum stew and squirrel gravy. And the possum stew was made with road kill."

"No way."

"Yes way. It was the Gambrells. Pete is one of my graduate assistants with the youth program. He's the one who brought in the possum. As long as it's still warm and not too squished, his mom can turn it into something delicious. She's a prayer warrior. Actually, that's where I'm headed for lunch now."

"I'd love to meet them. Do you think they'd mind if I just come say hi? I won't stay to eat since I haven't been invited."

"They won't mind, and I'm pretty sure they'll invite you for lunch. Follow me. And stick close. These roads can be a little tricky."

Ten minutes later, after the twisting, turning mountain roads I'd grown accustomed to, we pulled into the clearing where the Gambrells' cabin sat. Nancy emerged from her car, wide-eyed. "That was amazing," she said. "A couple of times I thought I was driving into the clouds. And look at that cabin!"

"That was my first reaction, too," I agreed. "Let's go in and introduce you. You game for whatever they feed you?"

She swallowed hard. "If they feed it to me, I'll eat it."

The hounds lumbered to their feet and bayed our arrival as we trudged up the steps. I knocked on the door.

"Come on in, Mark." I heard Liz's voice from inside. "My hands are floury."

I eased open the solid wood door and we stepped into a scene that could have been from a hundred years ago. I tried to picture it through Nancy's eyes, and it was easy—I'd just seen it for the first time myself about a year ago. Solid wood furniture. Hand-woven rugs. Old-time iron cookware over a wood stove. Two women moving about in their aprons, getting a meal ready.

"I brought someone to meet you," I said. "This is Nancy Mahoney. She's with the North American Mission Board. She's the one we're working with for the World's Fair."

"It's all Pete's been able to talk about. It's so nice to meet you." Miss Ina dried her hands on her apron, took Nancy's hand in both of her tiny ones and looked into her eyes in her soul-piercing way. "You'll stay to eat, of course."

"If you'll have me, I'd love to. You have to let me help, though. Put me to work."

So for the next hour, in the way of the mountaineers, I sat on the porch and looked out over the mountains with Pete, Todd, and Pete Senior while the women cooked. Through the open door I could hear the low voices of Liz, Miss Ina, and Nancy as they worked together to put a meal on the table. The toddlers rattled their toys and occasionally one of them put up a fuss, which Liz immediately quieted.

Before long the nine of us were seated around the huge wooden table, which as usual was groaning with food. Steaming bowls of home-grown greens, sweet potatoes, and corn, alongside platters of golden fried chicken and homemade biscuits. A stew steamed in a large pot. In smaller bowls was honey that I knew had come from the bees at the edge of the yard. Sliced home-grown tomatoes completed the meal.

"That chicken looks really good," I said as I helped myself to a crispy drumstick.

"It should be fresh. I wrung their necks just this morning," Miss Ina said. "Pete Senior just finished plucking them when y'all drove up."

I looked sideways at Nancy to see how she'd take this news, but she just kept filling her plate. "My dad died when I was young, so I grew up helping my mom cook," she said. "I like it."

"You did a good job," Liz said approvingly. She pointed to the sweet potatoes. "Nancy made those. Said it was her mom's special recipe."

"What's this stew?" Nancy asked as she ladled some into her bowl.

Miss Ina chewed and swallowed. "Rabbit," she said. "We raise them for food in a pen near the edge of the woods."

Nancy gamely went on with her meal, but I'd seen the hesitation in her eyes and I noticed she took only one ladle of the stew. I stifled a grin as I realized she must be thinking of cute little cottontailed bunny rabbits. But the stew was rich and savory. It reminded me of the moose stew Denise used to make in Alaska.

The meal went on as most family meals do, with chatter, side conversations, and a lot of laughter. Being the newcomer, Nancy was the target of many questions, and I learned a lot about her as I listened to her answers.

She grew up in Florida, went to Florida State University, and was a staunch, rabid Seminole. Ugh. I guessed I'd have to get used to that over the next year or so, especially with football season about to start. She had a brother who was currently a youth minister at one of the largest churches in Florida, with aspirations to be a senior pastor. He and her mother were both still in Florida. Their dad had died several years before when Nancy was in her early teens. She and her mother had leaned heavily on each other and were very close. Nancy had finished school and gone to work immediately for the North American Mission Board. Her first assignment was the World's Fair, and she'd been working on it for several months already from Atlanta.

"What did your mom think when you moved to Atlanta?" Miss Ina asked, as usual sensitive to the hurts of others.

"She misses me, and I miss her, but I'm doing what I've been called to do. Mission work."

"What happens after the World's Fair is over?"

"That's still a year away, so I really have no idea." She shrugged. "I'll get another assignment, somewhere else. Or maybe I'll find someone special by then. That's what I really want. To be a minister's wife and to share in the missions of the church. Get heavily invested in one group of people and try to help them. I'll follow wherever the Lord leads."

I could feel Miss Ina's eyes boring into me from across the table, but I didn't meet her gaze. I knew what she was thinking, and it was something I had no interest in. Just like with Janice in Alaska, my life was too full right now to be thinking long-term unless I found the one. Being with someone and having fun with her was one thing, and I was definitely enjoying being with Nancy. But at this point, that was it.

Besides, when I thought that far down the road, it wasn't Nancy's face that came to mind. It was a face framed by wispy blonde curls, highlighted with brilliant blue eyes, accompanied by a slim, lithe body that most people, I supposed, would find skinny. I thought it was perfect. When I closed my eyes, I could still feel her soft skin under my palms.

That girl was still out there, and I hoped it was the Lord's plan for us to meet again. Next time, I wouldn't blow it.

*   *   *

As the months went on, my involvement with Nancy grew. Her Sunday lunches with the mountain people became a weekly occurrence, and she fit in seamlessly. She jumped right into my work with the youth, and her ideas made our ministry even stronger. The kids were starting to tease me about her, calling her my girlfriend. The idea spread to the BSU, and the other guys began to give me knowing, sidelong glances whenever Nancy walked into the room. It was an unspoken assumption that we were a couple.

I took my own advice, though. I was committed to wait until after marriage for sex, so I was careful to avoid temptation. Nancy and I sometimes held hands as we walked, or maybe I'd drape my arm around her shoulders if we were sitting side by side. Sometimes, if my back was hurting even worse than usual, she'd give me a back rub to ease the pain. But nothing else.

One weekday in October, when the weather was unseasonably warm, I dropped by her apartment to drop off some paperwork and ideas for the World's Fair. I planned to just slide it under the door, when I heard music coming from the back of the building.

Nancy lived in an apartment complex right beside the site of the Fair in Knoxville. The complex had its own pool, which was situated perfectly to give the residents privacy, with a fence and shielding trees. The fence, however, was slightly ajar, and I gave it a slight nudge. If Nancy was outside, I could just hand her the paperwork.

But as I came near the pool, I also caught sight of Nancy. She was a modest person, and I'd never seen any part of her body that wasn't covered by very decent shirts and shorts, which didn't give any details whatsoever as to her build. Now, though, she was stretched out in the sun, taking advantage of these last rays of summer. Her bathing suit was a simple one-piece, but it left no doubt as to her curves. She lay on her back, eyes closed, and earphones in her ears as she basked in the warmth. I realized with a jolt that she really was a very shapely young woman. Her legs were toned, her stomach flat, and she had a full bust that was usually downplayed by the tops she wore. Her arms were deceptively slim, but I knew from watching her that she could toss a toddler in the air one second and help lug in a cord of wood the next. Underneath the slimness was quiet muscle that could do whatever it wanted.

I watched her and pondered. Maybe I was being too picky. Maybe those few minutes with the girl at the beach weren't what I thought they were. The blonde hair, blue eyes, and slim body that still haunted me might forever be a part of my past because I'd missed that opportunity. And maybe, just maybe, the girl lying beside the pool was the one meant to stand beside me while I did the ministry I wanted to do. It was something I needed to think and pray about.

Not wanting to embarrass her, I silently crept out the way I'd come, slid the papers under her door, then headed back to the BSU.

40

October became November, and the calendar edged its way toward December. Now Nancy had met my family. My dad and sisters loved her, but my mom was more reserved. I put this down to the fact that, of course, no one would ever be good enough for her only son. Bob Hall was nearly bursting with pride that Nancy and I seemed to be hitting it off, and he was the one who'd introduced us. I still hesitated, and no one could figure out why. What more could I possibly want in a woman?

I tried to explain it to Vernon Douglas. "I've always wanted someone special," I told him. "I know that what I want is out there because I've seen it with the Leos and the Chandlers. They're one unit. Neither would be complete without the other. Their love is so complete that you can feel it. They're different than any other marriages I've ever seen in my life. So I know it exists, and that's what I want."

"What makes you think you can't have that with Nancy?"

"It's nothing I can put my finger on." I had told him the story about the girl at the beach. "If I'd never met that girl at the beach, I probably wouldn't be hesitating now. But I did see her, even touch her, and look into her eyes. What I felt then . . . well, that's what I've always wanted to feel."

He gave me a level look. "Be honest, dude. You've already told me the rest of the story. How much of it is physical?"

"Some, obviously. But that's part of what I'm trying to tell you. I don't feel that with Nancy. She's pretty, and she has a great body—"

"How do you know that?"

"I accidentally saw her in a swimsuit."

"And?"

"Nice and tanned like you'd think a girl from Florida would be."

"Sounds good so far. Go on."

"And she's good with the kids, and she can cook, and she wants to be a minister's wife." I looked at Vernon in desperation. "So she's perfect for me. Why don't I feel it? Why am I not hightailing it to Markman's for a ring? We could be engaged by Christmas. I'm pretty sure she'd say yes."

"Have you kissed her?"

"Not the way you're talking about, no. Our relationship just hasn't gone in that direction, and that's a conscious decision on my part. I believe what I've told my young people. God expects us to stay pure before marriage, and that means not putting yourself in a situation where you could be tempted."

"Then you don't know if you're physically attracted to her or not."

"I know I don't feel for her what I felt for the girl at the beach."

"Maybe you should try putting sunscreen on her legs and see what happens."

I punched him. "Seriously, dude."

"Seriously? I think you need to be asking the Lord these questions, not me."

Over the next few weeks I did just that. Often. If God wanted me to be with Nancy, then so be it. I begged Him for guidance but got no answer whatsoever. And tomorrow, Nancy was planning to spend Thanksgiving with my family. I knew there would be sly looks and suggestive remarks. I had to figure this out.

So, the night before Thanksgiving, I shut my door and painfully, stiffly, knelt beside my mattress in my small room at the BSU.

"Lord," I prayed, "I've got a big decision to make here. Everybody seems to think Nancy's perfect for me, and I should be putting a ring on her finger. If that's what You want me to do, then that's what I'll do. Tell me, Lord."

Silence. Not only in my room but also inside myself. I knelt there for a long time, listening for that small voice inside me that never failed to lead me in the right direction. Nothing. So I headed for the Scriptures. Sometimes I found that voice in the words of the Bible.

I turned to Paul's epistles in the New Testament, to all the places where he describes how women should dress and act in public and how they should treat their husbands. Nancy was a strong Christian, and the Bible says husbands and wives should be equally yoked. Check. Cherish the children and lead them to Christ. Check. She was an invaluable help to me with the youth and even the small children. Women should conduct themselves with dignity, grace, and mercy, and not be malicious gossips. Check. They are to dress modestly and not draw attention to themselves. Check. And, it wasn't in the Bible, but it was pretty important to me that my wife be able to cook. She was constantly bringing me my favorite foods as I studied and worked. Another check.

In several places, the Scriptures say that wives should respect and be completely subject to their husbands, and husbands should take their responsibilities as head of the household—and their wives' spiritual mentor—seriously. Husbands are to teach and sanctify their wives, to love them as Christ loved the church. I couldn't quite picture this in my relationship with Nancy. She liked and respected me, but she didn't seem the type to completely subject herself to anyone.

I was getting more and more anxious until I came upon an underlined, well-loved passage in Philippians. "Be anxious for nothing, but in everything by prayer and supplication with thanksgiving let your requests be made known to God. And the peace of God, which surpasses all comprehension, will guard your hearts and your minds in Christ Jesus."

My spirit quieted instantly. No decision needed to be made right now. Let people talk. I'd keep praying, and keep watching and waiting, and sooner or later the answer would be made clear to me.

"Thank You, Father," I said. "You'll let me know what to do when the time is right. I trust You and I love You. Amen."

* * *

My resolve was put to the test the very next day when, in the middle of our Thanksgiving dinner, my dad pointed his fork at me. "So, Mark, when are you going to put a ring on this girl's finger?"

My mom choked on her macaroni and cheese. My dad's parents, who had come for the holiday, looked back and forth from me to Dad to Nancy with their mouths open. Lisa and Mellie looked on with interest, smiles beginning to dawn on their faces. Lisa was already planning her wedding, and I could tell she was bursting to share her ideas. Her fiancé sat beside her, obviously enjoying watching me squirm. Nancy put down her fork and waited to see what I'd say. Her lips curved in a half-smile.

My grandfather winked at me. He was a master electrician who'd helped build the nuclear Secret City of Oak Ridge, Tennessee, which had helped build the atomic bomb and end World War II. Now, he stoked the fire by nodding his head and waggling his hand at me. "See this?" He pointed at his Masonic ring with its huge diamond. "This diamond is for you when you're ready." He took the ring off and handed it over to Nancy. She gaped.

"This is absolutely beautiful," she said, and handed it back. "But we haven't really talked about marriage."

I looked at her gratefully. "She's right," I said. "The subject hasn't actually come up."

"Well, you better get on the stick," Dad announced. "This girl won't be on the market very long."

"I'll take that as a compliment." Nancy laughed and relieved the tension. "And who knows? Anything could happen."

She smiled at me, and something inside me loosened, something that had been balled up in a tense knot. Would Nancy be one of my many friends who just happened to be female? Or would she be more? Time would tell.

41

Life suddenly seemed to pick up its pace and fly along like an eagle. The application deadline for next summer's Nome trip came and went. Evidently word had gotten out, because we had double the number of applications this year. I checked with Will West, and he agreed to take three missionaries. Daniel Bowman, I was sure, would be one of them. He'd submitted his application like everyone else and was working hard to polish his Siberian Upik so he could communicate with the adults better.

Angie and Randy were among the others who'd applied, and I thought the competition would be interesting. Although he was the mission chair, Daniel would have to recuse himself because of his own involvement, so I would again have the lead role in picking the missionaries.

Over the Christmas holidays, I visited the seminary my dad attended—The Southern Theological Seminary in Louisville, Kentucky—and knew this was the place I wanted to go. The teachings here were very liberal, but that was fine with me because I didn't want to go to a place that taught everyone the same cookie-cutter theology. I wanted to be forced to ask, and answer, tough questions. Dinosaurs? Evolution? I had been through that constantly at UT. They didn't challenge my faith in the least, but I wanted to be put on the spot. Southern would do that, with its philosophies and world-renowned theologians from every faith, who came from everywhere to speak to these students.

I sent off my application for the next fall, and received my acceptance in early January. One more semester at UT, and I'd be off to the next phase of my life, whatever that turned out to be.

Between now and then, though, I had a big mission. The World's Fair, where my youth would be performing and the BSU would be a hub. We had less than five months now. Thankfully, my course load in my last semester would be light. I was actually taking beginning tennis, for goodness' sake, so that I could concentrate on the Fair.

Just looking around, it was obvious that this was a very big deal. Knoxville's very skyline had changed. The Sunsphere now stood 266 feet tall, shiny and new, a symbol of the big event that was about to bring people here from around the world. It was a steel tower topped with a five-story golden globe. It still stands today and, for many, is a symbol of the city of Knoxville.

The fair was built on a 70-acre site between downtown Knoxville and UT. The core was primarily a deteriorating railroad yard and depot, which had been demolished except for a single rail line that was converted into a restaurant.

Nancy, of course, was ahead of the news reports, and she told us gleefully every time a new nation agreed to participate. We were expecting people from Australia, Belgium, Canada, China, Denmark, Egypt, France, Greece, Hungary, Italy, Japan, Luxembourg, Mexico, the Netherlands, Panama, Peru, the Philippines, Saudi Araba, South Korea, the United Kingdom, and West Germany. Every time a new country was added, the eyes of the kids in our youth group got bigger. They were confident but nervous, and they worked harder and harder to get ready for this opportunity.

Nancy was a whirlwind as she packed the schedule with good, wholesome entertainment that would deliver a solid message. I worked alongside her, and it became more and more obvious that we were a good team. Sometimes our eyes met, and there seemed to be something there. Something more than friendship. But we still didn't talk about it, until one day when we were at the BSU taking a break from our frenetic preparations.

I had been thinking about it more and more, and praying about it. Still no direct word from the Lord, either from my prayer time or my Scripture study. This was only the second time since I'd begun to grow spiritually that the Lord had been silent. The first was when I hurt my back and prayed for healing, but I could understand that. My injury was because of my own pride, not through any action of His. Now, though, as I thought through my current situation and pondered the Lord's silence, I was remembering something else. There had been many times in my life when God had spoken to me through trusted mentors. Dr. Charles Stanley. Bob Hall. Will West. Charles Chandler. My parents. And there'd been others. Maybe this was one of those times. Maybe I had to trust in the counsel of the people who'd been put on this earth to guide me. Everyone seemed absolutely certain that Nancy was perfect for me, and I should grab her before it was too late. With that in mind, before I lost my nerve, I turned to Nancy and took her hand.

"Remember Thanksgiving at my house?" I asked. In the close friendship we'd developed, she knew instantly what I was talking about.

"Sure. Your face was priceless. I've almost never seen you at a loss for words, but that was one of those times."

"What do you think about it?"

"About what?"

"Us. Long term."

She leaned forward and looked me in the eyes. "I've thought for a long time that we'd be perfect together. I was just waiting for you to realize it too."

I stared at her. "Really?"

"Really."

"You'd be open to making that kind of commitment?"

"Being a minister's wife is what I've always wanted. Then you came along. I knew it from the beginning. It's perfect. So yes."

"But I'm heading for seminary in August, and you'll still be in the middle of the World's Fair."

"Mark." She looked at me with amusement. "Nothing says it

has to happen immediately, or that we can't be apart for a little while. I'll be done in October. Either you delay going to seminary until January, or I'll come join you in Louisville when the Fair is over. That is, if you're serious."

I thought about it for a minute. "Yes, I'm serious. I think we could do a lot of good things together for the Lord."

We shared a short kiss—our first—and just like that, I was sort of unofficially engaged.

It didn't occur to me until much later, when I was getting ready for bed that night, that neither of us had uttered the words "I love you."

42

"Mark, are you sure?" Miss Ina had a worried tone in her voice. She'd sought me out after church one day, after Pete spilled the beans about my unofficial engagement. It was still unofficial because the ring was still up in the air. My grandfather still wanted me to take his ring for Nancy, but we were a little uneasy about that. Masonic rings are a big deal, and most men want to be buried with theirs on their fingers. So we were still thinking about it, and as a result Nancy had no ring on her finger.

We were considering all sorts of scenarios, including getting married as early as September. But nothing had been decided. People, however, were now assuming our marriage wasn't a matter of if, but when.

We had also made no definite plans about timing, but I was leaning toward her suggestion that I delay seminary for a semester and stay around to help her finish the World's Fair. Bob thought that was an excellent idea and offered me a position as associate director at the BSU beginning immediately after graduation—even if I decided to go on to seminary as planned. I'd still be AD for the summer. Everything looked like it was falling into place perfectly, but I was still troubled by the silence I felt from the Lord.

"I'm not sure about anything, Miss Ina," I told her frankly. "I've asked and asked the Lord for guidance on this, but the only thing that's happened is that everyone I trust, everyone who's been a mentor to me in the past, seems convinced that Nancy's right for me. So I figure God's answering my prayers through my mentors, which has happened to me before."

She looked at me without speaking for a full minute.

"On something this big, I wouldn't be 'figuring' anything," she said. "God will put it on your heart if this is the girl for you. You will feel it and know it. You'll be unable to imagine life without her. If you don't feel those things, then don't give her a ring until you do."

I had a memory flash of vivid blue eyes and soft blonde curls, and resolutely pushed the memory away.

"I don't exactly feel those things, but everything I do feel is good." I thought for a moment and tried to explain. "She's one of my best friends. We click, and we make each other better. And she's always wanted to be a minister's wife." I paused, then told her something I hadn't told anyone. "And I think maybe God sent me a sign. You know we've all been praying for my back ever since I got hurt?"

She nodded.

"Well, Nancy gave me a back rub one day, and my back felt better. And she can cook." Listening to myself as I talked to Miss Ida, even I could hear the weakness in my thought patterns. She looked at me with pity.

"Mark, you can't live by signs. Sometimes they're from the Lord, and sometimes they aren't. Marriage is forever. You need to pray some more."

"Will you pray for me, Miss Ina? For discernment and wisdom?"

"Every day, until you're sure."

43

Things went from bad to worse. Time on my knees and in the Scriptures didn't help. My back was still killing me. Over the past eighteen months I'd had hands laid on me and tongues spoken over me. I'd been to faith healers who told me I just didn't have enough faith. If I did, they said, then God would take the pain away. The pain was debilitating, even with the strong painkillers. The Lord had never answered that prayer either, and now this quandary with Nancy.

The stress was starting to wear on me. One night at our youth group meeting, a young man came to visit, and it seemed to me that he was there for the wrong reasons. That feeling seemed justified when I spotted him in the corner during social time, making what looked like a very obvious pass at Jessica Hammond.

The temper that has always boiled hotly in my blood, just under the surface, came gushing out. In a flash I was across the room, grabbing the boy by the front of his shirt and hauling him away from Jessica.

"This is a serious Bible study, buddy," I told him as I shoved him out the door and he sprawled in a heap in the front yard. "Until you understand that, you stay away." I slammed the door behind him.

I strode back into the living room, where all the kids stood staring.

"He won't be bothering us again," I said. "Time to split up into our groups." The kids looked dubious, but we went on with our evening and had a successful Bible study on Revelation. These young men and women were spiritually mature enough to handle a very meaty subject, and I put the incident with the young man out of my mind and concentrated on doing a good job.

But the whole time, Martha Galyon watched me from the next room, where she was teaching the girls. When everyone had left and we were cleaning up, she cornered me.

"Mark, I don't usually question anything you do, because you've done such a good job until now," she said. "But I have to know why you did what you did earlier this evening."

"You mean with that young boy? He was messing with Jessica. He wasn't here for the right reasons."

"And how do you know that? She was handling things just fine, and he would have been in my group, away from her, in just a few minutes. Maybe God was using us to reach him, and now that's a lost opportunity. What you did was seems like the wrong way to handle it. There were other ways. It's just not you."

I thought about it and knew she was right. My temper had always been an animal, barely leashed under the surface. Whenever I saw a child, or a woman, or even an animal, being victimized, that temper tore free. Jessica hadn't been in danger. I could have pulled that young man aside and talked to him. Now I had no way of making it right, because the boy was a visitor and I didn't even know his name. As Martha said, an opportunity lost. And that was definitely not why I was here. I seemed off track—distracted.

Something had to give. This stress was making me crazy.

* * *

Right before spring break, we chose the missionaries for the summer trip. The method we'd used last year had worked so well that I used it again. The ones chosen were Daniel, Randy, and Angie. Normally, a freshman would be an unusual choice, but Angie was no usual freshman. She had a fresh sincerity about her, along with an unwavering commitment to follow the Lord, that convinced the EC that she would be an effective missionary—especially with the native kids.

When spring break came, I knew I had to have a break. My stress was mounting. Nancy was out there picking wedding colors and flowers, not realizing the turmoil in my heart. I was trying to make the toughest decision of my life, my back was still killing me, and the Lord had been silent on both subjects so far.

Plus, I had graduation, the World's Fair and seminary coming up. Usually Doug Taylor was my partner in adventure, but he was unavailable because his spring break and mine didn't line up. But I needed to get away. I mentioned it to Daniel Bowman, and he snapped up the idea. He was feeling a little stressed as well, with graduation and his mission trip coming up.

"Let's get out of here," he said.

My high school graduation gift had been a canoe, and I had rigged my little Chevette so I could lash the boat on the top. That way, I could go fishing whenever I wanted. Slide into the water anytime, anywhere. I'd found some of my best fishing holes this way. Slip up on a spot, drop a minnow, and start a feeding frenzy.

We decided to take a canoe trip, but where? Somewhere new, we decided. In the end we simply lashed the canoe to the car and took off, headed south, bound nowhere in particular. We ended up in central Florida, at the Ocklawaha River. I'd had the vague idea of going to Lake Okeechobee in southern Florida. When I was in high school, my dad took me out of school for a week and we went fishing at Okeechobee. My typing teacher was furious that I missed a week of school to go fishing, and I got a bad grade as a result, but I had some priceless memories with my dad.

Daniel and I didn't get quite that far. When we reached Ocklawaha, it seemed perfect, so we stopped and made camp.

We didn't make it onto the water the next day, as high winds and lashing rain pelted the area. We sat, huddled in our tent, eating freeze-dried meals and beef jerky, and looked at each other. And it hit me.

"Daniel, do you realize that here Nancy and I are talking marriage, and I haven't even met her family?"

"Dude, really?"

"And do you know where they are?"

"Where?"

"Orlando. Her brother, Chuck, is the youth minister of one of the biggest Southern Baptist churches here. Her mom is here too."

He looked at me with a smile. "I think you just figured out why we stopped in Orlando."

I grinned back. Maybe, finally, I was getting some much-needed guidance from God. Why else would we have just happened to stop in Orlando? And why else would the gorgeous weather all of a sudden be gray and soggy? Miss Ina had said not to put much stock into signs, but this seemed a little too coincidental.

The next morning Daniel and I marched into the main office at the church where Chuck worked. The receptionist looked up with a cheerful smile.

"Can I help you?"

"Is Chuck Mahoney in?"

"I'll check. Can I tell him your name?"

"Mark Smith. But he's not expecting me. I'm sort of engaged to his sister, and I just wanted to say hello."

Her cheerful smile turned into an ear-to-ear grin, and she grabbed the phone and spoke in low tones. She hung up almost immediately.

"He'll be right out," she said.

Moments later, a tall man with short, dark hair and an air of self-confidence came striding out. I knew from Nancy that he wasn't much older than me, somewhere in his mid-twenties. His career had skyrocketed from the moment he graduated from seminary, and he was leading an exploding youth program here in Orlando. There was a lot I could learn from this guy, I decided.

"Chuck?" I stepped forward and held out my hand. "Mark Smith."

He grasped my hand in a firm handshake. "So you're Mark.

About to be my brother. I've been wanting to meet you."

"I've heard all about you from Nancy," I said, and pulled Daniel forward. "This is Daniel Bowman." They shook hands. "He's a good friend, and we just happened to be in the neighborhood."

"You did? Nancy didn't tell me."

"She didn't know. We didn't know ourselves. We came to Florida for some canoe fishing, and our car just kind of brought us to Orlando."

"That's really interesting. You'll never guess who got here right before you."

"Who?"

"Nancy."

"She did?"

"Totally unplanned. And you'll never guess what we were just talking about, right when you got here."

"What?"

"We were trying to schedule a time for me to come to Knoxville and do your pre-marital counseling. It's required, and she wants me to do it. Is that okay with you?"

I stood there, stunned and unable to formulate a coherent sentence. "Sure, why not?"

"We can get that out of the way right now, if you're up for it."

So Daniel took an hour to sight-see while I followed Chuck to his office at the back of the church. Nancy jumped up and hugged me.

"What are you doing here?" I asked as I hugged her back.

"Since you weren't around, I decided to come see my mom. But I can't believe you're here too! This is the most amazing coincidence ever."

"We weren't planning to come," I explained. "If it weren't raining, we'd be in my canoe on the Ocklawaha River."

"God sent the rain," she said with conviction. "I really wanted Chuck to do our counseling, and now it's just worked out perfectly."

Many churches require counseling that lasts for several weeks, but Chuck put us on the speed plan and an hour later, certificate of completion in hand, we were leaving the church and headed for her mother's house.

"My mom is going to be so surprised," Nancy said. "She's been planning to come to Knoxville to meet you, and now here you are. Do you like gator?"

"Gator?"

"As in alligator. That's what's for supper tonight."

I'd never had alligator, but I was game to try it. After whale blubber and rancid seal oil in Alaska, and road kill possum stew in East Tennessee, how bad could it be?

Daniel and I got into my car and followed Chuck and Nancy to a modest home on the outskirts of Orlando. It nestled between several others that looked just like it, but Nancy's mom had decorated it to be unique. Flowering plants hung from the edges of the porch. Hummingbird feeders were placed strategically between the plants. A wind chime picked up the breeze and made pleasant music. Grapefruit trees, with their ripe fruit dangling from the branches, caught my eye.

And a plastic pink flamingo sat impudently on the lawn. Somehow, it looked just right.

We got out of our cars, and Nancy all but dragged me to the door, so excited was she. She burst right in, which was unusual for me. In our family, we always knocked or rang the bell. Families were different, I supposed.

"Mom!" Nancy called out. "Mom?"

"I'm in the kitchen. Come on back."

We all trooped to the back of the house, Nancy in the lead.

"That sounds like more feet than just you and your brother," her mom said as we approached the kitchen.

"We've brought a couple of guests for dinner."

"Do tell."

We entered the kitchen and Nancy's mom looked up from flouring chunks of meat that I assumed were gator. She was shorter than Nancy and plumper, with curled brown hair and soft green eyes. "Who's this?"

"This is Mark and his friend Daniel. Mark and Daniel, this is my mom, Mary."

"Mark? *Your* Mark?"

"Yes, he just showed up at church today while I was there. Isn't that incredible?"

"It's quite a coincidence." She wiped her hands on her apron and gave us both big hugs. "No hand shaking here. You're about to be family."

Before long we were all seated in the kitchen, with Nancy and Mary bringing dishes to the table. Gator with butter sauce, soft rolls, and fresh vegetables. Chuck asked the Lord's blessing on the food, and we began to fill our plates. The gator was a little too spongy and chewy for me, but it seemed delicious after whale blubber. With whale blubber, you have to just decide when to swallow, because you can never chew it up. Daniel eyed the food and looked a little green, but he gamely dug in.

"I've heard all about you from Nancy, but you have to tell me about yourself," Mary said as she passed plates around the table.

Between bites, I told her an abridged version of my history. I was a preacher's kid, a missionary, a college student, and about to be a seminary student. I told her about my spiritual journey, including some details about my year in Alaska that had her alternately hooting and gasping.

"What do you want to do after seminary?" she asked. This was a very astute question, because most people simply assumed that if a person goes to seminary, he intends to be a pastor. That wasn't my goal at all. I would follow where the Lord led, but I didn't feel—had never felt—that my gift was in preaching or even evangelism. I felt most effective when I was equipping and teaching others. Sowing and watering but not necessarily reaping. I wanted to be in the ministry, but not as a pastor, not unless the Lord made it very clear that that was what He wanted of me. I said as much.

"You're not going to be a pastor?" Nancy asked, startled.

"Not unless God tells me to."

"But you're going to work for a church."

"I hope so. Maybe in youth ministry, like Chuck here. I'm really enjoying that."

"That's a lot of fun. Your kids are doing a great job," said Nancy.

The conversation drifted from here to there, and I felt completely comfortable with Nancy's family. I seemed to fit right in, and for the first time I began to feel that all my mentors were right, and marriage to Nancy was the right thing.

When Daniel and I left that night, I hugged Mary, kissed Nancy, and shook Chuck's hand. "Thanks for a great evening. Really."

"I'm so glad you came by. Welcome to the family."

"You made me feel like family. I appreciate it."

"You'll be at the World's Fair?"

"For opening day. We wouldn't miss it."

"Then I'll see you in May."

"See you then."

44

The weather cleared the next day, and Daniel and I spent the next few days lazily cruising in my tiny canoe along the murky, grassy river. Huge bass lurked in the shallows, and gators lazily slid in and out of the water. We caught more than enough fish to feed ourselves every day, and we feasted beside the campfire at night. It was just what we both needed to relax and unwind before the final push when we got back to school.

I was feeling better about Nancy. I still didn't have a real answer from within my heart and spirit, but I couldn't ignore the coincidences in Orlando. Surely, God had a part in that. I put aside the advice Miss Ina had given me and decided that in this case, the Lord had made Himself clear through the signs. Every time I remembered blue eyes and blonde hair, I pushed the memory away. That was a momentary thing on the beach. Nancy was solid, here and now. I was seriously considering getting my grandfather's ring as soon as I got back, making it official, and setting a date for September. I could help her finish the World's Fair, and we could head for Louisville together in January.

Daniel and I were heading back to Knoxville when we stopped for our last night at a coastal state park near Savannah, Georgia. It was dark when we got there and curiously deserted for this time of year. We had our pick of campsites, and we chose one far away from the main road, close to the water, and set up camp. Since we'd been eating fish every day, we hadn't touched the cooler full of hot dogs we'd brought. We roasted them and some marshmallows over the fire, stuffed ourselves, and put the leftovers in the cooler.

We would have slept in hammocks strung between trees, but the weather was a little cool and misty tonight so we set up a two-man tent. It was a simple canvas structure with screened sides, lashed tightly to the ground to keep out skunks and other curious critters. Once it was set up, Daniel and I sat inside, leaning back against convenient, ground-level chairs called backjacks.

We sat in the darkness, a small lantern hanging from the tent supports, and opened our Bibles at random to a familiar passage in Mark. In this passage, Jesus came upon a man who was uncontrollable and lived in a cemetery, homeless and naked. No one would go near him, because he was too dangerous. Whenever anyone tried to handcuff and shackle him, he broke the shackles, smashed them and walked away. All day and all night, he wandered among the tombs and in the wild hills, screaming and cutting himself with sharp pieces of stone.

We turned to the gospels of Matthew and Luke, who had both told the same story, nearly word for word. When the man saw Jesus, he immediately recognized Him as the Son of God. "What do you want with me?" he screamed to Jesus. "Please, I beg you, don't torment me!"

"What is your name?" Jesus asked.

"Legion," he replied, for there were many demons inside this one man. He begged Jesus not to send them into waterless places.

A herd of pigs was grazing on the mountainside nearby, and the demons begged Jesus to let them enter into the pigs. Jesus granted their request, so they left the man and went into the pigs. Immediately, the whole herd—two thousand of them—rushed down the mountainside and fell over a cliff into the lake below, where they drowned. The herdsmen, of course, rushed to the nearest city and told everyone they saw what Jesus had done.

This is one of Jesus' more well-known miracles, but at this moment it had personal significance for Daniel and me. Because as we finished reading it, we heard the unmistakable sound of pigs snuffling outside our thin-walled tent. Anyone who spends time in the woods knows that feral hogs are just as dangerous as bears and other more well-known predators. They are huge, fierce, and constantly hungry. And when they gather into packs, they are almost unstoppable. Daniel and I looked at each other and froze.

"Do you hear what I hear?" Daniel whispered.

"I hear it," I whispered back. I knew the danger, and my heart was pounding. But all our food was outside the tent, so hopefully the hogs would find the food and leave us alone.

These swine, however, seemed intent on us and our tent. For the next half-hour, they shoved their snouts against our canvas walls, snuffled, and dug at the foundation of the tent. We had staked it firmly to the ground, but it was designed to keep out skunks, not boars. If they decided they really wanted to get into our tent, nothing could stop them from knocking it down and trampling us beneath their huge hooves. Nothing but Jesus. So we turned to Him.

I didn't know then, and still don't, if those pigs were really demon-possessed, but they were dangerous either way. And since Jesus Himself is the Creator of the world and everything in it, only He could make them go away. So Daniel and I knelt, Bible still open between us, and prayed loudly.

"Lord Jesus, deliver us now," I shouted. "Please turn these pigs away from us. Send them somewhere else, somewhere they can't hurt anybody." The pigs became even more aggressive, some of them snorting weirdly now, trying to dig their way under our walls, pressing their snouts against the thin canvas screen of our tent. All it would take would be one tusk to rip that screen, and we were done for.

"Jesus, we beg you!" Daniel cried. "Send these pigs away! Please protect us! Only You can. We are powerless here and are depending on You. Only You. Please send them away and don't let them hurt us."

I added my voice, talking to the pigs now. "In the name of Jesus Christ, the Son of God, and through His power, I command you to leave us alone!"

A slight pause in the mayhem outside. Encouraged, but still

shaking from head to toe, I shouted louder. "In Jesus' name, go away!"

Slowly, gradually, the snuffling ceased and the boars began moving in the direction of the river. After a few minutes we heard them splashing across to the other side, and we knew we were safe.

"What if they come back?" Daniel whispered.

"They won't. Jesus sent them away. He won't let them come back."

Indeed, the night was completely quiet now, except for the natural sounds of night birds, crickets and cicadas. No noises to warn us of anything amiss.

We lay down in our sleeping bags to try to get some rest, but my mind was whirling and finally, finally, I felt answers in my spirit. Those hogs had come just in time for me to avoid making a huge mistake. Maybe marriage to Nancy was still the right thing to do but definitely not in September as I'd been thinking. God didn't want me to change my seminary plans. I was supposed to go in August as planned.

The rest, I knew, I could comfortably leave up to Him and follow His lead.

"I hear You now, Father," I prayed in silent gratitude. "Those pigs were pretty scary, but thank You for sending them. I was hearing from everybody that one obvious path was the right one. Now I'm convinced that the devil was using this to distract me all along. You allowed those hogs to turn my attention back to You. Thank You." Then I snuggled down in my warm sleeping bag and went instantly to sleep, totally at peace.

The next morning we found our cooler, which had been securely shut and stuffed with our leftover hot dogs, several hundred feet away. It was covered in pig snot, hoof marks, and tusk marks. The hogs had never managed to get it open, but they'd almost destroyed it in the process. We loaded it into the car—it would make a great illustration when we told this story—and headed home.

As we left the park, we saw vividly why there had been no other campers that night. Clearly posted near the entrance were signs saying, "Park closed due to wild hogs." Daniel and I looked at the signs and each other, and collapsed in hilarity.

In the daylight, we could see those signs just fine. But in the dark last night, we had not. I thought it was ironic that on a day when I'd finally decided that God was speaking to me through signs, I'd missed the most obvious one.

45

"You're calling off our wedding?" Nancy asked, aghast. "I thought things were going so well. You just met my family. They're ready to adopt you."

"Not to put too fine a point on it," I said, "but we were never officially engaged. And I'm not calling it off. You said at the beginning that there's no hurry. We talked about me going ahead to seminary and you staying behind to finish the World's Fair. That's all I'm saying. When you finish your work, then we'll see where we are."

"What do you mean, we'll 'see where we are'?"

"Just what I said. We're only twenty-one, and we're both insanely busy. Let's let things calm down. If this is right, it'll work out. We pray about it and go from here."

Nancy wasn't happy, but finally relented. "January," she said. "If it doesn't happen by January, we seriously need to consider getting on with our lives on our own."

I agreed. January should give us both time to be sure, one way or the other.

*   *   *

Other people in my life weren't as easy to convince. Bob Hall warned me that I was giving someone else a chance to move in on a wonderful girl. My dad said I was insane for letting her get away.

266

My cohorts at the BSU were shocked; our wedding was a foregone conclusion by that time. The Pleasant Grove crowd, all of whom loved Nancy, had been looking forward to helping with our wedding and were horribly disappointed.

The only two people who seemed happy with my decision were Miss Ina and my mother. My mom took me aside and told me frankly, "I felt uneasy about this from the beginning. If this had gone any farther, I was going to tell you that."

Miss Ina patted me on the back and congratulated me on being strong enough to follow the Lord. "It was a near thing, Miss Ina," I told her frankly and described the situation in Orlando. "It all looked like things were just falling into place. Like one sign after another. But you were right and you gave me good advice."

She smiled. "And the answer might not be 'no.' It might just be 'not now.' You're strong enough to figure that out as you go."

"God had to hit me upside the head with a two-by-four," I said. "I didn't realize it at the time, but His silence was the answer to my prayer. By saying nothing, He was saying no. I know that now."

She hugged me and kissed my cheek. "I'm proud of you, Mark," she said. "We're going to miss you here, but you're ready to take the next step in your ministry."

My eyes stung. Hearing those words from her meant the world.

"Thank you, Miss Ina. And I'll keep praying for Pete. No one's a lost cause until the Lord says so."

"You do that. God might reel him in yet."

46

The last weeks before the World's Fair flew by. Like last year, I personally trained the Alaska missionaries, this time with Bert's help and considerable input from Daniel. His Siberian Upik was now flawless, and he was enthusiastic about reaching more adults. Angie couldn't wait to meet Prissy and the other kids she'd heard so much about. She planned to spend most of her time at the group home. And Randy was just so glad to be a part of this trip that he would do whatever Will West asked him to.

I also worked on the committee to identify and train my replacement at Pleasant Grove. The one finally chosen was an enthusiastic young man named Ken Newman, from Kentucky. Rather than being intimidated by the challenge, he looked forward to it. He was exactly the kind of go-getter we needed to take up the reins when I left for seminary in August. It would be right in the middle of the World's Fair, and there could be no down time.

Knoxville was spit and polished, awaiting its guests from around the world. Six-month passes were gobbled up at a price of $100 each. Television made much of the upcoming spectacle. And the closer opening day came, the more nervous and excited the kids became.

The opening ceremony was broadcast on local and regional television. President Reagan was in town to open the Fair. Dinah Shore was the master of ceremonies. Porter Wagoner and Ricky Skaggs performed.

Knoxville made its own kind of history when a new restaurant was born that has since become a multi-state chain. Petro's opened a stand in the food court and offered bags of Frito's corn chips, slit open and topped with chili, cheese, onions, sour cream and other choices. It was a handy, portable meal served with a plastic spoon, and it became an instant hit.

Each participating nation had a pavilion. The Peruvian exhibit featured a mummy that was unwrapped and studied at the fair. The Egyptian exhibit had ancient artifacts valued at more than $30 million. Hungary, the home country of the Rubik's Cube, erected a large, automated Rubik's Cube with rotating squares at the entrance to its pavilion. That cube is still present in downtown Knoxville, where it has been displayed since 1982 in the lobby of the Holiday Inn World's Fair Park.

And every night of the Fair, at ten o'clock sharp, the sky lit with a ten-minute fireworks display that could be seen over the entire city.

Our youth would be performing in the amphitheater near the food court, in the United States' pavilion. It was a perfect spot to draw huge crowds, and we'd bought microphones so the kids could be heard without shouting in the open-air arena. As we watched the city's final preparations, my youth worked harder and harder. They also had their plates full with four Vacation Bible Schools in June and July.

And at every turn, there was Nancy. Watching her work so fluidly and professionally with all aspects of the Fair, there were moments when I wondered if I'd made the right decision. Then I reminded myself that we'd left the door wide open. If she and I were right together, it would happen in the Lord's timing.

47

My youth had their first performance the Wednesday night after the Fair opened. We were gathered backstage, and my biggest job at this point was to calm this group down. They were alternately excited, nervous, and just plain terrified. They'd had some good experience over the past year and a half, but this? This was why we'd ordered the Muppets to begin with. This was why we'd done everything up to this point. And now it was about to happen.

My team looked to me for guidance. Sitting here with me were at least two kids who wouldn't be with this group much longer. Angie would be leaving for Alaska in two weeks. She was sorry she'd miss three months of being Miss Piggy, but she'd trained Jessica as her backup. Now, Jessica was skilled at changing her voice so she could operate both Bert and Miss Piggy. Jonathan planned to leave for Vanderbilt in mid-August. Jimmy was still undecided, but Samson knew he'd be staying on his family's farm. He could join Pete as a graduate helper until the end of the World's Fair.

I sat there on a padded stool, the kids gathered at my feet. What could I say that hadn't been said already? We'd been through so much together. It was incredible to think about where they'd been spiritually just two years ago, and where they were today. Martha Galyon had been there with me through it all. She stood beside me now, waiting to hear my final words before this first performance.

"Well, this is it," I said. "This is what we've worked for, practiced for, trained for, and dreamed of. Remember the first day we talked about this? You didn't think God could use people like you, just a small group from a little country church, but just look at what He's already done through you. People are headed to heaven because of how God's used you and this ministry. We've followed His will, and He's had His hand on us."

The kids were quiet, but I heard a couple of the girls sniffle. One dabbed her eyes with the back of her hand.

"Now," I continued, "you're on a bigger stage. Staying right there . . ." I made a small O with my fingers, "in the center of His will, is going to be more important than ever. You do that, and people will hear the good news of Jesus for the very first time, and they will hear it through you. Let's pray."

We all knelt and I prayed for God's guidance, calm spirit, and wisdom to be on these young men and women as they sought to reach people in His name. I prayed for their health and their ability to do whatever they had to do. And I prayed that people would be drawn to this little corner of this huge event, at just the right time.

When I finished, everyone looked up with fire in their eyes.

"Okay guys, here we go. It's what?"

"It's all about Him!"

"That it is. Head out and have fun!"

*　*　*

That first performance set the stage for all the rest to come. The place where we were performing was perfect, right in the center of all the action and directly in front of the food court. People had to pass us to get wherever they were going. The times we were scheduled to perform were perfect—Wednesdays at six o'clock and Saturdays at noon. People brought their families for a meal at the food court, and the kids saw the Muppets and came running. Families ended up staying for the entire show, and the kids got some valuable Bible teaching.

Every performance was a little different. They had to be, because we had some repeat visitors. I started everything off with a specific lesson, usually one we'd taught at children's sermons or at Vacation Bible Schools. There were plenty to choose from. Often the Muppets would play off of something that was happening in the audience. This was where our spotters were invaluable. Pete, Martha, and any kid who wasn't operating a Muppet stood where they could see and hear what was going on in the audience, and they would send cues to the hidden Muppeteers. Greg Wilson was at most every performance, helping the kids get the most out of their voices. Ken Newman soaked it all in and was an invaluable resource, as he learned what he would need to know when I handed off this baton in August.

At the end of every performance I had a kids' version of an invitational, telling them that it was simple to ask Jesus Christ into their life, and I'd be there for anyone who had any questions. A lot of kids did come up, usually to meet their favorite Muppets in person and get autographs. But a few, at least a couple every week, came up and either asked questions or said they wanted to give their lives to Jesus. Most were kids, but a few were adults. With each and every one, I prayed with them and counseled them on what should happen next.

And the pattern was set for the summer.

48

In mid-May, I graduated with honors from UT, and Bob made good on his promise. I immediately went on the payroll as the BSU's associate director for the summer. The missionaries left for Alaska right after UT graduation.

Days later, Jimmy, Jonathan, and Samson graduated from high school. The entire youth group was in enthusiastic attendance, whooping and hollering as the boys' names were called. Everyone knew that Jonathan would graduate with highest honors, medals, stoles, and such, but it was a surprise to see an asterisk beside Jimmy's name. An honor graduate. I knew how hard he'd worked for every good grade he got, and seeing that asterisk made me swell with pride.

The summer flew by, and being AD at the BSU was more than I had thought it would be. The top item on our agenda was to pick seven new residents for the coming school year. Everyone currently living there had graduated and would be clearing out at some point over the summer. Daniel Bowman, when he returned from Alaska, would choose a seminary and then enter the mission field full time. Bert Gibson had started a two-year missionary training program right after graduation. He would be going to secret places, places where missionaries would be executed if they were discovered. Susan Bryant was getting married to her long-time sweetheart, Mickey Roberts. Vernon Douglas already had a job lined up as a teacher and assistant coach for a high school in North Carolina.

Kenny Duncan and Brandon Payne were going to stay here at the BSU for the summer while they looked for jobs. Both had offers and were trying to determine the right fit. And Kelsey Rhodes already had a job secured as a church administration assistant and was about to get her own apartment here in Knoxville.

So, come August, the BSU would be empty, and it was Bob's and my job to fill it up. We sat in his office, piles of applications on his desk, and sifted through them. Some were obvious, like Angie Galyon and Randy Barnette. We chose Allison Bedford, the girl who'd come to me for counseling about her boyfriend last spring, to share the apartment with Angie. She had turned out to be a sweet, energetic worker here. She and Angie, we felt, would get along well.

Others were kids who'd spent a lot of time here, and we knew them well—it was a just a matter of choosing the right mix of personalities and spiritual gifts. We needed people who, if they worked together as a team, could continue and expand on what we'd been doing. We sifted and sorted, and after hours of solid work we finally had only one slot to fill.

Then I picked up one of the final few applications, and my jaw dropped.

"Bob," I said as I scanned it, "do you know who this is?"

He took it and looked at it. "Well, may the Lord be praised."

The name hit both of us immediately. The applicant was Joe Barton, the young man who'd held a knife to the throat of a young girl right here in this building, just a little over a year ago. He had obviously been possessed by a demon, and Vernon and I had called on Jesus to cast the demon out. Joe had been fine ever since. Bert, with counselors from Calvary Baptist and Campus Crusade for Christ, had been working with him. I'd kept away from that situation, because Bert had told me frankly that Joe was embarrassed to be around Vernon and me. The hurt over what he'd done was still too deep. He knew Jesus had forgiven him, but he was still working on forgiving himself.

Now, Bert and the counselors had made such a difference in his life that he wanted to be part of the team here.

"What do you think?" Bob asked.

"I think we take him. With what he's been through, he would have a powerful testimony."

"I completely agree." He put Joe's application in the "accepted" pile. "Done," he said. "We have our residents."

"It's a good group."

"It is. They'll work well together. As they move in, we'll decide who we think would be right for which job. You want to call them and tell them they've been accepted?"

"I'd love to," I said.

For the next couple of hours I placed calls to the new residents, most of whom had been waiting and hoping that this particular call would come. They had dorm space lined up, but this was much better than dorms, not to mention free. They all said they'd come by over the next few days to stake out their rooms.

With anticipation and pleasure, I picked up the phone to call Joe Barton. The phone was answered on the first ring.

"Hello?"

"Hi, may I speak to Joe?"

"This is Joe."

"Joe, this is Mark Smith at the BSU and I've got some good news for you."

"I got in?"

"You got in, and it wasn't even close. Congratulations."

Silence on the other end of the line. A long, in-drawn breath. "I'm so grateful," he said, "and amazed that you'd take me."

"You deserve it, Joe. And you have a powerful testimony. God will use it if you let Him."

"I've never told you and Vernon thank you. So I'm telling you now. Thank you."

"Don't thank me. Thank Jesus."

"I have, and now I'm thanking you too. You knew the right things to do to get my life on the right track."

"It's all about Him, Joe."

"It sure is."

I waited until last to make the call to Alaska. I calculated the time difference and called at two o'clock, hoping that Randy and Angie would still be at the pastorium.

The phone began to ring as the call went through, and shortly a woman's voice came on the line. Denise, I realized instantly. Tears sprang to my eyes and rolled down my cheeks before I could even say a word. I got control of myself quickly.

"Denise?"

"Yes, this is Denise. Is this Mark?"

"Yes, and I'm so glad to hear your voice. I didn't realize how much I'd missed you until I heard your voice."

"We miss you too, but you sure have sent us some excellent workers this year and last," she said. "These kids are special. We've never had one that can actually speak the native language before."

"He's worked hard on it for a year now."

"Well, it's paying off. He's communicating with the guys at the jail, and all the other adults, in ways we've never been able to. He says he wants to go into the mission field, and he'll be a natural."

We chatted companionably for a few minutes, catching up on each other. She told me that Connie's baby had been born in the spring—a little sister for Prissy and Paul. Thomas—now eight years old—had fallen naturally into the leadership role at the group home as soon as Paul left to join Connie and Jack. Atka's little brothers were now regulars at the Lighthouse, and Angie had helped them accept Jesus just a couple of weeks ago.

"And Darren?"

"I saved the best for last," she said. "He's in high school now and already has a full-ride scholarship locked in at the University of Alaska Fairbanks."

"The Nome campus?"

"No, sir. Our Darren is going to the big city. The main campus in Fairbanks. He's going to study to be a doctor and come back here to practice. He's going to minor in counseling, so he can directly address alcoholism and treatment of the diseases it causes. His mom passed, you know."

"No, I didn't know."

"Darren thought he didn't care about her, but her death hit him hard. Now he wants to help people like her."

I sat amazed, tears streaming down my face. God can use anyone, anytime. I'd already seen ample evidence of this, and here was more. God had used an alcoholic mother who, as far as anyone knew, had never given Him a second thought in her life. Good for Darren for picking himself up and using his experience in a positive way.

"And how are you and Will?"

"Better than ever. The Iditarod ministry is turning into a full-time thing, all year round. A lot of the things we do during those three weeks can be done anytime. So now we do them. The missionaries you send are a big help."

"Speaking of which, are they around?"

"They sure are, sitting here eating eggs and moose sausage. Here's Angie."

A pause. Then, "Hello?"

"Hey Angie, how's it going?"

"Fabulous. These little kids are amazing. Being Miss Piggy is fun, and I can't wait to get back to it, but this is just tremendous. I'm so glad I got picked for this."

"You earned it. Angie, I've got some good news for you. Can you share the phone with Randy? This is really for you both."

She called him over and said, "We're both here."

"You've been picked as BSU residents."

A squeal, from Angie I hoped. A squeal like that from Randy would cost him some man points. "Really?"

"Really. You'll be the last ones to get there, but there will be rooms ready for you to move in before fall term."

"That is so awesome," Randy said. "So much better than the dorm."

"It is, but you're going to have to work your tails off on the BSU ministry. You both know all about that."

"We do, and I can't wait."

"Let me talk to Daniel for a minute."

He came on the line and greeted me in flawless Siberian Upik, so perfect that I thought I was talking to a native. My jaw dropped.

"I'm impressed. What did you say?"

"That I'm so happy to be back here and I'm more confident than ever that this is what I want to do."

"Well, that's really good," I said. "How are the guys at the jail?"

"They're all good. There are a couple of new ones that Hank's been working with. There was a baptism at the jail last week. It's amazing to just sit back and watch God work."

"It really is. He's doing some mighty things here, too. We could use you at the World's Fair."

"I'll help when I get home, which will be about the time you're leaving, right?"

"That's what I was going to ask you about. Would you be willing to step in as leader of the BSU's involvement with the Fair? You don't need any training; you've been there from the beginning."

"Absolutely. Now I can't wait to get home!"

We chatted for a few more minutes and I hung up, smiling. *God has a way of putting everything in place,* I thought. Everything I loved and had worked so hard for over the past two years was going to be in good hands.

49

On Saturday, July 31, I sat in my office at Pleasant Grove and pondered. I usually preached the fifth Sunday of each month, but there hadn't been a fifth Sunday in July and I had some things I really wanted to share with the people at this church before I left. So Pastor Dunkel had agreed to let me preach the next day.

Now, though, sitting here and preparing to actually write this sermon, my thoughts and feelings were jumbled. What in the world could I share with these wonderful mountain people who'd meant so much to me over the past two years? What message could I leave them with as I went on to the next phase of my life? I wanted it to be something profound, something deep, something that let them know how very important each and every one of them was in God's overall plan. Just look at what He'd done through the youth! He could do the same with anyone.

And I wanted them to know how much they meant to me, and how hard it was to leave them.

I looked out the open window at the mountains and smelled the spicy scent of spruce that always hung in the air here. How I loved it! It would always be home. Just like these people would always be family. We all were different colors in the same divine portrait, different threads, weaving little by little into one immeasurable tapestry of infinity.

And that, I realized, was the point. God had just given it to me. I bent my head to my notebook and started to write.

The next morning, sitting on the front pew and waiting for time to preach, I felt very much like I'd felt two years before, sitting in the Athens church where I'd grown up, waiting to tell the congregation about my year in Alaska. This was the same but different. I'd had another life-changing experience here in these mountains. Who'd have thought you could drive a few miles and be in a totally different culture? I'd learned that, and so much more, from these people.

The last notes of "O for a Thousand Tongues to Sing" faded away. I stood and climbed up to the pulpit and gazed out at these faces: Henry Roberts, the head of the search committee who'd hired me for this job . . . Bob DeLozier, who'd met me in the parking lot that first Sunday and welcomed me in . . . Greg Wilson, who'd been hired the same time as me, and who'd grown and learned with me . . . Robert and Martha Galyon, who'd become precious friends and had helped me so much, especially in the three months after I got hurt . . . All my youth, who sat together and waited to hear my final words to them. Last, my gaze lit on Miss Ina, the prayer warrior who'd taught me so much about communicating with God.

Two years ago, they'd all been strangers. Now they were my brothers and sisters.

"Last night," I began, "I sat down to write what I would say today. I couldn't imagine how I could ever begin to express to you how much it's meant to me, every day, over the past two years." I pulled out a piece of paper from my pocket and glanced at it, then held it up for them to see. "When I came here, I had to preach a trial sermon. This is it. I wrote it about thirty minutes before that service. God made me wait that long before He let me know what He wanted me to say to you.

"I said I would do my best to teach your children about how to have a relationship with Jesus Christ. I said I would give everything that was in me to do my best by your children, and that I would actively strive and pray every day for Him to work through me for them. I said that my goal was to teach and inspire them so well that they would all be saved and baptized before they left this youth group."

I put the piece of paper away, then gazed out at them again. "We've had some success in this youth group, but it hasn't been because of me. It's been because of your kids and their willingness to follow where God has led them. God has used them in a mighty way, and they're touching people from literally around the world. People who've never heard Jesus' name in their lives are now hearing it from the kids in this church. That's an amazing gift and an awesome responsibility. These kids are handling it with humility, knowing it's not—ever—about them.

"Many of you know that I've also served in a leadership position at the BSU at UT over the past couple of years. The two experiences have interwoven inside me in a way I can't even explain. The best way I can describe it—it's like a master puzzle, or portrait, or a tapestry. Each and every person has a role in God's plan. We can only see a tiny piece of it, and almost all of us cry at one time or another that we just don't understand. Why is my friend cheating and getting top grades, and I'm working hard and being honest, and barely getting Cs? Why does my dad beat my mom? Why do people hurt each other at all? Why are there earthquakes in Mexico and tsunamis in Japan? Why do people get cancer? And why does God allow it?

"Those are all questions way bigger than me, and none of us will know the whole story until we get to heaven. Then, we'll be able to see the whole picture. The whole tapestry. Because each of us has our own color in the painting or our own thread in the tapestry. Without that color or that thread, the whole work wouldn't be complete. But somehow, because of the Master's hand of genius and sovereignty, it will all fit together into one perfect picture that will glorify Him."

I paused. "I'm not even twenty-two and headed off to seminary in a couple of weeks, so you can take my advice any way you want—but here it is. Realize that the world is not all about you. It's about Him. We all just fit into His picture. We each need to do our best to figure out how we fit in and live our lives accordingly. We all have gifts we're expected to use, gifts we may not even know we have until we start living for God—really living for Him. But once you figure that out, and you know you're walking in His will, you will be at peace. A peace beyond all understanding. You'll know that you're in the palm of His hand, and no one can ever pluck you away from Him.

"It doesn't take away the bad teachers, the illness, and the earthquakes. But if you belong to the Lord, you've got His Spirit in you and you know He'll help. He promised, and He never breaks His promises.

"Think you don't have wisdom? Ask. He'll show you.

"'Trust in the Lord with all your heart, and lean not on your own understanding. In all your ways acknowledge Him, and He will make your paths straight.'

"Or my favorite verse—my life verse—'He will accomplish that which concerns me.'"

I paused and looked down at my notes.

"One of the questions I've gotten most over the past three years—how can you know God's will for your life? I wish I could tell you, but I have no clue myself, only parts. Just start with the Bible. Take a step every day and follow where He leads. As you begin to know the Scriptures better and better, you will love them and deepen your love for Him. Then you will know that the things you want are not just your desires. He put them there. They are of Him and they are His will.

"He never promises it will be easy. He never promises He'll show the whole path in front of us. He does promise that His Word will be a lamp to our feet and a light to our path. Not a spotlight or a beacon that shines a long way in front of you but a lamp that just shows you the next step. And if you're living in the Lord, that one step is all you need. When you're His, and you have that perspective, this world all starts to make sense because you begin to realize, in some tiny way, how temporary we are. Our time on this earth is just a short adventure. It's a sliver of eternity, and then we're on our way home."

I put my notes down and looked out at the congregation again.

"Bottom line—don't worry about everyone else. What are you doing about *you*? You may not ever have all the answers, but you can deal with yourself. And as you do that, you fulfill your part of God's tapestry. I can't wait to get to heaven and see the whole picture.

"If you remember anything I said, remember this: It's what, kids?" I pointed at my youth group, seated together in the pews.

"It's all about Him!" they shouted in unison.

* * *

After the service I stood at the front of the church and shook everyone's hand as they left. It would still be a week or so before I left for seminary, but this was my last Sunday at Pleasant Grove.

Jimmy waited until everyone had left, then he took me aside. I shook his hand, then pulled him into a big hug. "I never told you, man," I said, "but I'm so proud of you for the way you made it through high school. Not only made it, but an honor graduate."

"It hasn't been easy, Mark. There have been other things going on that you don't even know about." He glanced around to make sure we were alone, and I knew exactly what he meant.

"I think I have a clue. And I totally understand. I've been right where you are."

"I kind of thought you did." He paused, looked down, then back up at me. "I wanted to tell you a couple of things. First, I've decided what I'm going to do after high school."

"You have? Tell me."

"I'm going into the Air Force. I've been accepted already. Jonathan decided to go with me instead of going to Vanderbilt."

"Dude, that's great!"

"And the other thing is that I rededicated my life to Jesus today, during your sermon. I did it years ago, but what you said made me realize that I needed to come completely clean with Him and give Him everything. My all. All the good and all the bad. So I did."

I choked past the lump in my throat. "How does it feel?"

"Incredible. Like you said, the peace of God surpasses all understanding."

"It sure does. Well, I'm so proud of you, Jimmy. Be ready to be used. Even more than you already have been."

"I can't wait."

50

I spent the next week officially turning over all the reins of everything I was doing to new, capable people. Ken Newman took the youth ministry and ran, never missing a beat. The new crew of people moved into the BSU. Joe Barton arrived in time to choose the room I'd lived in for two years. Daniel got home right before I left and, with barely a flicker, took over the BSU's involvement in the World's Fair, with plans to go to the seminary he'd chosen in January. Angie came home and resumed her role as Miss Piggy. And Randy Barnette now had even more fire for the Lord than before. I knew that the dorm Bible study program we'd started two years before would now explode.

Nancy came by as I was packing. She poked her head into my room. "Got a minute?"

"Sure." I rubbed my aching back. I needed a break anyway.

"I just wanted to say goodbye and tell you that you were right."

"About what?"

"That getting married in September, and you waiting to go to seminary, wouldn't have been the right choice. For either of us. I'm perfectly okay with figuring it out as we go."

"Letting God lead, and being happy with wherever He leads."

"Exactly. I just wanted to tell you that."

"I'm glad you did."

She gave me a light hug and a kiss on the cheek. "See you."

"See you later."

I finished moving out of my room, taking special care to pack a sarong that Brandon had brought me from Indonesia. I'd learned to tie it as he'd suggested, and it's still a staple in my dresser—one of the most comfortable things I have. I loaded everything I owned into my little Chevette, canoe securely lashed to the top, and went by the lumber company to pick up my last check. I drove north, windows open, wind in my hair, free of everything except what lay ahead of me. Thanks to the jobs the Lord had provided, and some smart investing, I had enough in my bank account to cover me until I finished seminary, even if I didn't work at all during those three years.

And what would come after that? What kind of ministry would I find myself in? Would I end up marrying Nancy after all? Or would God put that blonde, blue-eyed girl who still haunted me back into my path? Or, maybe, someone else entirely?

Only the Lord knew. And I was fine with that.

ABOUT THE AUTHOR

Until 2013, Frances Smith spent her professional career in journalism, corporate communications, and public relations.

In 2011, God used match.com, an online dating service, to bring her to Mark Smith. Almost instantly they knew they were meant to be together. They married in 2012, and God called Frances to write full-time for Him in 2013. Her first book, *Cleft of the Rock*, was published in 2014. *Thorn in the Flesh* was finished in 2015, and the third book in the trilogy, *Lamp to My Feet*, should be complete by mid-2017.

Frances has also been active in church leadership, serving as wedding director, Presbyterian Women moderator, and Presbyterian deacon. Today she is a baptized member of Pleasant Grove Baptist Church, where she is part of the Sunday School teaching team.

She holds a Bachelor of Arts in English and a Master of Arts in English education. She and Mark live in East Tennessee and, between them, have four sons and a daughter. They enjoy fishing, hiking, and nature.

Visit Frances at www.cleftoftherock.org, or email her at fran@cleftoftherock.org.